Military Executions during World War I

Military Executions during World War I

Gerard Oram
Department of History
The Open University

palgrave
macmillan

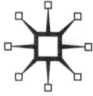

First published 2003 by
PALGRAVE MACMILLAN
Houndmills, Basingstoke, Hampshire RG21 6XS and
175 Fifth Avenue, New York, N. Y. 10010
Companies and representatives throughout the world

PALGRAVE MACMILLAN is the global academic imprint of the Palgrave Macmillan division of St. Martin's Press, LLC and of Palgrave Macmillan Ltd. Macmillan® is a registered trademark in the United States, United Kingdom and other countries. Palgrave is a registered trademark in the European Union and other countries.

ISBN 1-4039-0694-7

This book is printed on paper suitable for recycling and made from fully managed and sustained forest sources.

A catalogue record for this book is available from the British Library.

Library of Congress Cataloging-in-Publication Data

Oram, Gerard.
    Military executions during World War I / by Gerard Oram.
        p. cm.
    Includes bibliographical references and index.
    ISBN 1-4039-0694-7
    1. Capital punishment–Great Britain–History. 2. Military offenses–Great Britain–History. 3. World War, 1914-1918–Great Britain. 4. Executions and executioners–Great Britain–History. 5. Deserters, Military–Great Britain–History
I. Title
    KD6333.O73 2003
    343.41'0143–dc21   2002192469

10   9   8   7   6   5   4   3   2   1
12   11   10   09   08   07   06   05   04   03

Printed and bound in Great Britain by
Antony Rowe Ltd, Chippenham and Eastbourne

For

Phyllis May Oram
(1905–2002)

and

Hope
(2001)

I miss you

Contents

List of Tables

List of Figures

Acknowledgements

I would like to acknowledge all the people who have assisted, advised or contributed in some form to this work. They are too numerous to list, but in particular I would like to thank my examiners Dr John Bourne and Professor Arthur Marwick, and my supervisors Dr David Englander and Professor Clive Emsley. Each deserves my unalloyed appreciation.

I also owe thanks to the staff at numerous archives and libraries, especially the Public Record Office and the Imperial War Museum. To Julian Putkowski I offer my most sincere thanks for making available his own personal archive, for feeding and accommodating me on my trips into London and for continuing to contribute to the debate in his own indomitable style. There are more: Dr Christoph Jahr assisted me with some of the German material and Dr Nicolas Offenstadt with the French, and Professor Gerry Rubin has clarified some of the more complex points of military law.

I have made every attempt to ensure that copyright has not been breached, by following the 'fair dealing' guidelines, but if I have inadvertently done so I offer my apologies.

Finally, I would like to acknowledge the ongoing support of my family and all my friends. During the past twelve months my wife and I have suffered personal tragedy and deep sadness, but also great joy. I cannot overstate how much I owe to Anna and now to our new baby daughter, Izzette. Life goes on.

Introduction

> The primary object of the infliction of the death sentence is that it
> shall act as a deterrent. . . . . After all, what alternative punishment is
> there, when troops are facing the enemy?
>
> Major-General Sir Wyndham Childs[1]

Writing in 1997, Professor Ian Beckett remarked that 'there is a seeming public obsession fuelled by some popular works with the relatively minor matter of 312 wartime executions [on the Western Front only]'.[2] The 'popular'
works to which Beckett refers are numerous, but most notably include
Anthony Babington's *For the Sake of Example*, and *Shot at Dawn* by Julian
Putkowski and Julian Sykes.[3] Until recently, these two works were the first
point of reference for historians concerned with British executions,[4] yet
both are deficient, though in different ways. Moreover, they both adhere to
a style and tradition the origins of which can be traced directly to Ernest
Thurtle's 1924 polemic, *Shootings at Dawn*.[5] Similar traditions are to be
found in fictional works such as *The Secret Battle* by A. P. Herbert (1919)[6] and
in the Alan Bleasdale television play *The Monocled Mutineer* (BBC, 1986).

There has been a backlash against these works – usually defending the
actions of the army. This approach is implicit in Beckett's own rejection of
the subject. John Peatty has argued that 'It is not the job of the historian to
sit in judgement on the past and second guess the action of our forebears –
although, frankly, many historians do it'[7]. Sadly, Peatty avoids any analysis
of the material, preferring instead to quote modern-day journalists in his
defence of the army's actions and, therefore, his essay amounts to little more
than yet another polemic, albeit from a different point of view. This
approach has also caused problems in the most recent work on the subject,
by Cathryn Corns and John Hughes-Wilson, where the infelicitous use of
evidence has detracted from a book that might otherwise have made a
meaningful contribution to the debate.[8] Fortunately, more erudite studies
do exist. Professor David French used the executions of the First World War
to provide a context for his study of discipline in World War II and David

1

Englander's work has provided an excellent comparative framework, which seems to invite future exploration of the topic.[9]

Unfortunately, until now the polemical works have clouded the issue, and consequently there has been little specific analysis of military executions during the war. This is a great pity because despite Beckett's dismissal of the subject, the death penalty formed a vital component in the British High Command's approach to discipline. The numbers involved, far from being 'relatively minor' were the equivalent of a whole infantry brigade: official sources record that the threat of the death penalty hung over more than three thousand men, but the real number probably exceeded four thousand.[10] This number far exceeds the number of civilians condemned by criminal courts during a comparable period of time, but studies of capital punishment in criminal cases have not been dismissed so lightly. Furthermore, the trial and review of cases would have occupied an enormous proportion of the time of very senior officers. The impact on those touched by executions, either as members of firing squads or as witnesses, has seldom been considered by historians. The works of David French and David Englander have shown how military executions can provide the basis for serious analyses of military discipline and morale. All armies engaged in the conflict carried out executions but some, such as the British, demonstrated less restraint than did others. Why this should be the case has not been adequately explained. It is my contention that in order to understand this last question we need to look beyond purely military considerations: social and cultural structures were every bit as important in defining the respective armies' approach to the death penalty.

Having considered the British Army's disciplinary structures within the greater context of other armies, we need to assess how those structures were applied: how were ideas about discipline formed and what events shaped its meaning to contemporaries? It is not within the scope of this study to analyse the evolution of the British Army as an institution, but we should note that during the second half of the nineteenth century and up to the eve of the First World War, the army had undergone considerable change. It was modernising. The nature of military discipline was also changing, although there was considerable resistance to any attempt to liberalise the military code. The advent of modern warfare, which the army had recognised before 1914, presented fresh challenges to commanders. Previous studies have concentrated on strategic considerations and the implications of new technology,[11] but manpower concerns and the discipline of a changed army was every bit as important to contemporaries. Although apparent to military pundits before 1914, this took on huge importance at the outbreak of war with the rapid and vast expansion of the army. The war, it could be argued, slowed down modernising reforms on matters such as discipline, at least in the first years. Faced with a desperate military situation almost from the beginning, British commanders, it seems, fell back on traditional ideas of control based on the principle of deterrence, and executions became commonplace in the years 1914–17.

The emergence, for the first time, of a 'mass' British army challenged existing ideas about troop morale, which had been defined largely in terms of individual character. Eventually, it also sounded the death knell for traditional ideas about control of the army following the recruitment of huge numbers of men, very few of whom intended to be professional soldiers. The creation of a 'citizen army' had altered the relationship between leaders and led, but also tested the organisational and administrative structures of the army. Traditional punishments such as the death penalty were initially applied with as much vigour as ever they were in the old Regular Force, but by the end of the war traditional approaches to discipline and morale gave way to forms consistent with the modernising voices of the pre-war era. By the final year of the war the army had altered its disciplinary policy, if not the actual code, and in practice at least it began to resemble some of its continental counterparts, though not all.

The process of change, however, was not universally consistent. There were great variations between different units. It appears that different traditions influenced practices in certain types of formation. It has been argued elsewhere that Regular divisions, for example, were subjected to harsher forms of discipline than Territorial Force divisions.[12] Was this trend reflected in the approach to the death penalty? The evidence suggests that, broadly speaking, it was. But the situation was far more complex, especially in the divisions of the New Army where practices varied enormously. Variations also existed in Regular or Territorial formations and we need to assess the role of divisional commanders in particular. Death sentences and executions were only a small part of the disciplinary process, but they formed arguably the most important component in an army dominated by ideas of deterrence. Executions might not provide an accurate barometer of discipline in any given unit, or army for that matter, but they do provide us with a unique sounding board – a framework on which to make comparisons.

A total of 361 executions of men serving with the British Army is recorded in official documents (29 of which were carried out after the armistice): 321 for military offences such as desertion and cowardice, etc., the remaining 40 for murder.[13] Additionally, an unknown number of Indian soldiers were also executed[14] and it appears that records relating to the execution of British soldiers are incomplete.[15]

Professor Beckett's assessment is correct in two respects. Firstly, when compared to the enormous number of casualties during the First World War the execution of 361 men might well appear to be of little importance. Secondly, the relevant literature has tended to be dominated by popular, anecdotal accounts which, consistent with public perceptions, have concentrated on apparent injustices. But these have overlooked potential areas for serious historical analysis – such issues as the use of the death sentence in the British Army as a disciplinary device and its impact on morale, as well as the social and cultural context of the death penalty. However, Beckett's comments underestimate the impact that the wartime executions had on soldiers in the trenches. The number of references to executions in diaries, letters and memoirs is surely testament to the nature of their impact and for many soldiers the experience of witnessing an execution or the fear generated by the rumours circulating in the trenches was a profound part of their wartime experience.

Professor Beckett is equally critical of the current campaign to gain pardons for those executed, which he views as applying 'modern morality to the past' – a line also taken by Peatty.[16] This does raise some interesting questions. What, for example, does one then do about approximately three thousand other men sentenced to death who were ultimately spared by the commander-in-chief? There is scant attention paid to these cases. Do they not deserve pardons too? The implications not only for those convicted by military courts but also for those convicted under the criminal code are too vast to warrant serious consideration by historians and are best left to the politician. Nevertheless, it appears that the approach and scope of many studies on executions have been dictated by the writers' concerns about injustice and a genuinely heartfelt belief that those executed should be pardoned. The inaccessibility of official records for seventy-five years has also contributed to concerns of a 'cover-up', leading to fears that the situation might have been far worse than it actually was. This has deflected attention away from the true historical debate concerning the use of the death penalty, or at least the threat of its use, as an instrument of control.

The death sentence was the ultimate disciplinary weapon available to British courts martial and there can be little doubt that the High Command considered it to be an essential component in the maintenance of discipline, a view supported by the Committee of Enquiry chaired by the Right Honourable Sir Charles Darling.[17] Interestingly, there was a contemporary campaign against the military use of the death penalty headed, as is also the case with the current campaign for pardons, by a Labour MP, Ernest Thurtle. It may well be the case that Thurtle was less concerned with the putative inequity of military justice but saw in the executions an opportunity to attack the army itself.[18] Nevertheless, Thurtle's role in the subsequent abolition of the death penalty for most military offences in 1930 cannot be overstated.[19] Principal among Thurtle's concerns was the power vested in the commander-in-chief, who, in the absence of any appellate system, acted as final arbiter in all matters of military justice. This differed from the French army's judicial process which placed the ultimate decision in capital cases on the shoulders of the President of the Republic. However, the report of the Darling Committee, published in 1919, not only supported the existing system of military justice but also concluded that the commander-in-chief had acted properly and judiciously.[20] His role was central to the whole process and we must gain a firm grasp of this if we are to understand the workings of military discipline.

In 1924 Thurtle published *Shootings at Dawn*, his own account of the wartime military executions.[21] This collection of supposedly eyewitness accounts set the trend that others were to follow. Anonymous witnesses recalled the details of several executions. The style is anecdotal and little in the way of analysis is attempted. Of course to be fair to Thurtle his purpose was to shock the public and thereby bring about a change in the law. The successive horror stories certainly achieve their aim. An account of the execution of three members of the Durham Light Infantry is typical:

> A motor ambulance arrives conveying the doomed men. Manacled and blindfolded they are helped out and tied up to the stakes. Over each man's heart is placed an envelope. At the sign of command the firing parties, twelve to each, align their rifles on the envelopes. The officer in charge holds his stick aloft and as it falls thirty-six bullets usher the souls of three Kitchener's men to the great unknown. As a military prisoner I helped clear the traces of that triple murder. I took the posts down . . . I helped carry those bodies to their last resting place; I collected all the blood-soaked straw and burnt it. Acting upon police instructions I took all their belongings from the dead men's tunics (discarded before being shot). A few letters, a pipe, some fags, a photo. I could tell you of the silence of the military police after reading one letter from a little girl to 'Dear Daddy,' . . .[22]

The horror of an execution has been explicitly recalled. The purpose of the account is clear and it is highly effective.

Unfortunately for Thurtle, his reliance on eyewitness testimony and liberal use of hearsay evidence together with the unavailability of official records has resulted in a document with many more than the usual problems. Many of the events described in *Shootings at Dawn* contain factual errors. Furthermore, the language is often over-emotive: references to shootings or murders in cold blood abound – a deliberate literary strategy to manipulate the reader's emotions. Even Thurtle's statistics are incorrect: he cites a total of 264 executions.[23] Rather than being an account of the executions carried out during the First World War, it would be more accurate to regard *Shootings at Dawn* as evidence of the impact executions had on morale and on certain parts of British society.

The unavailability of official records, which were closed to the public for seventy-five years, also hampered William Moore's 1974 publication *The Thin Yellow Line*.[24] Most of the book is concerned with exploring the military and medical responses to fear and cowardice. Executions were dealt with in this context. Not surprisingly, the result was an interesting appraisal of the main topic but an altogether unsatisfactory account of courts-martial that could only hint at the impact of executions and death sentences in the British Army, without making very much sense of them. However, a useful comparison was made with the justice system employed by other armies. This clearly showed that the British Army was far more frequent than were the armies of France and Germany in its use of the firing squad to maintain discipline. These comparisons were themselves hindered by the absence of official records of French or German executions. The French records, rather like the British, were closed to public scrutiny and the German records had apparently been destroyed in World War II. Nevertheless, Moore was able to make use of secondary accounts such as Guy Pedroncini's study of the French mutinies of 1917.[25]

Without the benefit of access to official records, Moore's book disappoints as far as executions are concerned, but the simple comparisons with other armies pointed the way forward. Most revealing is the short section on the United States Army, which was the only army to make a medical examination a legal requirement in capital cases. Before a sentence of death could be carried out a second opinion about the condemned man also had to be sought. Unfortunately, Moore does not analyse why such a different and seemingly enlightened approach existed only in the American army, and the apparently lower number of executions in the French and German armies are not sufficiently explained.

In 1981 Judge Anthony Babington was granted access to the still-closed files of the Judge Advocate General, including all the proceedings relating to the executed soldiers. The result was *For the Sake of Example*, first published in 1983. It is the first comprehensive study of military executions during the war and, as one might expect from a judge, the focus is firmly on the legality and justice accorded these men by the courts martial. However, his claim in the preface to the second edition that his work is 'a definitive study of the capital courts martial in the British Army during the First World War'[26] is not realised. Babington provides a useful narrative of the executions and of Thurtle's role in the abolition but little in the way of analysis. His comparisons between the various armies achieve little more than Moore had a decade earlier.

One of the conditions upon which Babington was granted access to the files was that he did not divulge the identities of any of the executed men. Consequently, names of individuals are not revealed nor is the identity of the units concerned. This appears to have seriously handicapped the work: references to the fighting experience of units and the circumstances of alleged offences are vague. Judge Babington, naturally, concentrates on the judicial process. In so doing he neglects to contextualise the cases and the relationship between morale and discipline is not sufficiently explored. *For the Sake of Example* follows the tradition started by Thurtle in focusing on justice in the courts martial and provides a link between Thurtle's politically motivated attack on the Army and the current media campaign for parliamentary pardons for those shot by British firing squads. Considering the unique access to files granted to Babington, his book is a disappointment.

Babington's later book, *Shell-Shock: A History of the Changing Attitudes to War Neuroses*,[27] is an ambitious attempt to explore the condition from ancient times to the present day. The most important section concerns the First World War. Here, Babington discusses many of the same cases that he dealt with in *For the Sake of Example* but, as the title implies, they are set into the context of the military and medical reaction to the condition. This makes for a much more satisfactory account of these cases, but it does not match the more erudite studies of the condition by Eric Leed and Martin Stone.[28] The latter is an invaluable aid to understanding the social and cultural as well as military significance of 'shell-shock' during the First World War. Nor does Babington's work come close to the original theses of Peter Lynch (1977) and Peter Leese (1989).[29] Surprisingly, Babington does not refer to any of these works, nor are they contained in his bibliography. The condition known as shell-shock was a factor in determining the approach to discipline in the army. It was also a factor in many of the capital trials. The Army's reluctance to accept the condition as a genuine one no doubt affected the outcome of many cases. The relationship between the condition and the death penalty needs to be explored, but Babington's work provides little of use here.

A far more incisive account appeared in *The Unknown Army* by Douglas Gill and Gloden Dallas in 1985.[30] Their examination of the working class and the British Army showed that there was more resistance to military authority than had previously been revealed. However, dissent had been spontaneous. Political and pacifist movements had made few inroads into the army. In this respect the authors reflected the earlier argument advanced by David Englander and James Osbourne.[31] Gill and Dallas were able to show how the death penalty, or the threat of it, was used by the British High Command to instil obedience to its will. An essential feature of this process was the reading out on parade of the names of executed soldiers, as recorded in General Routine Orders, to deter would-be deserters. Reactions to this practice varied. In particular, it seems the Australians, who were exempt from the death penalty, were appalled by the harsh treatment meted out to British soldiers while some German commanders appear to have been envious of the extent of their British counterparts' power. This became an essential feature of the 'stab in the back' legend after the war, whereby during the inter-war period German military commanders and politicians on the right (including Hitler) claimed that the German Army's effectiveness had been undermined by politicians at home. But could the military authorities inculcate in their men a blind obedience on threat of death alone? I will argue that it could not. Most armies developed alternative strategies, and while the threat of the death penalty was a potent weapon in securing the obedience of the men it was not the only one. The citizen armies of France and Germany differed markedly from the British, but by the end of the war even the British Army had come to realise that it needed to gain and maintain the *consent* of the troops if it was to continue fighting the war.

The identities of all the executed soldiers were finally revealed six years after *For the Sake of Example* first appeared. Julian Putkowski and Julian Sykes, the authors of *Shot at Dawn*,[32] had put names to each capital case even though the records had still not been opened to public scrutiny because of the seventy-five-year rule. As a result, references to individuals and their units were more specific and greater analysis was possible. Extensive appendices, the result of meticulous research, provided vital statistical data of the ages of those executed, their units, dates and locations. Comparisons between units, theatres of the war and the various phases of the war were now possible. Reliance on sources other than official records resulted in some errors. Many of these were corrected in the revised edition, published in 1992, and an updated edition is due in 2003. However, the authors' main concern remained that of justice. Included in the first edition was a call for 'the exoneration of all those who fell victim to British Army firing squads during the First World War'; it was repeated in a statement in the revised edition.[33] It appears likely that the publication of *Shot at Dawn* has been a major factor in the campaign for parliamentary pardons for all capital cases, which resulted in a review by the Blair government in 1998.

Part of the legacy of the work of Babington, Putkowski and Sykes has been the inclusion of references to executions in general histories of World War I. There are few references to executions in the British Army to be found in general histories published prior to 1989, when Putkowski and Sykes first revealed the identities of the condemned men.[34] This has now changed and historians such as Martin Gilbert and John Bourne have considered the executions sufficiently important to be included in their works.[35] Unfortunately, the former appears to have drawn his material entirely from the works of Babington, Putkowski and Sykes, with the result that his references have not done justice to the subject matter. The analysis remains superficial and the only attempt at an explanation is to quote one soldier who stated 'I cannot stand it'.[36] The inclusion of a map in Gilbert's *Atlas of the First World War* showing the home towns of 20 executed men is even more puzzling.[37] Bourne's reference, although brief, considers the impact of the threat of execution on soldiers in an incisive and succinct manner. He highlights the impact of the influx of millions of civilians, adding that 'there was neither a real understanding of its [the Regular army] values nor a desire to share them'. The army's sociology and long-established methods of operation, he argues, faced the threat of revolutionary change.[38] The death penalty and other disciplinary practices, I will show, eventually became victims of this force for change.

For the historian, the true value of *Shot at Dawn* probably lies in the possibilities that it opened up. The extensive amount of data contained in

Putkowski and Sykes's publication formed the basis for part of my own statistical analysis of the British executions. From this base I extended the research to include all the death sentences passed by courts martial during the war whether or not they resulted in an execution.[39] This 'wider' study produced some surprising results. Firstly, the performance of all the commanders-in-chief in the various theatres of the war remained remarkably consistent: approximately 10 per cent of the cases referred to each of them were confirmed. Most importantly, this percentage also remained consistent when viewed in the context of the country of origin for each unit. Men sentenced to death from English, Scots, Welsh, Irish, Canadian and South African units all stood a one in ten chance of having their sentences confirmed by the commander-in-chief. The exceptions to this were the Australians, whose own regulations practically forbade executions, and New Zealanders, who were more than twice as likely to have their sentences confirmed. When viewed together, men serving with ANZAC units fared the same as others. It appears that New Zealanders paid the price of Australian immunity from execution.[40] The consistency achieved in the imposition of the death penalty warrants further attention. It is argued in this study that the proportion of one execution in every ten condemnations was no coincidence, but rather a managed figure which it was believed would achieve its military purpose – deterrence – without appearing excessively harsh. This last consideration was most important because, it will be argued, the military authorities needed to retain the support of politicians and troops alike. The army did not want to have its power to discipline its men compromised by political interference, nor could it afford to lose the consent of the troops. This, therefore, casts some doubt on the generally held belief that the commander-in-chief (C-in-C) was personally responsible for confirming sentences. Although nominally the role of the C-in-C, it is highly unlikely that he could devote the amount of time necessary to review each case, let alone maintain a ratio of one execution in every ten condemnations.

Some of these ideas were developed in the published version of my thesis, which appeared in 1998.[41] Particular reference was made to the influence of pre-war attitudes and beliefs concerning 'race' and degeneration. The research indicated that Irish soldiers were statistically more likely to be sentenced to death than were other soldiers. This was explained in the context of concerns about the quality of the Irish 'race'. Although considered natural warriors, especially during the time of the Boer War, by 1914 concerns about Irish loyalty had reactivated nineteenth-century ideas of Anglo-Saxonism over supposed Celtic inferiority and indiscipline. The war in South Africa had also focused attention on the physical quality of British recruits and this in turn had given additional stimulus to the eugenics movement. I have argued that while the disproportionate condemnations of Irish soldiers merely reflects a more general British concern about the Irish, the influence of eugenics is often explicit. During the process of reviewing death sentences and making recommendations senior officers' concerns about degeneracy *could* be a crucial factor.[42]

Interestingly, it has been argued elsewhere that these same groups, the Irish and the degenerate, were widely believed to be predisposed to suffering from the condition known as shell-shock. In peacetime these 'outsiders' were considered abnormal and as such were often deemed to be a threat to society. During the war, it has been argued, this was considered a threat to military efficiency and discipline.[43] Timothy Bowman has also shown how Irish troops were tried by courts martial more often than were other soldiers in the British Army. Although most cases were relatively minor infractions of discipline such as drunkenness and absence, Bowman has also suggested that concerns about the loyalty of the Irish units lingered throughout the war even though the evidence suggests that these fears were unfounded.[44]

Studies of the Dominion armies under British command have also taken account of the question of discipline and the death penalty. Principal among these are Christopher Pugsley's study of discipline in the New Zealand Division, *On the Fringe of Hell,* and a number of studies about the Canadian Corps by Desmond Morton.[45] A key feature of these works is the analysis of the relationship between the Dominion unit and the *British* command as well as other units in the army. Pugsley has shown that the use of the death penalty against New Zealand soldiers, including two Australian nationals, was more frequent than for other soldiers in the army commensurate with the number of condemnations; a conclusion supported by my own research (see above). Pugsley focuses particular attention on the role of the commander of the New Zealand Division, Russell. Pugsley argues that it was he who was responsible for the harsh code of discipline imposed on the New Zealanders, and that the excessive zeal shown by the courts martial, staffed by New Zealand officers, was actually moderated by the British High Command. The death penalty became an instrument by which Russell sought to rid the New Zealand Division of the ' "incorrigibles", the 10 per cent of his New Zealanders who were always in trouble'.[46] Pugsley's central argument is that the harsh approach resulted in the emergence of the New Zealand Division as a highly disciplined and efficient fighting force, arguably the most effective unit in the British Army by the end of the war.[47]

Morton's work on the other hand conforms more closely to the 'British' pattern of anecdotal narratives that tend to pose questions rather than providing answers. This is a pity for in the Canadian Corps there was an easily identifiable minority: French-speaking Canadians. Morton quite correctly identifies that the number of French-Canadian soldiers sentenced to death by British courts martial was disproportionately high. But he makes little attempt at an explanation beyond the reaction of Lieutenant-Colonel Thomas Tremblay, the commander of 22nd Battalion, who insisted on five executions to purge his unit of 'tramps and ne'er-do-wells'.[48] The war effort had never been well supported by French-speaking

Canadians and recruitment was particularly poor among that section of the population. Those who were recruited were concentrated into two battalions, 22nd and 14th. These two battalions alone account for 36 of the 222 death sentences against soldiers of the Canadian Expeditionary Force's 258 battalions. This is an aspect that warrants further study and a more considered explanation.

What the works of Pugsley and Morton do have in common is that both authors assess the use of the death penalty within the wider context of an increasing sense, on the part of the respective Dominions armies, of independence from British control. Morton finds it paradoxical that 'in a period when Canadians were expanding their autonomy in many other areas of military administration and authority, there seems to have been no question of the right of a British Commander-in-Chief to order the execution of Canadians'.[49] His conclusion that the Canadian authorities were satisfied with the situation is not borne out by other developments, namely the insistence on Canadian officers being present at Canadian courts martial. It seems more likely that the Canadians did not entirely trust the British and that what eventually emerged amounted to a compromise. By the time of the Second World War Canadians were no longer under the jurisdiction of the British commander, which is hardly indicative of complete satisfaction with the previous arrangement.

Morton does, however, make the very astute observation that 'the avowed purpose of military law is not to do absolute justice to the individual but to maintain discipline'.[50] In this brief statement he sums up the main problem with many of the works discussed here. The impact of the death penalty needs to be measured by its effect on groups, not just individuals. That is not to suggest that the concerns about injustices are irrelevant, for the impact on morale, *esprit de corps* and unit esteem need to be analysed. The fear and pity, not to mention shame, felt by the comrades of men executed by firing squad has never been fully explained by historians. Significantly, this aspect of military discipline, often present in the papers of rank-and-file soldiers, is usually absent from senior officers' published memoirs.

If concerns about apparent injustices have dominated most accounts of British executions then the influence of these concerns has been less noticeable in studies of executions in the other armies. Studies of the French Army tend to focus on the mutinies of 1917. As a consequence there is a greater emphasis on the political rather than the judicial significance of executions. Guy Pedroncini's study of the 1917 mutinies was concerned with the judicial process, but the context remained a political one.[51] Pedroncini was mainly concerned with the rehabilitation of the reputation of Pétain and the mutinies of 1917 provided an ideal platform for this. Pétain's understanding of war and of soldiers, Pedroncini argues, enabled him to reassert control over the army by introducing sensible reforms and improving morale without merely giving in to the mutineers' demands.[52]

The execution of so-called leaders of the mutiny is symbolic of Pétain's command of an army that was otherwise degenerating towards anarchy.

Pedroncini compiled statistics from the *Archives de la Justice Militaire* which suggest that 49 executions followed the mutinies of 1917. Prior to that it appears that the execution of approximately seven *poilus* each month was typical.[53] This may seem a lot, but it is far lower than the British total. With a far larger army than the British, the reputation for harshness acquired by the French upon comparison appears unfounded. The introduction in 1916 of a right of appeal to the President was never matched by a similar development in the British Army (although something like it did exist in the American Army on its entry into the war in 1917). This is indicative of a political dimension to the use of the death penalty in the French Army.

Leonard Smith further developed the 'political' theme. Smith has explored the nature of the relationship between the rank and file, their officers and the High Command against the background of the social and political concerns of 1917. The result is a highly compelling and incisive argument that the parameters in the 'power-relationship' were in a state of constant change. The balance of that relationship shifted throughout the war in favour of the *poilus*, so much so that the nature of discipline itself can be regarded as negotiable to a certain extent. So too it seems was the conduct of the war after 1917 when Pétain, the new Commander-in-Chief, temporarily abandoned the large-scale offensives. In return, Smith argues, the *poilus* accepted a limited number of executions of their own number.[54]

Forty-nine men were selected for execution from the original number of 554 death sentences following the mutinies of 1917. These were 'token' displays of authority. So-called leaders were selected, tried and sentenced by *conseils de guerre*. The identification of the 'leaders' of the mutinies, those destined to pay the price of the mutiny and, therefore, of the concessions gained, raises interesting points. Military courts convicted approximately 10 per cent of the 40,000 mutineers, with 554 receiving death sentences. Most of these were subsequently commuted but the selection of 49 *poilus* for execution does not appear to have been entirely arbitrary.[55] According to Smith the 'leaders' were variously selected for their 'poor spirit', poor antecedents or because they were intelligent. Another, it seems, was selected merely because he was a local man.[56] The implication is that unit commanders took advantage of the opportunity to remove unwanted men as well as any that they found difficult to deal with, such as those identified as 'intelligent'. Selection was far from random.

The absence of any real opposition to these 'token' executions, Smith argues, amounts to a tacit approval by the 'citizen-soldiers' of the reassertion of discipline by the commander-in-chief. The 'political' relationship was, therefore, a two-way arrangement. The executions amounted to a symbolic gesture of reinstated control of the army. In return, many of the *poilus'* grievances were addressed: the High Command acquiesced on the issues of extra leave, rations and the abandonment of the costly large offensives. In this respect, Smith argues, it was the *poilus* who manipulated the course of the negotiations, not Pétain who remained 'more reactive than active, in a situation he never fundamentally controlled'.[57] It is on this point of Pétain's command of the situation, and by implication of the army, that Smith most seriously deviates from Pedroncini's argument. Smith asserts that 'the courts martial served to display the theoretically (and only theoretically) absolute power of the command structure'.[58]

Smith and Pedroncini do agree that there is little evidence that the mutinies were the result of outside political subversion. The demands of the mutineers reflected tangible concerns about their immediate welfare and that of their families. It was the frustration of unrealistic expectations, particularly the hopes raised by Nivelle's over-confident claims, rather than doctrinaire idealism, that ignited what was essentially a spontaneous though highly infectious mutiny involving large sections of the French Army.

Pedroncini has tabulated the occupations and trades of the convicted men.[59] The results are reflective of an army conscripted from within a society which was still largely agrarian. Farmers and labourers are the most common 'trade' while craftsmen and artisans make up the majority of the remainder. Smith concurs with Pedroncini's statistics adding that a mere 10 per cent were industrial workers, 'using the most generous definition'.[60] Social elites and the bourgeoisie are absent. This suggests that the discipline and its enforcement by the elite in the French Army might have reflected peacetime class divisions and tensions. According to David Englander the 'iron' nature of discipline did nothing to enhance officer–men relations and *poilus* resented the continuance of authority of the 'bosses in uniform' drawn almost exclusively from the upper and middle classes.[61] In this context it is surprising that there was seemingly little opposition to the ultimate statement of authority, namely the executions that followed the mutiny. Smith does not adequately deal with this aspect and it is conceivable that the *poilus* were less in control than he asserts.

There are limitations in Smith's work. Most significantly, the study is limited to the 5th Infantry Division which Smith admits was not typical of the French Army as a whole. Beyond the presentation of statistical data, there is little in the way of comparisons with other French divisions and only limited reference, mainly in the conclusion, to the armies of the other belligerents. However, his assertion that the *poilu* was unique is interesting. As a 'citizen-soldier', Smith argues, the *poilu* had more in common with soldiers in Bolshevik Russia than with the 'subject-soldiers' of Britain and Germany.

Nicholas Offenstadt has examined the executions and their relationship with collective memory of the Great War. He regards the campaign for pardons essentially as a matter of how the war is remembered in Britain and France. He also considers the absence of a similar campaign in Germany in the same context. Given unrestricted access to sensitive military records and drawing from works published in each country, Offenstadt found that eugenics might also have been a factor in French army executions. 'La thèse d'Oram', he states with reference to *Worthless Men*, 'trouve quelques éléments de confirmation dans l'armée française.'[62]

Comparative assessments such as this are surprisingly rare. Another recent one compares desertion in the British and German armies.[63] The author, Christoph Jahr, is dismissive of the military perspective of morale and discipline which, he argues, is impossible to quantify or define. Instead he prefers a social and cultural approach that contrasts the traditions and practices of the German and British armies, arguing that one of the reasons for the lower number of German executions in comparison to British ones lay in fundamental differences in the respective legislation.[64] German military law required a high degree of proof to sustain a conviction for desertion and there were many acquittals. In the British Army on the other hand desertion was relatively simple to prove, often being preferred to a charge of cowardice for that reason. Very few British soldiers were acquitted of desertion, or any other offence for that matter. German soldiers it seems had more rights than their British counterparts and prosecutions were seldom attempted in the German Army as a consequence. This feature of military justice needs to be examined within a wider comparative framework. Was comparative harshness, for instance, present only in the military code or was there a parallel in English criminal law? If so, why should this be the case in a country that considered itself to be the most progressive of nations?

The lack of comparative histories leaves a gap in our understanding of the power-relationship, as Smith would put it, or even of officer–men relations of which discipline was a crucial factor. Inflicting the death penalty was the ultimate statement of authority and control. Its use was designed to ensure compliance by the rankers to the will of the commanders. In the British Army at least, this message was often reinforced by compelling the condemned man's own comrades to deliver the fatal volley. Every major army of the First World War used the death penalty (if one accepts that the Australians were a component part of the British Army and not a separate force). Yet there were many differences in their traditions, laws and practices. For example, a simple act of desertion was not a capital offence in the French military code. Only the offence of abandoning a post in the face of the enemy (similar to the British offence of cowardice in the face of the enemy) had attracted a death sentence in the 5th Infantry Division before the mutiny of 1917.[65] This contrasts markedly with the British Army, where death sentences for desertion were frequent.[66] The similarities and differences between the military law of the respective armies have not yet been analysed in any great depth.

Accounts of British executions have been deficient simply because most authors have failed to recognise that military law was not as concerned with justice as it was with maintaining discipline. That is not to suggest that the apparent injustices are not important, because they are. Rumours of unjust executions did much to spread fear through the ranks. Ultimately, it was this fear that commanders hoped would ensure compliance from their troops. The death penalty was highly valued for this reason. Douglas Haig, for example, not only wished to retain the death penalty but also pressed unsuccessfully for its extension to the Australians under his command. The concerns expressed about injustices, together with the campaign to pardon those executed, have much to do with our present-day perception of the First World War and little to do with understanding discipline and morale in the trenches.

Contemporary observers understood this more clearly than have present-day writers. If justice alone was the purpose of military law then the final decision in capital cases would have been entrusted to a judicial figure, but this was never the case. The French, from early 1915, preferred a political figure to a military one and the final decision lay with the President of the Republic. In the British Army, where military concerns were considered paramount the decision remained with the commander-in-chief. In common with many other facets of wartime Britain, higher value was placed on winning the war than on individual rights or liberties. The overriding concern of courts martial was the state of discipline in the army. For evidence to support this view we need look no further than the report of the Darling Committee which concluded:

> In regard to sentences, we consider that, subject to the right to petition for clemency, the decision ought to be left, as at present, to the military authorities, who *alone* are in a position to form a correct judgement as to what sentences the state of discipline in the army, or in a particular force, requires [my italics].[67]

Discipline was considered to be *the* determinant factor in such matters and justice does not even warrant a mention. It is this fundamental point that has eluded so many writers.

The history of executions during World War I has been written in a style that reflects concerns that can also be detected during the war. French histories have conformed to the 'political' tradition whilst British studies have been dominated by concerns about apparent injustices, which originated with Thurtle's attack on the power of the commander-in-chief. As a result the current literature is extremely limited in its scope.

Military discipline was a complex issue and the simplistic view that soldiers were repressed by incompetent generals located far away from the front line is no longer good enough. Troops were able to negotiate, within certain parameters, their continued support. David Englander and Leonard Smith have emphasised this point – the latter perhaps overly – but most writers have missed it. The changing relationship between men, their leaders, repression and the death penalty requires further examination. One historian has recently suggested: 'If the men at the front had not somehow defined the war they were waging as their war also, it is doubtful whether sheer repression could have prevailed, because in such a case the total collapse of motivation would have flooded the dams of military justice.'[68]

In order to examine this it is first necessary to analyse the legal and cultural dimensions of army discipline which, as I have suggested, cannot be understood in military terms alone. This will provide us with an analytical framework in which comparisons can be drawn. The starting point of any study of military executions must surely be to locate their origins. These can be found, I will argue, not so much on the battlefields of the Western Front, but in the traditions (military, legal, cultural and social) of the respective armies. Why did the British Army value the death penalty so? How were ideas about discipline and morale shaped and where did they come from? How did these compare with practices and ideas in other armies and how did they alter over time? Military concerns and strategic considerations were only one part of this process – usually the final component. We need first to consider how the law was constructed and to understand contemporary ideas about discipline, deviance and obedience before we can examine the specifically military factors.

One final note of caution should be emphasised here. Not only can statistics be interpreted in a number of ways but also the relationship between discipline and punishment is extremely complex. The high incidence of punishments, including the death penalty, in any military formation does not necessarily indicate high levels of crime or indiscipline in that unit. In a study of the 48th Division – one of the formations examined closely in a later chapter – one historian has suggested that type of formation and rank were two factors that could affect the outcome. He also suggests – more cautiously – that relatively low levels of prosecutions and lenient sentencing in a particular unit (1/8 Battalion Royal Warwickshire regiment) indicated little in the way of disciplinary problems.[69]

With so little data available to the historian this can be a difficult area and the cautious approach is entirely justified. Yet this is a problem familiar to criminologists who have developed three different approaches to the historical study of criminal statistics: positivist, interactive and pessimist. The first holds to the belief that statistics do tell us something about levels of crime, the second that quantitative data tells us *something* about crime, but only in the context of the law and its enforcement, and the third that crime statistics are wholly unreliable and often manipulated.[70] Military crime does differ: it is normally victimless and is not usually reported by the public. Normally, it first comes to notice at the point of detection – when a man is missing from parade or an attack. Records are sketchy and tell us more about prosecutions than about offences committed, most of which were dealt with by extra-judicial means. It is difficult to see, therefore, how the quantitative data available can be interpreted in a positivist manner.

There is some evidence that statistics for military crime during the First World War were manipulated. In particular, the number of death sentences passed on Australian troops was highest in early 1917 – a time when senior commanders were pressing for the abolition of Section 98 of the Australian Defence Act, which forbade the execution of any member of the Australian forces.[71] This, it might be argued, was intended to put pressure on the Australian authorities by its implication of serious disciplinary problems in the Australian Imperial Force. Similar trends can be detected in other formations, particularly the 35th Division, which suffered a spate of condemnations and executions at the same time that concerns were raised about the 'low physical and moral standard of the infantry in this Division'.[72] One also has to question why in an army whose two commanders-in-chief were both cavalrymen there were only ten condemnations and no executions in the cavalry divisions. Some of the evidence does support a pessimist interpretation. But, broadly speaking, much of the analysis in the following chapters follows the interactive model and argues that the available statistical data tell us more about approaches to discipline (by the army or particular commanders) than about levels of offending.

1

'The administration of discipline by the English is very rigid': British Military Law and the Death Penalty 1868–1918

In a recent study of military discipline during the First World War David Englander rightly asserted that 'British and Belgian soldiers were more at risk [from capital punishment] than either their French or German counterparts'.[1] This contradicts both existing ideas on Prussian militarism and popular notions of French military justice – or more accurately injustice – such as those conveyed by Stanley Kubrick in his film *Paths of Glory*. A comparison of statistics on discipline in the British, French and German armies, the three main combatants on the Western Front between 1914 and 1918, supports Dr Englander: the British condemned more than three thousand men, compared with two thousand in the French army and only 150 in the German army.[2] Indeed, the comparative harshness of the British was especially marked in the case of deserters on the Western Front.[3] While it should be noted that the number of French soldiers executed (approximately 600[4]) exceeded that of the British army (officially 346, but probably many more[5]) the two remain comparable given the relative size of the armies. Only 48 of the 150 German soldiers condemned by military courts were shot. Putting aside for a moment the apparently more oppressive military regimes in Eastern Europe and the Italian army, which executed 750 men, the British soldier was especially vulnerable among those serving on the Western Front.

On the face of it the British Army was not beset by disciplinary problems any more than were the other major armies, yet no historian has adequately explained this striking difference. This is even more surprising given pervasive British attitudes of the time: Germany was castigated as authoritarian and militaristic and France was viewed from across the channel as decadent. The French army, so it appeared, was not immune from this and its collapse at Sedan was regarded by many in Britain as evidence of the moral degeneration of the French, a view seemingly confirmed by the chaos of the Paris Commune. Accordingly, when discipline in the French army collapsed in 1917, the British commander, Field-Marshal Sir Douglas Haig, emphasised what he considered the lack of 'moral qualities' in the French army as its major cause.[6] Paradoxically, German authoritarianism and militarism had,

18

according to some, been a major factor in securing the Prussian victory in 1871: British generals had a high regard for the discipline of the Prussian army if not their tactics.[7] Yet these continental armies exhibited more tolerance of their soldiers than the supposedly more progressive British. Paradoxically, therefore, it was in the country that believed it most espoused liberal values that military discipline appears to have taken on its harshest form.

None of this was lost on contemporary observers. In his diary Prince Rupprecht of Bavaria commented that:

> The administration of discipline by the English is very rigid. Whilst on our side there is known to me only a single case in which a soldier on account of aggravated refusal of duty in the face of the enemy was shot, I gather from a compilation of the British orders which have been found, that at least 67 English soldiers have been shot under martial law in the period between 27 October 1916 and 30 August 1917.[8]

This was an underestimate of British executions during that period, which actually numbered 81. Ludendorff famously recorded his envy of Douglas Haig's power over matters of discipline and punishment, estimating that the real loss to the German army in terms of manpower ran to tens of thousands.[9] Indeed, that entry in his memoirs, published in 1929, reflected a variation in the stab-in-the-back legend, widely held by former military commanders, that Germany's comparative leniency had cost her victory.[10]

However, the old-fashioned view that British disciplinary harshness was attributable to an oppressive and ultimately incompetent High Command will no longer do. British commanders, like their German and French equivalents, worked within a disciplinary and judicial framework inherited from the nineteenth century.[11] For too long historians have ignored this inheritance, most especially the influence of the parent societies of armies: military discipline, law and organisation should be related to the parent societies. It is no longer sufficient to separate military law from the criminal code as if it had developed organically, isolated from contemporary views on criminal behaviour, deviance, punishments and penal policy. It is the development of the respective military codes, the context for military discipline and punishments during the First World War, which must now be analysed.

In this chapter we will discuss the evolution of British military law from the mid-nineteenth century to the outbreak of war in 1914, within the wider context of military law in other European countries, in particular that of the French and German armies, and America. It will be shown how the variations in numbers of capital punishments inflicted by each army between 1914 and 1918 reflected military traditions and pre-existing social structures as well as more general concerns about crime, punishment and control of the army. It will also be shown that in terms of its military code, far from being progressive, Britain lagged behind its continental equivalents in key areas. The process by which men were selected for execution is analysed in a later chapter. Here we must focus on the role played by the lawmakers in the history of British military executions. British military law was surprisingly stagnant during the war years, but other belligerent countries – most significantly Germany – modified their codes, suggesting once again that Britain was relatively less progressive.

The judiciousness of the respective military codes often reflected the status ascribed by societies to both the army and to soldiering as a profession. This in turn was greatly influenced by the traditional method of recruitment.[12] In Britain in particular obedience was often deemed to be attainable only through traditional concepts of punishment based on fear and deterrence. Indeed, an over-reliance on this type of control meant that, come the Great War – by which time corporal punishment had been abolished – senior commanders all too readily fell back on capital punishment as the sole means of maintaining discipline, rather than exploring alternatives.

Background

The harsh nature of military discipline in Britain owed much to tradition. The earliest armies were regulated by Articles of War issued on the prerogative of the Crown and valid only for the duration of any given conflict. This power, introduced by William I, was not superseded until the nineteenth century. But if military law seemingly became more the concern of parliament than of the Sovereign, the Crown was still able to exert considerable influence in this area, playing the 'apolitical' card to great effect – the army shared with the Crown a (mythical) status that supposedly transcended politics. The nature of these earlier Articles was pejoratively described in a military manual of 1914 as being 'of excessive severity, inflicting death or loss of limb for almost every crime'.[13] Ironically, a certain amount of this severity was to return in the years that followed.

The peacetime army – thanks to the British aversion to a standing army – originating during the late seventeenth century,[14] did not exist in a modern sense and no regulations were thought necessary beyond what was covered by criminal and civil law. This changed, however, shortly after the so-called Glorious Revolution whereupon the Mutiny Act was passed in 1689. The object of this annually renewable act, which made mutiny and desertion a capital offence, remained largely unchanged until 1878. It did, however, undergo a series of refinements, each reflecting the circumstances of the time. The Act, often allowed to lapse during times of peace, was frequently reintroduced, usually with an extension of its jurisdiction to include overseas territories as the army's garrison duties expanded around the globe. The Mutiny Act finally superseded the prerogative power to make Articles of War towards the end of the Peninsular War in 1813 and remained in force, largely unaltered until the First World War, despite ongoing debates about the nature and origins of military crime during the early nineteenth century.[15]

Increasingly concerned by what it perceived as a drunkenness problem in the army the British government ordered an inquiry into military discipline in March 1868 under the tutelage of the Right Honourable John Wilson Patten MP, colonel of the Royal Lancashire Militia. It is clear from the evidence, however, that the Committee was uncertain about how to maintain discipline and control of the army in the event of the abolition of corporal punishment. Flogging (the usual nomenclature) had been partially abolished in 1867 following the death of Private Robert Slim from such punishment,[16] but it remained available as a punishment during peacetime for crimes of mutiny or insubordination involving violence, and during wartime it was extended to cover desertion and even drunkenness. For a decade the army used flogging sparingly, but its re-emergence as a common punishment in Zululand in 1879 attracted the attention of Liberal politicians, including Gladstone, who rejected the 'necessary deterrent' argument and denounced the practice as anachronistic. The number of lashes was initially reduced by Parliament before its final abolition in 1881.[17]

The shift away from traditional style punishments such as flogging during the late 1860s reflected a similar trend favouring a more progressive penal policy, which, aided by a statistical reduction in the crime rate, can also be detected in the criminal code.[18] Public whippings for criminal offences had been abolished in 1862 and the last public execution was carried out in 1868, largely thanks to growing public disquiet at the effects on society of such punishments.[19] The effects on offenders were, however, of less concern and in the 1860s penal policy did assume a harsher character once again, especially with the introduction of the draconian 'Garotters' Act 1863, which allowed for the administration of up to fifty lashes on prisoners convicted of violent offences. This was partly a response to the virtual end of transportation in the 1850s and a corresponding perceived rise in violent crime.[20] Britain was the last Western European country to cling to whipping as a punishment and in both the criminal and military codes we must look to Eastern Europe to find parallels. The number of floggings in English local prisons remained fairly constant (approximately 155 per annum) during the late nineteenth century, although a significant reduction was noted in 1894.[21] There was considerable concern about the number of corporal punishments and it was becoming increasingly clear to British military observers that the days of flogging in the army were also numbered. But concerns about how to control unruly soldiers closely mirrored the fears aroused by the end of transportation – pundits believed, after all, that most troops were drawn from that same criminal class. The need to find a suitable alternative became the focus of the subsequent report.

The report, published in two parts during 1869,[22] set in motion a process of yet further inquiry and eventually reform, culminating in the annually renewable Army Act of 1881 – the basis for the regulation of the British, Dominion and Empire armies during the Great War. This process coincided not only with the changing attitude towards crime and punishment, but also with a growing realisation among military pundits that the changing nature of warfare would necessitate an enlargement of the army, control of which became a serious concern. Although the report provides a unique insight into perceptions about army recruits, discipline and punishment in Victorian Britain, it has received little attention from historians. Before arriving at its conclusions the Committee examined military law in other countries, including France and Prussia, and while this evidence tells us more about how the British Army viewed its continental neighbours, it remains a useful starting point for a comparison of military codes across Europe.

Inquiry and reform 1865–81

The various European military codes had much in common. Nowhere was the final arbiter of military justice a judicial or legal appointee. In some countries (Britain, Austria-Hungary, Italy) the commander-in-chief of the army performed this function during wartime. In others, France for example, the head of state theoretically held this position. Of course in some cases (Russia, Prussia) the head of state was also the commander-in-chief of the army, making such distinctions superfluous. This had important implications in Britain where the role of the Judge Advocate General (JAG), who oversaw the process of military justice, had come under considerable scrutiny in the mid-nineteenth century. Army commanders had become increasingly concerned at the growing influence of the JAG and saw a threat to their authority if judicial considerations were given priority over disciplinary ones.[23] This too was common in other European armies. In Russia, for example, a Judge Advocate (*procureur militaire*) attended courts martial to prosecute only and did not act in a judicial capacity.[24] Typically, in the late nineteenth-century Habsburg army, where courts were composed of representatives of all ranks – an exceptional practice not continued after the turn of the century – a *Militärauditor*, who was a qualified lawyer, performed a range of legal tasks, but could only make recommendations to the *military* judges. According to one historian 'the [Habsburg] army managed to prevent any serious tampering with its [judicial] privileges'.[25] This reflected practices in almost every other European army. The role of non-military persons or departments was invariably restricted to purely administrative duties. Nowhere did these civil servants wrest a modicum of judicial authority from the military no matter how well qualified they were.[26]

The British Army always resisted any suggestion of political interference. Invariably, this was cloaked in the notion of the army's apolitical status, but in reality it amounted to a rejection of external control. The army's judicial processes were not immune from this. For instance, Lord Wolseley (Commander-in-Chief 1895–1900) 'repudiated the idea of civil rights for soldiers as essentially mischievous and misconceived'.[27] Wolseley's successor, Lord Roberts, faced accusations of exercising 'despotic power' by removing Colonel Kinlock from his command of the 1st Battalion, Grenadier Guards, in a way that had circumvented the normal rules of procedure. It was not, the Duke of Bedford told the Upper Chamber on 28 April 1903, merely 'a matter of military law or military procedure. It is a question of the infringement of the provisions of an Act of Parliament'.[28] But political interference, from whatever quarter, was invariably resisted to preserve the Army's putative independence. As Lord Harris retorted one week later:

> The whole object of the authority which is given to the commander-in-chief, and to commanders of units, will, it seems to me, be imperilled if noble Lords [such as Bedford] are encouraged to take the opportunity of membership of this House to call in question the decisions of the commander-in-chief on military matters.[29]

By 1914 the disciplinary power of the commander-in-chief remained unalloyed, having survived threats from lawyers and politicians alike.

Other similarities between European armies included a hierarchical system of courts martial with varying jurisdiction. Officers were normally only tried by the highest form of military court. However, in Italy there was no permanent court with jurisdiction to try officers, reflecting the rarity of such trials. This casts some doubt on the principle enshrined in the code that the 'private and general are equal before the court-martial'.[30] It was also universally accepted that judicial procedure gave way to military expediency during wartime when it was usual for courts, often known as drum-head courts, to be convened in the field.[31]

Courts martial in the Habsburg army operated on a three-tier system with the second and third tiers acting as a court of appeal and a supreme court of appeal respectively. The uppermost court did not possess any power to increase sentences, but acted purely as a safety valve. Prisoners did have a right to make any 'reasonable objection' to members of the tribunal – a provision also available to British troops.[32] The court was also obliged to provide an interpreter if proceedings were not held in the language spoken by the accused. This reflected the sort of problems faced by the multi-ethnic army, but masks the racial aspect of discipline in the Habsburg army during the war. Attempts to 'Germanise' the Austro-Hungarian army in the reforms of 1912 revealed deep-seated mistrust of other troops, particularly ethnic Serbs and Croats who tended to experience a harsher form of discipline in much the same way as Poles in the German army suffered most from military authorities.[33] Sentences passed by Austro-Hungarian courts were announced with much ceremony. Usually, the president would draw his sword and trumpeters sounded a call three times. If a sentence of death was promulgated then the president was expected to break a staff in front of the condemned man. This was usually done away with during times of war when military expediency took over and the military code allowed for individuals to 'be tried at once by "drum-head" court-martial, and the sentence carried out on the spot'. The importance of ritual, including its special significance for military executions, has been explored by Michel Foucault. According to Foucault, it was through ceremony that authority manifested itself. The formal ceremony might on occasion be dispensed with, but the ritual of the firing squad remained a spectacle.

Interestingly, the Austrian code allowed for decimation, that is 'death by shooting, inflicted on every tenth man by lot'.[34] Russian courts martial were also hierarchical, but appeal – directly to the Emperor – was only allowed on grounds of illegality. During wartime sweeping powers were granted to the commander-in-chief 'for the purpose of facilitating the administration of justice in cases of necessity'.[35] One such measure adopted by the Russian Army during the war was the reintroduction of flogging in 1915. This, according to a survey of mail censorship, caused deep resentment among the troops.[36]

The Italian military code was passed in 1869 and was based on its Sardinian predecessor (1840). It was particularly harsh, particularly with its very broad definition of desertion. During the First World War, Cadorna, the Italian Commander-in-Chief, made ample use of this in imposing a brutal disciplinary regime on his troops.[37] Military crimes, which included desertion and insubordination, were punishable by being shot *in front,* but so-called 'dishonourable' crimes such as treason or murder were punishable by being shot *in the back.* Sentences were normally carried out within twenty-four hours, but sentences passed by extraordinary drum-head courts – including death sentences – were carried out summarily and *'ad modum belli'.*[38] This allowed Cadorna to apply strict discipline from the moment of Italy's entry to the war. In July 1915 he warned that 'every soldier . . . must be convinced that his superior has the sacred duty to shoot all cowards and recalcitrants immediately'.[39] This was not an empty threat and during the war a total of 4028 men were condemned with 750 executed.[40] Summary executions were not uncommon, especially after Caporetto, and Cadorna resorted to sacking generals (217 of them) and decimation among the troops.[41]

Despite the common heritage of much European law – not to mention military tradition – differences did exist and these often reflected the parent society. British observers reported, with apparent envy, on the French system which allowed for the removal of the persistent offender into a *compagnie de discipline* and the reputed bad character into light infantry units in Algeria 'so that he may not taint his old comrades by going back into their ranks'.[42] This aspect of French military justice, enshrined in the 1857 code, reflected the concept of the 'dangerous classes' familiar to those concerned with national security in France since 1840. This is now most usually associated with the period of the Paris Commune when police and army alike were fearful of 'an uncontrollable and destructive rising of the "lower depths" '.[43] Control of the army in such circumstances was understandably considered crucial, and the military code allowed for the swift removal of soldiers who fell into this category. Extensive use was made of this provision and executions were certainly not unheard of during the revolutionary decades in the middle of the nineteenth century: 84 men were executed between 1833 and 1851. Significantly, most of these executions occurred in units in North Africa. On the other hand about a third of French courts martial resulted in acquittals[44] – a rare finding in the British army.[45]

The British army possessed some experience of penal battalions, but it had not been good. For a period of ten years beginning in 1816 commanders could send troublesome individuals to serve in so-called 'condemned corps'. These were located in unhealthy locations such as West Africa where disease was rife and such a posting was tantamount to a death sentence. Concerns about the inhumanity of the practice led to it being abandoned in 1826 in favour of transportation. There was a growing feeling, however, that transportation was increasingly seen as rewarding offenders rather than as punishment. It was abandoned in 1857 and penal servitude introduced.[46]

The severity of the Prussian code was viewed with some envy from Horse Guards. Undoubtedly there was a genuine regard for Prussian-style discipline, but it is also likely that Prussian military prowess during the 1860s had boosted the army's reputation. This admiration increased after the Franco-Prussian War when the draconian Prussian code was contrasted with the lenient French code, seemingly confirming the view that linked military efficiency to strict discipline. The British military attaché responsible for the compilation of the report on the Prussian code was impressed by the sentence of 'loss of nobility' and all that it implied. He was equally impressed with the power granted to commanders summarily to inflict corporal punishments and the life-long disgrace that went with dismissal from the army.[47] Indeed, notions of honour pervaded the Prussian code and only executions for military offences were performed by the honourable method of a firing squad. Otherwise, death was inflicted by beheading.

Such comparisons and the envy they provoked in British military observers took no account of the differences in attitude towards the army in each society. In Prussia soldiering was considered a noble and worthy profession – hence the disgrace resulting from dismissal from the army. The French Army inherited much of its identity from its revolutionary and Napoleonic predecessors: the *poilu* was ideally an 'Intelligent Bayonet' – a concept partly formed from a reaction against so-called Prussian automata – and the State assumed a paternal responsibility towards those it compelled to serve in the ranks.[48] In Britain the difference could not be more marked.

Far from being an honourable profession, soldiering was considered worthless by most classes, but most especially among the working class who regarded the army as a refuge for drunkards and criminals rather than a respectable trade. Hunger was the most effective of recruiting-sergeants and it was no coincidence that the Irish disproportionately filled the ranks even of nominally English regiments.[49] The Duke of Wellington's comments that 'the French system of conscription brings together a fair sample of all classes; ours is composed of the scum of the earth – the mere scum of the earth'[50] remained equally relevant at the end of the century.

The resentment felt by some towards the army was magnified by the deployment of the military during the industrial disputes before the First World War, particularly following the shooting at Featherstone colliery in 1893 and again in 1911, when soldiers shot dead two protesters at Llanelli. This latter incident enlivened the subsequent debate over the annually renewable Army Act. Labour MP, George Lansbury, told the Commons that 'the Army was being used in a murderous manner whenever the capitalist class became too much alarmed'. Other members pointed to the misuse of the army: radical Liberal MP, Josiah Wedgwood, accused the government of using troops as 'blacklegs to run trains'. The mistrust of the army towards their working-class recruits was also revealed with Keir Hardie, Labour MP for Merthyr Tydfil, informing the Commons that Territorial troops who were also colliers had their rifles taken from them when deployed at industrial disputes.[51] An atmosphere of mutual suspicion hung over the relationship between the army and the working classes from which the former sought its recruits.

It was in this context that British army discipline had evolved. The result was a form of discipline that was particularly harsh as this was believed to be the only effective means of ordering men drawn from the very bottom strata of society. However, the challenge to traditional ideas on punishments such as flogging was forcing the army to explore alternatives. There were three forms of serious punishment available to Victorian courts martial: imprisonment, flogging and marking (known also as branding, this was abolished in 1871) – whereby the prisoner was 'marked' with a letter 'D' for deserter or 'BC' for bad character. Analysis of punishments handed out by British courts martial during the three years prior to the abolition of flogging for most military offences in 1867 shows a shifting of emphasis towards imprisonment at the expense of flogging (see Table 1.1).[52] However, it is apparent that the army was still making wide use of flogging despite its imminent abolition.

Interestingly, the practice of marking had increased. Possibly some men who would otherwise have been flogged found themselves marked instead, but the most likely explanation of the dramatic rise in marking soldiers is that this represented an attempt by the army to ensure that unwanted recruits did not re-enlist after flogging had been partially abolished in 1867.

Table 1.1 Punishments inflicted by British courts martial 1865–1867[53]

Year	No. imprisoned	No. flogged	No. branded
1865	16,804	601	1,636
1866	19,257	510	1,584
1867	19,854	150	1,805

The commissioners unwittingly alluded to this when they attempted to justify the unpopular practice, stating 'the real object of marking is not the punishment of the offender but the protection of the public'.[54] More striking, though, is the comparatively little use made of the power to discharge offenders: there were only 106, 122 and 184 discharges in each respective year,[55] reflecting ongoing concerns about poor manpower levels.[56] The British Army's reluctance to give up corporal punishments contrasts with the French Army where corporal punishment had long been interdicted, and the Austro-Hungarian Army where the flogging of recruits was abolished in 1868.[57] István Deák has shown that a high proportion of courts martial in the Habsburg Army concerned cases of brutality against subordinates.[58] This might suggest a general move away from violent disciplinary punishment during this liberal era in the Dual Monarchy.

This clinging to flogging and the branding of offenders was not exclusive to the British. Russian courts martial could order corporal punishments to be administered summarily in the presence of a soldier's company or battalion.[59] Elsewhere corporal punishments were less apparent: most armies only allowed for some form of restraint rather than flogging. The procedure adopted in the Dual Monarchy after 1868 was to fix prisoners to an object such as a post or a tree by way of rings attached to the ankles and wrists.[60]

The Courts-Martial Commission concluded that existing punishments needed to be strengthened with more use being made of military prisons. Imprisonment, they suggested, 'should be made as severe and deterrent as a due regard for the health of the prisoner and the laws of humanity will permit'.[61] Otherwise fines, which could be used to fund 'rewards to well conducted men' and greater use of the power to discharge men who were 'beyond the power of reformation' were proposed.[62]

However, no immediate alterations were made to the manner in which the army was regulated and the Mutiny Act remained the key statute, continuing to reflect traditional ideas about discipline. For example, the 1876 version outlined a number of military offences for which the death penalty could be applied. These included mutiny, sedition, desertion, cowardice, sleeping at or leaving a post, striking or using violence towards a superior officer and disobedience.[63] It also established rules for the constitution of courts martial and laid down procedures for the execution of sentences. The power of any court martial to inflict corporal punishments was retained,[64] but only during times of war and with an upper limit of 50 lashes.[65] Such a sentence could be commuted to not more than 42 days' imprisonment or 20 days and 25 lashes.[66] Clearly corporal punishment continued to be considered an essential element in the maintenance of military discipline.

The legislators had recognised that special powers were required in times of war and special provision was also included with regard to the death penalty. Only the highest form of court – the General Court Martial – was granted the power to impose a sentence of death. This type of court was constituted of no fewer than nine commissioned officers (no upper limit), at least two-thirds of whom had to concur for a sentence of death to be lawful.[67] Provision was made for these powers to be transferred to a Detachment General Court Martial during wartime with a reduced constitution of at least three commissioned officers. To avoid any political involvement sentences had to be confirmed by the Monarch or, during active service, the commander-in-chief. There remained no right of appeal and, therefore, no appeal court.

The Army Council reconsidered military discipline in 1879, ordering another report on punishments in other armies. Little had altered in the decade separating the two reports, but one significant change had occurred in Germany. The Prussian code, so admired by British generals, had been replaced with an altogether more progressive German one in 1872. The death penalty was retained, but soldiers received greater protection from the new code. The administration of law was the responsibility of the *Kriegsgerichtsrat* (Judge Advocate), under the jurisdiction of the *Oberquartiermeister* (Administrative Staff), attached to the General Staff.[68] Furthermore, German soldiers were granted legal rights, *Rechtsstaatlichkeit,* as protection from abuses of authority. However, for some reason this information was not considered worthy of inclusion in the report.

The report, compiled by General Sir Charles Ellice, largely confirmed the findings of the 1869 Inquiry, but had to take account of the new German code and the American one. Ellice identified twelve capital crimes in the German code including *repeated* desertion. A sole act of desertion, however, even if committed in the field, was punishable by a maximum of ten years' imprisonment.[69] Curiously, he omitted the offence of leaving a watch, contained in the German code (a similar offence, abandoning a post was a capital crime in the French army only if it was committed in the presence of the enemy). Like its French equivalent the German code allowed for the removal of individual offenders to penal battalions but, unlike the British, in neither the French nor the German armies was the offence of sleeping on post considered sufficiently serious to merit the death penalty.

The existence and use of penal battalions remained an important feature of the codes of a number of continental armies during the war. The French and German armies made considerable use of them. But they were never reintroduced by the British, who preferred to allocate transportation and menial and dangerous tasks such as digging trenches and clearing ordnance to labourers recruited from Africa, India or China. Even black West Indian troops, who had volunteered to fight, found themselves more often than not allocated to these unpopular duties. It seems likely that ideas about 'race' had clouded the view of many in charge of organisation and the distribution of manpower in the British army.[70] Significantly, the British were unable to learn from their alliance partners. The Belgian army, which had executed 13 soldiers during the first year of the war, introduced penal battalions to avoid the need to carry out more.

British policy, though, exhibited a continuing faith in deterrence which predated the war. General Ellice's report of 1879 had drawn attention to Article 54 of the 1874 American Articles of War, which prohibited both flogging and branding, adding with apparent satisfaction that previously the United States had been forced to reintroduce flogging for deserters. Although corporal punishment was finally abolished in the American army in 1861, Ellice drew attention to the Judge Advocate General's remarks which allowed for other physical punishments:

> courts-martial must needs often draw upon the customs of the service for a penalty which shall insure the description of a corporal punishment. Thus, the accused may be adjudged to carry a loaded knapsack for a certain time, stand on a barrel, or suffer any other ignominy which would naturally result in a degree of bodily pain or fatigue, provided the same were not excessive and physically injurious.[71]

American military law at this time can still be regarded as a direct descendant of the British code. As such it was not as tightly constructed as the German code. Wide-ranging powers were bestowed on the commander-in-chief in times of war. For example, capital punishment was permissible, but the restrictions imposed by Article 47 could easily be bypassed:

> No sentence of a Court-Martial or Military Commission, inflicting the punishment of death, shall be carried into execution until it shall have been confirmed by the President; except in the cases of persons convicted, in time of war, as spies, mutineers, deserters, or murderers, and in the cases of guerrilla marauders convicted in time of war, of robbery, burglary, arson, rape, assault with intent to commit rape, or of violation of the laws and customs of war; and in such excepted cases the sentence of death may be carried into execution upon confirmation of the Commanding General in the field, or the Commander of the geographical division or department, as the case may be.[72]

However, there were signs that the American code was detaching itself from its heredity. Unlike the British code, the American Articles did at least envisage a role for a political person such as the President. This represented the start of a movement away from an old British tradition and towards a military code with a distinctly American identity – a process not completed until 1916 when a new military code was approved. Perhaps Ellice was unaware of this development or had attached no importance to it, but other 'modernising' provisions were present in the 1874 Articles. As well as an allowance for adjournments there was an increased role for the Judge Advocate General who could be appointed to any court martial. This direct role for a judicial rather than a military figure was a sure sign that the emphasis was beginning to shift from the disciplinary function of the court martial to one of a dispenser of justice. This was not a painless process and a bitter dispute erupted during the First World War between the American JAG and his deputy. The latter interpreted his role in a far more interventionist manner, which was viewed as a threat to military discipline by the commander of the American forces in France, General Pershing, and from Washington by Secretary for War, Baker.[73] Nevertheless, David Schleuter has remarked that these provisions 'marked to some extent an increased realization by Congress that due process considerations should apply'.[74] The exigencies of the war forced the British Army belatedly to introduce similar provisions, but not by Act of Parliament. However, the Army Council's creation of 34 Court Martial Officers[75] (CMOs) – legally trained personnel who could attend trials to ensure their legality – in 1916 had little impact: condemnations continued apace during 1916 and 1917.[76] Nor did the creation of the post appease critics in the Labour Party – arguably its true purpose.

Developments across the Atlantic passed by the British legislators, who clung firmly to tradition. The Army Discipline and Regulation (Annual) Act of 1879, which parliament had to approve annually, rationalised the disparate military law under one statute, but it was not until the 1881 version that flogging was finally abolished (Section 6). Other punishments – bearing an uncanny resemblance to those of the Austrian army – were introduced instead (Section 4), revealing the influence of other European models.[77] These entailed handcuffing offenders to a cart or wagon or requiring them to carry extra weights known as 'burdens'.[78] However, here the army was clearly out of step with the criminal code where the use of irons or other mechanical restraints as punishments had been forbidden by the Prison Act, 1865, except in exceptional circumstances – themselves the subject of further restrictions in 1893.[79]

Laying the foundations 1881–1914

The Army Act, also passed in 1881 and renewable annually, was the culmination of the process of inquiry and was intended to reform and modernise British military law. Yet it bore a closer relationship to earlier British models and to those of the old empires in Eastern Europe than it did to the more progressive ones in Western Europe. The Act outlined a total of 27 capital offences – 12 were punishable by death at any time and 15 were so punishable on active service only. These are summarised in Tables 1.2 and 1.3:

Capital punishment remained available for a wide range of offences, both military and criminal. Of particular interest here is the inclusion of certain criminal offences such as housebreaking, which had ceased to be a capital crime in the criminal code some decades earlier. This is an unambiguous indication of the status ascribed to British troops and the nature of the concerns about their anticipated behaviour. Indeed, during the First World War there were a number of death sentences passed on British soldiers for house-

Table 1.2   Offences punishable by death

Section	Offence
4 (1)	Abandoning post
4 (2)	Shamefully casting away arms in the presence of the enemy
4 (3)	Corresponding with the enemy
4 (4)	Assisting the enemy
4 (5)	Whilst a prisoner of war, serving with enemy forces
4 (7)	Cowardice before the enemy
7 (1)	Causing a mutiny
7 (2)	Inciting others to mutiny
7 (3)	Joining a mutiny
7 (4)	Failing to inform CO of mutiny
8 (1)	Striking or threatening to strike a senior officer
9 (1)	Disobedience

Table 1.3   Offences punishable by death only if committed on active service

Section	Offence
4 (6)	Commission of an act which imperils H. M. Forces
6 (1) (a)	Leaving CO to go in search of plunder
6 (1) (b)	Leaving a guard, picquet, patrol or post
6 (1) (c)	Forcing a safeguard
6 (1) (d)	Striking a soldier acting as sentinel
6 (1) (e)	Impeding Provost Marshal
6 (1) (f)	Act of violence towards person bringing provisions
6 (1) (g)	Housebreaking
6 (1) (h)	Causing false alarms
6 (1) (i)	Treacherously revealing the parole or watchword
6 (1) (j)	Misappropriation of provisions
6 (1) (k) (i.)	Whilst sentinel: sleeping or drunk on post
6 (1) (k) (ii.)	Whilst sentinel: leaving a post
12 (1) (a)	Desertion
12 (1) (b)	Inciting others to desert

breaking, robbery and even four (unlawfully) for being drunk.[80] The Army Act also created a greater number of capital offences than existed in the French or German armies, illustrating what is perhaps the most important difference between European military codes: the fundamental question of offences and punishments. These varied more widely than is often thought by historians. Therefore, simple comparisons of death sentence statistics without some analysis of the respective codes are wholly unsatisfactory. What was a capital offence in one army was not necessarily punishable by death in another: sleeping on post, abandoning a post or single acts of desertion most notably.

Furthermore, capital offences were variously constructed and defined in different armies. Take, for instance, the crime of desertion, which according to a British pamphlet of 1916, was 'at any time a serious one, but more especially so when the deserter's regiment is on active service'.[81] In fact desertion accounted for approximately 75 per cent of the executions in the British army between 1914 and 1920. A British soldier was guilty of desertion if he:

a) Deserts [that is *intends* to avoid a particular duty] or attempts to desert Her [or His] Majesty's service; or
b) Persuades, endeavours to persuade, procures or attempts to procure, any person subject to military law to desert Her Majesty's service.

And:

if he committed such offence when on active service or under orders for active service, be liable to suffer death, or such less punishment as is in this Act mentioned.[82]

The French code was not so straightforward and broke the offence into two types: *désertion à l'ennemi* and *désertion à l'intérieur*. Only the former was punishable by death with the lesser offence of *désertion à l'intérieur* attracting a maximum penalty of five years' penal servitude even in time of war. The German code of 1872, as opposed to the Prussian code, also regarded desertion as a more complex affair than the British: in the German army offenders could only be sentenced to death in the case of recidivists who had previously been convicted of the offence.[83] Like the Italian code, British military law constructed the crime of desertion in very broad terms. Like the Italian army, British commanders took advantage of this in strictly enforcing discipline during the war.

Paradoxically, therefore, Britain had adopted a harsher military code than the mass armies of its European neighbours with Germany and France legislating for a greater degree of tolerance, particularly in the case of desertion. The reasons for this are not so elusive as might appear. Britain had retained the voluntary principle as the basis for recruitment and with it came a crucial difference in attitudes towards absenteeism. In France and Germany a certain degree of desertion was tolerated, expected even, among soldiers who had been compelled to serve. This was reflected in the separation of the different types of desertion identified by the French code and the corresponding leniency of sentence in the case of men convicted of *désertion à l'intérieur* and in the German principle of *Rechtsstaatlichkeit*. For the British, however, no such tolerance was considered necessary for men who had enlisted of their own volition.

This relationship between the voluntary principle and the brutal nature of military punishments themselves was also the subject of parliamentary debate. Those responsible for army discipline argued for the efficacy of such punishments based on the assumption that deterrence was the most effective means of regulating working-class recruits – an assumption frequently challenged by those on the Left. On 10 April 1912 Joseph King, Labour MP for Somerset North, told a House of Commons Committee:

> Moreover, we practically alone among the nations of the world have volunteer forces, and by that means are guarded against possible dangerous offences which may be even common in other armies. In view of the state, not only of public opinion, but of our army in particular, I venture to say that offences under the Army Act might well be met by lighter penalties than at present.[84]

Colonel Seely's reply for the Government reflected traditional concerns about a standing army. He stated that severe measures, although rarely applied, needed to be available because of 'the danger to the community that would occur from insubordination on the part of any body in the army'. John Ward, Liberal MP for Stoke-on-Trent and Chairman of the National Democratic League, added that the 'death penalty was, perhaps, the *only* penalty for mutiny on active service' [my italics]. But according to Sir F. Banbury, Conservative MP for the City of London, it was not necessary to subject officers to such punishments. The threat of dismissal, he said, was sufficient for an officer because 'dismissal meant disgrace and ruin for the rest of his days'.[85] Differentiation such as this reflected long-established military traditions and was reminiscent of the 'loss of nobility' sentence contained in the old Prussian code that had so impressed British observers decades earlier.

Other traditions also influenced the nature of military law. In its criminal code Britain was consistently more reliant on capital punishment than most other European countries. During the period 1900–14 there were on average 27 death sentences passed annually by criminal courts in England and Wales, with an average of 15 executions carried out. By contrast, in France, where juries could accept mitigating circumstances in order to avoid the death penalty, the figures were 23 and five respectively. Capital punishment was not practised in nineteenth-century Prussia and in other German territories executions were rare although the penalty was reintroduced by Bismarck in 1878. Despite the change during the Wilhelmine era, when clemency was generally refused as a matter of state policy,[86] Britain remained exceptional in its reliance on the death penalty. Even in Tsarist Russia the death penalty was rarely used in criminal cases – although continued use of the knout resulted in many deaths and little restraint was shown in the army. Nineteenth-century abolitionists castigated Britain as 'the most merciless of Christian countries' with a 'backward and unsatisfactory' criminal law.[87] In America too, many states had abolished the death penalty.[88] Britain, though, clung on to capital punishment – a practice reflected in its military code. In 1908 there was a significant alteration to the criminal law: those charged with murder and facing a possible capital sentence were granted a right of appeal. But there was no corresponding development in the military code where the power of life and death rested firmly in the hands of the commander-in-chief.

The concentration of power in the office of the commander-in-chief, although common in most European armies, was effectively unfettered in the British army. There is a parallel here with the role performed by the Home Office in the nineteenth century, which acted to mitigate capital convictions especially where insanity was suspected. The process of assessing a condemned prisoner's sanity to prevent injustices and avoid adverse publicity, in spite of the assumption of adult responsibility established by Common Law,[89] anticipated the role the commander-in-chief later performed in relation to soldiers suspected to be suffering from the condition known as shell-shock. What singled out military law, however, was the absence of any appellate system: other officers and indeed the JAG made recommendations, but the commander-in-chief was the only authority who could set aside the sentence of the court. In the German army soldiers were protected to a certain extent by statutory rights and French soldiers had the theoretical protection of the President of the Republic.[90] Even Russian and Austrian soldiers were not theoretically denied a right of appeal to a higher court.[91] But British soldiers had to place their faith entirely in the hands of a commander-in-chief who was required to put discipline above justice. *The Manual of Military Law* was explicit that: 'The object of military law is to maintain discipline among the troops and other persons forming part of or following an army.'[92] The role of the commander-in-chief has to be understood in this context.

Most soldiers who appeared before British courts martial were expected to defend themselves. During the First World War this was common practice, even in capital cases: prisoners had a right to be represented by a 'friend', but this was rarely taken up. Although this was also standard procedure for those appearing at so-called police courts, there was not really a criminal parallel because these courts did not preside over capital charges. This feature of military justice has already been the subject of much analysis.[93] Here, it is sufficient to draw attention to it, but also to point to the resilience of military tradition. Just as the right of appeal in capital cases had passed by the military code, so too had the practice of representation.

The impact of modern warfare 1914–18

By 1881 all the countries that would be at war in 1914 had formulated the rules that were to regulate their armies. Tradition had been a major factor. So too had varying attitudes towards crime and punishment. For these reasons the British army adopted a code more closely resembling those of the old authoritarian empires of Eastern Europe than those of Germany or France. The British code remained effectively unaltered during the war: the only changes made were procedural rather than legal or judicial. These procedural changes, which are further discussed in the following chapter, had little actual impact on the administration of discipline through the courts martial. In other respects Britain was less progressive than other west European armies: in France the President's intervention, although not strictly a legal change, had a real impact and curbed the early excesses of French military justice. The most significant change, though, was in the German system. Already progressive by British standards, the German code was further liberalised during the war. It became increasingly difficult for German commanders to secure capital sentences as the rules of trials and evidence were gradually tightened and by 1917 field punishments had effectively been abandoned.[94] That same year the British Army carried out more executions than in any other year in its history – a total of 110, more than twice the German total for the entire war. It was only in 1918 – when conscripts filled the ranks – that the number of condemnations and executions in the British army was reduced, although the number in that single year was still more than the larger German army managed in over four years of war.

In fact amendments made to the German code during the war warrant some attention here. The first significant alteration was actually made during the crisis which followed the assassination of Archduke Ferdinand in Sarajevo. On 14 July – just a few days after Germany had affirmed its support for Austria – the code was modified to reduce minimum sentences for desertion and absence during peacetime.[95] The next important alteration occurred at a critical moment in the war – the spring of 1917, which saw the collapse of the Tsarist armies and the failure of Nivelle's offensive on the *Chemin des Dames*. The new law,[96] which made it possible to pass considerably more lenient sentences in cases of desertion, absence, disobedience, striking of superior officers and mutiny than was previously the case, was frequently made use of. At this time it might have appeared to the German army that they retained the upper hand in the war. However, despite the optimism of the spring offensive, by the early summer months of 1918 hope had turned to despair. On 18 July a French counter-attack at Villers-Cotterêts not only threatened the German position on the Marne, but also propelled Ludendorff into a deep psychological crisis, which prevented him from performing his duties satisfactorily. This caused many senior German officers to consider Ludendorff's position no longer tenable.[97] Yet just one week later the military code was further liberalised. The new law, which abolished restraint of prisoners,[98] suggests that the military command did not possess the authority that is often supposed during this period. Attempts to liberalise the German code further still, however, were abandoned during the autumn of 1918, as Germany's situation became more turbulent. After the war Ludendorff himself laid the blame for Germany's defeat partially on the modifications made to the military code, claiming that liberal politicians had undermined his authority and unnecessarily blunted the army's mettle – a significant element in the formation of the 'stab in the back' legend:

> Verhängnisvoll wirkte es, daß die militärische Rechtsprechung ganz unter dem Einfluß des unklaren Denkens der Heimat stand, die fortwährend auf Straferlaß drang und die Militärgesetze milderte, während sie der Feind verschärfte. Sie konnte sich nicht zu schweren Strafen, geschweige denn zur Verhängung der Todesstrafe entschließen.[99] [It was disastrous that military jurisdiction came totally under the influence of the blurred thinking in the homeland. Those in the homeland constantly pushed to liberalise military law while the enemy stiffened his. They simply couldn't accept the necessity to inflict heavy sentences let alone the death penalty.][100]

It is a real paradox, therefore, that in Germany, which was effectively under military rule by 1917, the military code was liberalised seemingly in the face of objections from the High Command. Yet in Britain, where democratic traditions were arguably stronger than in Germany, the military code was left effectively unaltered. Given the relative severity of the respective codes at the beginning of the war this is even more surprising. The British Commander-in-Chief faced no challenge to his authority and position as sole arbiter in matters of military discipline: a situation that Ludendorff was envious of. In Germany it appears that politicians were able to moderate the power of the High Command even at critical moments of the war. This was in part, no doubt, thanks to the constitutional state – the *Rechtsstaat* – which not only preserved rights of individuals but also led to a more restricted bureaucracy, which required the military to act within a judicial framework. This was not so in the British army, where senior commanders were able to manipulate proceedings in their attempt to enforce discipline.[101] The judicial process amounted to little more than the legitimisation of the disciplinary authority of the commander-in-chief.

Unwittingly, the legislators had laid down the very conditions which ensured that, in terms of capital punishment, the British soldier was more vulnerable than his French or German counterparts. This does not appear to have been the intention of the legislators who, by removing the old practices of flogging and branding, were attempting to change what had become the unacceptable face of military discipline. However, the new code reflected much of the criminal law, which itself placed enormous emphasis on the death penalty as a means of deterring crime. During the First World War most military commanders adopted just such an approach and the law encouraged them to do so.

Why was military law so framed? For the answer we must again look to the criminal code. The parallels are not so elusive and tradition remained an important influence. Military law, as represented by the Army Act 1881, simply followed earlier British models and reflected traditional fears about control of the army and the quality of recruits. In fact it was highly unlikely that the British could have envisaged a military code such as existed across the Channel or the Atlantic. The result was a code that placed additional responsibility on the commander-in-chief during wartime. His function as the final arbiter in legal matters bore a marked similarity to the role of the Home Office: both were expected to mitigate condemnations from the courts to an acceptable level. One had to balance public opinion against public order, the other troop morale and discipline. Yet in practice this judicial role was not compatible with the commander-in-chief's overriding responsibility for army discipline. Unlike the French or American armies, which theoretically placed ultimate judicial responsibility on their respective presidents, British tradition dictated that politicians were not to be trusted with a modicum of control over the military. In peacetime the Crown fulfilled the role that was delegated to the commander-in-chief during wartime. No doubt his role was delegated further, but the important feature of the system was that British soldiers had to rely on the benevolence of senior officers who were virtually unaccountable, at least for the duration of the war.

It seems likely that the army got what it wanted from the legislators: a code that reflected army traditions. Like the Crown, the Army was not as apolitical as it was usually painted. Despite the reforms it retained its traditional approach to discipline in a code that remained immune from interference from civil servants such as the JAG or from politicians. The Army's reputation as a non-political organisation is indeed mythical. As Hew Strachan has shown, the army was indeed capable of political intervention and not always was it subtle about its actions: the Curragh incident of 1914 was the most glaring example.[102]

French and German soldiers on the other hand had a legal apparatus constructed around them as protection from the excesses of military discipline. The law was framed in a manner that offered at least a degree of tolerance of desertion. It is no coincidence that such a view existed in Germany and France, but not in Britain where there was no tradition of compulsion, and where it was not thought necessary to show leniency to men who had accepted the regulations when they volunteered. This is an important theme, which I have dealt with elsewhere. In short it is worthy of note at this point that shortly after British conscripts arrived in large numbers at the front there followed a sharp decline in the number of condemnations by courts martial.[103] German soldiers also benefited from statutory rights while French *poilus* enjoyed the theoretical protection of their President, which although slow to be enacted doubtless saved many from the firing squads after 1915. Pre-war attitudes and traditional military practices were also markedly different in these continental armies with commanders accustomed to other forms of managing discipline such as the penal battalions. Alternatives were limited in the British code.

British commanders were imbued with notions of authority rather than management. In this they were aided by the law, which was constructed around the concept of deterrence. It is hardly surprising, therefore, that when confronted by a stalemated war, British commanders invariably grasped at traditional ideas rather than exploring less well-trodden paths. This approach was epitomised by General Sir Horace Smith-Dorrien, commander of the 2nd Army, when reviewing a case in 1915:

> There is a serious prevalence of desertion to avoid duty in the trenches, especially in the 8th Brigade and I am sure that the *only* way to stop it is to carry out some death sentences [my italics].[104]

In short the British went to war in 1914 with a military code that allowed a proliferation of capital punishment to go unchecked. Paradoxically, the abolition of flogging – one of the few progressive features of the reforms – was a contributory factor. Lacking alternatives, British commanders were simply bereft of ideas short of capital punishment when it came to controlling the army during wartime. This had not proved to be a major problem in the minor wars at the end of the nineteenth-century – not even the war in South Africa. But the intensive nature of warfare on the Western front in particular cruelly exposed the inadequacies in the rules for management of the army. Commanders, fearful of losing control of a much-enlarged army, were encouraged, expected even, to resort to capital punishment. Complicit in all this were the legislators who followed draconian criminal as well as military traditions when they acquiesced and allowed the army to maintain its grip on such a harsh and rigid system.

2
Military Discipline and the Nation at War

Executions in the First World War were justified by that tenet of military discipline *'pour encourager les autres'*. It was a widely held belief in all the armies that examples were necessary to maintain discipline and to underpin soldiers' commitment to the war effort.[1] What little debate there has been among historians has centred on how the examples were selected, rather than why.[2] The maintenance of discipline was perhaps the most important factor in the commander-in-chief's considerations throughout World War I. This was based on the assumption that discipline was the keystone of military efficiency and its collapse meant military defeat. Writing in 1967, John Baynes, himself a battalion commander during the Second World War, argued that the engagement of two highly disciplined armies (British and German) ensured that the First World War lasted as long as it did.[3] Conveniently, he makes no mention of the French army, which survived a collapse in discipline. Typically, the French army's response to the crisis of 1917 was a reimposition of military authority by carrying out a number of executions. Yet the relationship between discipline – or at least perceived acts or instances of indiscipline – and executions is surprisingly complex.

In the next chapter we will consider troop morale, arguably an even more obscure concept than discipline. Here, though, it is necessary only to note that the relationship between military discipline and troop morale was never fixed and was constantly redefined according to the circumstances. Tim Travers has argued that the British army was in a transitional stage during the First World War and that the exigencies of the war exposed some of the faults of the old traditional army and facilitated the emergence of a 'modern' professional army and all that it entailed.[4] As we shall see, part of the modernisation and restructuring of the army entailed adopting new methods to monitor troop morale.

Commanders were particularly conscious of potential charges of poor discipline in their units. To be regarded as being soft on discipline was an especially serious charge with grave implications for the career soldier. Naturally, this concern was passed down the chain of command, with the result that each rank was eager to avoid the censure of the one above it. This sense of being monitored was even felt by those who made up the courts martial. Commanders of divisions were expected to exercise a certain amount of control over courts operating under their command. The barometers by which discipline was monitored were often vague and complex. Sickness returns undoubtedly played an important role here as did assessments of performance in battle, but the most tangible of criteria was often the dreaded visit of or inspection by more senior commanders. In many cases the number of death sentences passed by courts martial, and for that matter the number of executions, can be attributed directly to remarks made by senior officers on inspections. In other cases death sentences and executions resulted from concerns that adverse criticism might follow certain incidents or even the general state of a unit, normally a division. Far from acting independently, courts martial often reflected the concerns of unit commanders, many of whom exercised a direct influence over trials in their divisions.

Assumptions about discipline also played a significant role. Different expectations – in terms of discipline and fighting ability – were made of Regular soldiers as opposed to 'New Army' volunteers or conscripts: even after the Regular army had ceased to exist in anything other than name, the disciplinary ethos in so-called 'Regular divisions' remained stricter than in other units. Similarly, less was expected from soldiers from the Dominions, at least initially. The differing approach to discipline in various units owed much to the character of the pre-war Edwardian army. The Regular army was a rigidly hierarchical institution and the men of the ranks, normally recruited from the lower echelons of society, had a harsh disciplinary code enforced upon them. By contrast men of the Territorial Force, established in 1908, and the other auxiliary units had to be handled with more respect to avoid their merely leaving. Therefore, a dual approach to discipline emerged. On the one hand strict control was achieved but individual initiative was stifled, while on the other greater flexibility in leadership relied on the development of self-discipline on the part of the troops. Regular army commanders were suspicious of their auxiliary counterparts and of the New Army troops who succeeded them. Their different approach to discipline, it was often assumed, diminished their ability as soldiers.[5]

Such assumptions were not, however, limited to military background: the Edwardian preoccupation with inherited characteristics formed the basis of many disciplinary concerns and correspondingly much of the army's policy as applied at divisional level. Certain 'races', for instance, were believed to be in need of firmer control than others. This was certainly true of the treatment of Irish soldiers who, while considered natural warriors by the British, were generally thought to be indisciplined and in need of particularly firm handling. Colonial, or 'black', troops were also less disciplined in the minds of their British commanders. In many cases this was the result of traits ascribed to certain 'races', but it was also the result of prevailing British attitudes, themselves sometimes shaped by particular incidents – such as the mutiny of the Indian Army in 1857. The same criteria were applied to native labourers, though in many instances with an even greater degree of severity. According to David Englander, 'This Brutality, perhaps, represents – albeit in exaggerated form – the authoritarianism of class relations in Edwardian Britain. The traits ascribed to Oriental labour form an uncanny mirror image of the perceived social character of the working class sharpened by a rampant racism.'[6] Consequently disciplinary measures varied from unit to unit, being defined by the type of unit and by the ascribed character of the soldiers within it. Assumptions about 'race' were remarkably resilient and many were still evident during the Second World War.[7]

Active service – usually, though not exclusively, on foreign soil – brought with it extra demands. Supply and logistics were immediately a more complex matter than for an army on home soil. But it was the enormous expansion of the army after 1914 that was the greatest challenge and raised most concerns. Uncertainty about the reliability of first the reservists, then the Territorial Force, followed by the citizen soldiers of the New Army and the Derby scheme, introduced by the Earl of Derby, Secretary of State for War, by which men attested to their willingness to serve before they too were succeeded by the conscripts from 1916 onwards, centred on the issue of discipline. In its simplest form the term discipline referred to the maintenance of control of the army by its commanders – obedience to the will of the commander-in-chief. Clearly there were several aspects to the form this control took, but central to the concept of discipline was the notion that soldiers were expected to follow orders. This was reinforced in the soldier's small book, issued to every recruit, which stressed:

OBEDIENCE IS THE FIRST DUTY OF A SOLDIER.[8]

It was the adherence to this most valued military principle by the new soldiers that most concerned leaders of the old army. Brigadier General Crozier recalled how he instilled into the men of his New Army battalion that 'the wish expressed by the C.O. is tantamount to an order – no matter what it may be'.[9]

The marriage of the old army to the new was not an entirely harmonious one. Most commanders believed that the best way to get obedience was through the threat of harsh punishments – the death penalty being the last resort, but nevertheless a very real threat.[10] This was merely a continuation of centuries of British military tradition. Although most First World War commanders had joined the army after flogging had been abolished in 1881, traditional views on punishments were resilient. In the absence of flogging only Field Punishments stood between imprisonment of offenders and the death penalty. This, it will be argued, resulted in an over-reliance on the extreme penalty when concerns about discipline were most heightened.

New recruits, too, had their concerns. According to John Bourne, 'Kitchener's men, in particular, were acutely conscious that they had volunteered for military service. They were there of their own accord by deliberate choice. They were deeply resentful of the belief that they could only be kept to their duty by the threat of being shot by their own side for any dereliction of it.'[11]

The regulation of the army presented a number of problems. First, by 1914 the main legislation was over thirty years old. This might not have been such a problem except that the nature of warfare and that of the British army had altered. Both France and Germany had older military codes, but were able to adapt them more readily to the exigencies of modern warfare. This was at least partly because, unlike the British code, theirs catered for large conscript armies. While the British Army Act 1881 anticipated some of the potential problems – and these were reflected by its content – it had never been intended to form the basis of discipline for an army the size of the British Expeditionary Force which, by 1917, numbered approximately two million. The legislation, drawn up with colonial policing in mind and never seriously altered, was adapted to the changing needs of an ever-expanding army by practitioners in the field. This process was not always a smooth one.

Discipline was variously defined according to its context. In terms of the general control and command of the army, senior officers were expected to exercise authority backed up by punishment for those who disobeyed. Commanders were expected not to shirk from ordering the death penalty should it be necessary to impose that authority. Baynes has argued that the death penalty was a necessary disciplinary tool, as it was by carrying out executions that the High Command was able to demonstrate its resolve that indiscipline would not be tolerated.[12] With few exceptions, there was a widespread acceptance of the deterrent value of the death penalty among the higher echelons of the army. At the other end of the scale men of the ranks were expected to conform and to carry out orders without failure. In other words they were expected to fight regardless of the apparent dangers. The inability or unwillingness of men to face these dangers was met with little tolerance by the army, which initially clung rigidly onto old disciplinary structures designed for the Regular army of the nineteenth century despite the irreversible changes in the composition of the army. The 'citizen-soldiers' of the Kitchener armies and the conscripts who followed them were subject to the same code as those who had gone before. This had serious implications for army discipline, which needed to be modified to cater for the different type of soldier now in the ranks. The code itself was not altered during the war, but the manner of its application gradually changed and in 1918 a shift in attitudes towards discipline in general and the death penalty in particular can be detected. In the final year of the war there was a substantial fall in the number of condemnations by courts martial and consequently in the number of executions carried out.

Table 2.1 Condemnations and executions in the British army, shown annually[13]

Year	Condemnations (monthly average in brackets)	Executions (monthly average in brackets)
1914	85 (17)	4 (1)
1915	591 (49)	55 (5)
1916	856 (71)	95 (8)
1917	904 (75)	104 (9)
1918	515 (47)	46 (4)

The emergence of a mass army, and eventually a conscript army, did not pose the sole threat to the traditional approach to discipline. Modern warfare brought with it new problems or at least it magnified pre-existing ones. Notable among these was the condition known as shell shock. Probably not experienced for the first time in World War I, the incidence of war neuroses became a major issue because of the sheer numbers affected by it. This was largely due to the development of long-range, quick-firing artillery which fired ever increasing calibre shells of high explosive. It might also have owed much to the 'de-skilling' of the role of the infantryman, the sheer inertia of the front line and the appalling conditions that soldiers had to endure.[14] From a disciplinary point of view, however, shell shock presented a major cause for concern. Commanders were never truly comfortable about recognising a condition that actually excused soldiers who fled the line. To its credit the British Army did absorb some of the ideas of psychologists such as Charles Myers. There is also evidence to suggest that the army was prepared to use shell-shock as an acceptable form of escape from duty in extreme cases – the poet Siegfried Sassoon providing a good example. Overall, however, shell-shock remained a disciplinary rather than a medical matter in the eyes of those who led the army.

Finally, military-style discipline began to creep into British society as the war continued. The military took on roles that did not come under its peacetime remit. In a few extreme instances there was even the threat of the military death penalty. Ireland and the cases of conscientious objectors are obvious examples of this, but military discipline infiltrated much deeper into society.

Regulating crime in the army

It was recognised in the Army Act that discipline did not only apply to the battlefield. As well as ensuring the efficient maintenance of the army by legislating against such acts as 'interfering with supplies', the Act sought to protect the civilian inhabitants of the area occupied and, therefore, the relationship between the army and the local populace. When the legislators drew up the Act they probably had some colony in mind, but during World

War I the land occupied by the British army was in most instances that of an ally, France. Relations between British troops and the French or Belgian civilians who continued to inhabit the areas close to the front line have recently been the subject of analysis by Craig Gibson.[15] After an initial 'honeymoon period' relations deteriorated as trench warfare set in. The failure to evacuate civilians, and problems concerning damage to property and crops caused by British troops, placed an enormous strain on the relations.[16] Here, it is necessary to concentrate on the more serious aspects of crimes against the civilian populace because we are primarily concerned with capital punishment. However, it is noteworthy that two of the factors cited by Gibson as affecting day-to-day relationships between the troops and the local communities – namely alcohol and prostitution – also had a major influence on the nature of capital trials involving British Empire soldiers.

Such massive occupation of allied territory had certainly not been anticipated and the Act did not stipulate a preference for allied (presumably therefore friendly) or enemy (and therefore hostile) civilians. Theoretically, behaviour towards both was expected to be of the same standard. The courts martial enforced this code, convicting 1709 officers, men and civilians attached to the British Army for an 'offence against an inhabitant'.[17] Although no record has survived to indicate precisely what each offence was, it is clear from the courts martial registers that the *type* of crime covered by this charge tended to be the more serious type of criminal offence such as robbery or rape.[18] Twenty-three of these crimes were considered serious enough to warrant a sentence of death, three of which were carried out. A further five men were condemned for crimes specified as robbery and another for rape. Three civilians were executed in Egypt for armed robbery.[19] A small number of death sentences can also be traced for relatively minor crimes such as theft and housebreaking but these too usually refer to convictions of civilians in occupied territory.[20] Remarkably few convictions were recorded against British soldiers for crimes against what we might term 'hostile' civilians: of the 23 condemnations for crimes against inhabitants 22 were on the Western Front, and the location of the other cannot be traced.[21] It is quite possible, therefore, that no soldier was convicted of crimes against civilians elsewhere, suggesting that all the victims of these particular crimes were almost certainly nationals of an allied country. A similar trend can be detected in cases involving the murder of civilians, where charged as such (see below). It is unlikely that there was an absence of crime by the army while occupying enemy territory and it is possible that different standards were applied to unlawful acts against hostile civilians.

There was of course a precedent here. Not only did the military authorities implement a very aggressive policy towards supposedly hostile civilians during the wars in South Africa, but there was also a history of tolerance towards certain unlawful acts committed by British soldiers, and this in spite of the army's tough line on discipline backed up by harsh punishments. The army's reluctance to take action against troops in certain circumstances occasionally resulted in local police having to restore order. During the Zulu War in 1879, William Russell, special correspondent of *The Times*, wrote:

> I think the military authorities have been culpably remiss and negligent in the discharge of their bounden obligation to maintain discipline and to protect the property and secure the peace of well-disposed loyal [?] citizens[22]. What the reasons or motive for their indifference may be I do not pretend to surmise, but I am sure they are pursuing a course which must lead to most serious consequences if they gloss over or pretend to ignore the excesses which in Natal and the Transvaal are covering the army with odium and disgrace. It is not of drunken frolics or of robbing henroosts or poultry yards that I complain – no, nor of orgies and street brawls which bring the soldiery into contempt in the eyes of Boer and Kaffir – but of housebreaking, burglary, assault and robbery, of a condition of things which fills the minds of dwellers in stations up-country with alarm and indignation, and the gaols and scenes of convict labour with men wearing the uniform of the queen. There is not a house in Heidelberg, close at hand, which has not been broken into, with two or three exceptions, and other stations are nearly as bad. Women are flying to the large towns, where there are some guarantees of safety in the shape of police, as though they were hunted out by Zulus or Swazies.[23]

Section 41 of the Army Act allowed for the trial of criminal offences by courts martial.[24] Unfortunately, it is unclear from the official records whether the victims of criminal acts such as theft (4604 cases) were other soldiers or civilians. The implication is that it refers to the former and that all offences against inhabitants are accounted for by the figure of 1709 recorded as such together with a further 1960 recorded simply as 'miscellaneous civil offences' (probably including the death sentences passed for housebreaking, etc). This makes the total number of recorded crimes against the civilian populace 3669 which, if it is to be believed, represents a remarkably low crime rate given the size of the army and the period of 'occupation' – approximately four years – fewer than 1000 crimes a year. This would have been equivalent to an annual crime rate of approximately one crime for every two thousand people. It is perhaps more likely that only the more serious cases such as robbery and rape were actually dealt with by courts martial, other crimes being dealt with by other means, if at all.

Behind the lines the army's two greatest concerns were drunkenness and murder; the former for its prevalence and its effect on discipline; the latter for its seriousness and the impact on relations with local communities and agencies. These problems were not mutually exclusive: most murders it seems were carried out by drunken soldiers. Once again, the evidence is sketchy, but the little that has survived suggests that the impact on discipline rather than concerns about a possible deterioration of relations with the locals was paramount to British commanders. This was consistent with pre-war attitudes in the army. Drunkenness, it will be remembered, was a persistent and major preoccupation of those commanders who examined army discipline before 1914. Significantly, in one case in February 1915 a soldier's execution for desertion was justified because of a perceived drunkenness problem. According to Brigadier General Congreve, commander of 18th Brigade (6th Division): 'There is a great deal of drunkenness and absence resulting from it in this battalion more than 2/3rds of it being composed of special reservists.'[25] The connection ascribed to drunkenness and absence could not be more explicit. Furthermore, the offence of drunkenness appears to have been associated in particular with the pre-war veterans who made up the special reserve and had been recalled to the colours at the outbreak of war.

The death penalty was obviously not available to courts martial for offences of drunkenness but other forms of punishment were, including the dreaded Field Punishment Number One. The rules of Field Punishment were set out in the *Manual of Military Law*. The 1914 edition stipulated that the prisoner could be kept in irons (or tied with straps or ropes if irons were not available) to prevent escape. He could then be attached to a fixed object, normally a cart-wheel or a post, for up to two hours daily. The maximum period allowed was twenty-eight days, but tying the prisoner to a fixed object was not permitted for more than three consecutive days out of any four.[26] Therefore, a prisoner could be tied to an object for a maximum of 21 days over a 28-day period. The punishment had been introduced to fill the vacuum left by the abolition of flogging and, in common with other military punishments, the nature of Field Punishments reflected the lowly status of British troops. Baynes justified its use on the grounds that the pre-1914 soldiers were tough individuals capable of savage acts when drunk, adding that 'one cannot believe that tying them [Regular soldiers] up for two hours to a gun-wheel did them very much harm'.[27]

There is little evidence to support Baynes' other assertion that many commanding officers dispensed with attaching the man to a fixed object because 'they felt that it was degrading and bad for morale'.[28] It was clearly a common practice even for minor offences throughout the war. Robert Graves' servant was one of many thousands of troops sentenced to 'crucifixion' for being drunk.[29] Drunkenness, considered a blight on the character of the pre-war British soldier, continued to be a major concern for the army between 1914 and 1918, attracting harsh punishments. On four occasions courts martial passed unlawful sentences of death on men charged with nothing more than being drunk, although none of them was confirmed by the commander-in-chief.[30] This was an indication of how far some officers were prepared to go in order to eradicate drunkenness. It also reveals the inadequacy of some courts martial that passed unlawful sentences.

There were over 35,000 convictions overseas for drunkenness.[31] Yet this, it could be argued, is low given the numbers and period of time involved and does little to support my earlier assertion that drunkenness was one of the army's major problems in respect of its relationship with the civilian populace. The figure probably obscures the true picture, which can be glimpsed by referring to trials for other offences, especially murder. In common with English criminal law, murder was punishable by death and the death penalty was mandatory. Courts martial convicted 64 men of murder, mostly of other soldiers – usually an NCO – but some involved the killing of civilians. Drink appears to have been a common feature in both instances. In approximately half the trials for murder evidence was produced which suggested the offenders were drunk at the time of the crime.[32] It seems quite possible that drunkenness played a part in the other cases but is not explicit in the evidence.

Another important trend can be identified. In the ten cases where the murder victims can be conclusively identified as civilians they were, without exception, women.[33] In fact in nine cases, all on the Western Front, the victims were identified as prostitutes, itself suggestive of a sexual motive. However, it is more likely that this was a reflection of the demographic impact of the war on French society with few men remaining in the villages and towns and those who hoped to profit from the presence of the British Army, such as prostitutes, moving in. This also shows that the civilian populace with which the British Army had closest contact was far from a normal one, and this partially explains the low opinion that many soldiers held of French civilians. Mail censorship had revealed that a common feeling about the French was that they were viewed as racketeers and crooks eager to 'rip-off' British troops at every opportunity. The humorous suggestion made by one censor that a common sentiment in the letters sent home was that there would be no shortage of volunteers for any future war provided that the enemy was France was not without an element of truth.[34] A similar sentiment was later extended towards the Italians, presumably for the same reasons.[35]

In England and Wales during this period there was an annual average of approximately twenty-five death sentences passed by criminal courts. On average roughly thirteen of these were carried out.[36] Given the comparative differences in the size of the civilian population of England and Wales and the British Army during this period, the army obviously made greater use of the death penalty than did British criminal courts. However, the two do not bear close comparison. Circumstances were entirely different. Not only were soldiers under fire but they also existed in a false community which virtually excluded women and where relationships between themselves and the civilian populace were far from normal. It must also be said that soldiers were armed and the stakes had been raised considerably when it came to sorting out their differences. These are obvious points but it should be emphasised that the evidence does not suggest that drunken British soldiers were running amok across northern France or other theatres of the war. Nor does it suggest that the High Command made more liberal use of the death penalty than would have been the case in British society: the commander-in-chief actually commuted a greater proportion of cases than did the Home Secretary.

What is perhaps more significant is that with just one exception those executed for murdering prostitutes were all Colonial (i.e. 'black') troops or labourers from China and Egypt. The only case involving a British soldier occurred in Le Havre. Corporal Wickens of the Rifle Brigade, who had strangled a prostitute in her room, was executed on 7 March 1918.[37] Unfortunately, detailed records of all trials where death sentences were later commuted have not survived and it is therefore difficult to make any meaningful and sustainable comparison between cases involving British soldiers and those involving Colonial troops. What can be asserted with confidence, however, is that of the ten executions where the victims can be identified as civilians (all women) only one offender (Corporal Wickens) was white. This suggests that assumptions about 'race' and women might have influenced sentencing but in the absence of more complete information such an argument remains tenuous. Certainly the proportion of death sentences confirmed and carried out against 'black' Colonial troops and labourers is only slightly higher than that of the 'white' British and Dominion troops (68 per cent and 61 per cent respectively). It should be noted, however, that the same number of murder cases were brought against each of these two groups, which, given the respective overall size of the army (5,955,514[38]) and the foreign labour corps (approximately 500,000), is indicative of a problem, whether real or perceived.

The most dramatic example was the case of three Chinese labourers who killed a prostitute and also her three children near Amiens. They all admitted their guilt and it is hardly surprising that the mandatory death sentence was confirmed. Two were executed and the other committed suicide to avoid the firing squad.[39] Elsewhere on the Western Front, two men of the Cape Coloured Labour Corps were executed at Lille for the murder of two Belgian prostitutes.[40] The only case that does not appear to involve a prostitute occurred in Palestine. The motive though was clearly sexual. Private James Mitchell, a 'black' soldier of the British West Indies Regiment, was executed on 22 December 1917 for murdering the husband of a woman he had attempted to rape.[41]

Discipline on the battlefield

A more obvious, and arguably overriding, disciplinary concern centred on the battlefield. The central feature of what may be termed battlefield discipline was that the troops would carry out the orders of the commanders, moving as and where ordered, taking up positions as ordered and holding the ground as required. As we have already discussed obedience was highly valued. Yet there was little point in commanders producing strategies or tactics that the troops would not carry out and herein lies the key to battlefield discipline. A degree of consent was required to control an army such as Britain put together during the war years. Discipline, especially at the warfront, was a two-way affair. Senior officers could not produce grand schemes based on battlefield maps or Staff College courses without giving some attention to what level of discipline could be expected from their troops. True, the threat of the death penalty and other forms of punishment could be and were employed to subjugate the men to the authority of the generals but even this was not a sufficiently strong weapon to allow for complete domination of the men. The image of the deferential British soldier was not consistent with reality. Plans for battle, even the big offensives such as the Somme in 1916, were made within the confines of expected rather than desirable levels of discipline.[42] The balance between these two positions, the achievable against the desirable, was not always accomplished. Perhaps it would be fair to say that a satisfactory balance was rarely accomplished, but a major mutiny such as most other armies experienced was nevertheless avoided. The army slowly adapted its pre-war position, whereby troops were treated as unintelligent loafers, to one which accommodated the citizen soldiers upon whom it came to rely, and this was no doubt an important development. The army was still wrangling with the same problem during the Second World War, as expressed by Lord Moran:

> Everywhere men are asking whether a system of discipline and training designed for the illiterate has been modified to meet the needs of an educated rank and file.[43]

But it was during the First World War when it had first recruited citizen soldiers that the army had been forced to reappraise its practices. One of the innovators in this respect was Sir Ivor Maxse, a wartime commander at brigade, division and corps level and Inspector-General of training from June 1918, who taught greater trust and respect for the average soldier than was traditionally exercised. The mood of the troops was another important factor in defining this relationship and the army went to great lengths in assessing it and producing regular reports on morale, a subject dealt with in the next chapter.

The key to unit discipline was widely believed to be the development of a strong *esprit de corps*. This was built into the structure of the pre-war British Army. Regiments were recruited on a local basis, adopting the county names to give them a sense of identity, and battle honours from previous campaigns adorned regimental colours. Rather than undermining this system those who rushed to the colours in 1914 and 1915 were absorbed into the old regiments. These new 'service' battalions, therefore, adopted the same identity and, it was hoped, the loyalty to the regiment of the Regular army. It was only after the introduction of conscription, by which time the disastrous effects on communities of the Battle of the Somme was realised, that this system was altered.[44] Even then the regiments kept their county names, their battle honours and the paraphernalia which tied them to the perceived glories of the past.

Esprit de corps, however, was not simply a matter of identification with a locality or with the past. It was actively engendered through day-to-day practices. Drill, it was thought, developed both teamwork and obedience which would then be transplanted onto the battlefield. According to Baynes, even though his unit, 2nd Scottish Rifles, did not emphasise drill as much as some other units, it was still held to be 'an important part of military training' and when out of the line 'everyone was put to drilling'.[45] Traditional forms of discipline such as these proved to be resilient to the changing demands of the war itself. In a pamphlet on training written in February 1918 and based on 'no less than 30 British missions in 1917', Major-General Ivor Maxse placed the emphasis on what might be termed traditional discip-line. He cited marching, regular billet inspection and saluting as being essential to the maintenance of discipline. This was achieved, he argued, by inculcating pride in each unit.[46] The concerns engendered by the thought of a collapse of discipline were clearly spelt out by Maxse:

> We are in for a long strain and must all pull together in 1918. The greater the strain, the more apparent becomes the need for discipline. Officers should tell their men what has happened in Russia through indiscipline, and the men will respond right well.[47]

The association between military defeat and the collapse of discipline is consistent with pre-war Clausewitzian ideas about army structure and authority. However, Maxse's suggestion that discipline might be a two-way affair and that the men should be trusted more represents a departure from the traditional view. This in itself was symptomatic of a general change in attitudes in the army towards disciplinary matters by 1918. The recruitment of men whose background was not that of the traditional infantryman and the absorption into the officer corps of men with experience, possibly of a managerial type, gained in commerce and industry, had resulted in subtle changes to leadership. This change in attitude is more obvious in Maxse's other recommendation:

> One fault is that our Officers do not take their men sufficiently into their confidence, but leave them at the mercy of false rumour and untruthful statements. The British soldier has never failed those who have really trusted him, and he will not do so now. But we must trust him and tell him the truth: we cannot drive him and ignore him too.

We should in fact deal with him as an intelligent and patriotic man, which is just what he is.[48]

It is unlikely that sentiments such as these could have been expressed earlier in the war and it is salutary to compare them with Travers' argument that British generals did not trust their own troops when planning for the Battle of the Somme the year before.[49]

There was a limited degree of continuity here with the pre-war army. Gary Sheffield has argued that, before 1914, Regular soldiers were viewed with mistrust by their officers. Traditionally, he argues, the Regular soldier was a poorly educated man of poor physique and 'urban provenance'.[50] In common with ideas prevalent in Edwardian society, such men were often regarded as degenerates and viewed with great suspicion by social commentators and their commanders alike.[51] The troops, Sheffield continues, were treated as if they were unruly children and punished if they stepped out of line. Men of the Territorial Force and other auxiliary formations enjoyed a wholly different relationship with their officers. Consequently, discipline was less formal and men were treated more as citizens than as children. This model was normally adopted in the New Armies, but Regular style discipline often crept in. Although the British Army during the Great War was a mixture of the old and the new, by 1918 the old Regular army had long ceased to exist except in name and the dominance of the New Armies was apparently assured. But the idea that there was no attempt to modernise the army until the exigencies of war forced the issue should be resisted. There were signs of a significant change in attitudes towards discipline early in the twentieth century: the military theorist Colonel G. F. R. Henderson argued for the development of 'intelligent' rather than 'mechanical' discipline following the embarrassment of the Boer War.[52]

Henderson embraced the lessons learnt from foreign generals, even French ones. He published works on the American Civil War and the Franco-Prussian War and was greatly influenced by the ideas of the generals of antiquity, by 'Stonewall' Jackson, Von Moltke and Napoleon, whom he described as 'the greatest general of them all'.[53] In his writings he placed the emphasis on training, leadership and troop morale rather than blind obedience. His work was part of a general debate about military practices that can be attributed to the period between the Boer War and the First World War.

There is other evidence to suggest that attitudes in the British army were changing prior to 1914. In 1913 the army had examined the system of special training for *sous officiers* in the French army who were considered suitable candidates for a commission, with a view to adopting a similar scheme for British NCOs. Major Earle was sent to France to study the scheme and report back. While his final report did not dismiss the idea of a special officers' school for NCOs, he did identify a number of potential obstacles, most notably the differing traditions and the legacy of the revolution that, he argued, rendered it difficult to learn anything from the French system. A more fruitful comparison, he argued, could be found in the system adopted by the Royal Navy for promotions from the lower deck.[54] The report is evidence of a lingering suspicion of the qualities of the French army and a reluctance to embrace its practices, but also of an increasing awareness in the British army of the need to modernise the selection procedure for officers.

The roles of various arms of the military were also debated during the pre-war era. Of particular note was the cooperation between artillery and infantry and the role of the machine-gun.[55] More mundane issues such as the deployment and training of relatively new units were also seen as needing to be addressed. In 1909 it was recommended that the Medical Corps should be integrated into the army's war games and that RAMC officers should be trained in supply and transport duties.[56] All were signs of an army slowly coming to terms with the changing nature of war before 1914: discipline was but one issue in this process.

Nevertheless, significant changes in disciplinary practice were forced upon the army by the experiences of the First World War. For example, the number of death sentences passed in 1918 was approximately 40 per cent lower than the total for 1917, which was itself merely a continuation of the trend started in 1915 and carried through 1916.[57] In other words the British Army had changed course and far fewer men were condemned in 1918 than in earlier years. The introduction of Court-Martial Officers (CMOs) and a greater understanding of shell-shock might have played a small part in this development, but it was a general change in attitude towards matters of discipline that had by far the greatest impact. The emergence of a citizen army, anticipated by Henderson after his study of American Civil War armies, initially made up of volunteers but latterly of conscripts, had crucially altered the nature of command. Most significant of all were the changing perceptions of the rankers by senior officers, as epitomised by Maxse, and a realignment of the relationship between officers and men. This latter development was an inevitable outcome of both the changing basis for recruitment into the army and the altered composition of the officer corps. The limited acceptance of the ethos prevalent in the pre-war auxiliary formations as the model for the citizen army probably ensured that discipline was not so inflexible that it would collapse. It is worth noting that Baynes, whose argument often appears to be at odds with this notion of command by (limited) consent, was dealing only with a Regular unit.

While it is important to view the death sentence in the context of these changes to the structure of the army, it cannot be overstated that the most important decisions regarding individual condemnations were usually made by pre-war commanders whose ideas had been shaped by tradition rather than by post-1914 developments. The ratio of executions to condemnations remained stable at roughly 10 per cent: it was the number of condemnations by courts martial that had fallen. Concerns about the quality of recruits and suspicions about the nature of discipline in Territorial as well as New Army and Dominion units were paramount and determined many an outcome. Assumptions concerning the fighting abilities of these troops coupled with pre-war notions of ineffective discipline in such units can be detected in many commanders' recommendations. For example, in reviewing a death sentence passed on a young Irish soldier, one brigade commander noted 'the discipline of the 9th R.I. Rifles is good *for a service battalion*' (my italics).[58] The implication that discipline in service battalions was generally poor is a misleading one. Of necessity discipline was different in pre-war auxiliary units to their Regular counterparts, but it remained effective.[59] New Army formations shaped their own approach to discipline and there is no substantive evidence to suggest that they were universally blighted by indiscipline. During the war the auxiliary battalions and their ancestor units maintained a similarly effective discipline, but the pre-war assumptions of the Regular army commanders lingered. During the Battle of the Somme General Sir Henry Rawlinson, Fourth Army commander, expressed surprise that both the New Army and Dominion units had 'fought with a bravery and determination which one had never dared to hope for'.[60] These notions persisted beyond the war. Writing in 1945 Lord Moran stated:

> The difference between a battalion of the professional army of 1914 and a Kitchener unit was not that years of training had made the actions of the Regular soldier automatic, but that they had implanted in the very marrow of the men the creed of the Regiment which blossomed into a living faith till nothing else mattered.[61]

Commanders were expected to take a close interest in matters of discipline, including the courts martial. This did not change between 1914 and 1918 regardless of any transition the army was undergoing and commanders remained responsible, and therefore answerable, for both the discipline and performance of their troops. In any case the latter was generally held to be inseparable from the former.

There was a fine line between the natural desire of a senior commander to oversee matters of discipline and interference in judicial decisions which undermined the independence of courts martial. After all, the courts martial were designed as an adjunct to discipline rather than overseers of justice. Regardless of their theoretical status, courts martial were not independent. They were convened by commanders to try cases which for some reason were beyond the scope of disciplinary measures available to more immediate superiors such as NCOs. In effect, then, courts martial were intended only to try more serious cases or cases which it was deemed desirable to be tried rather than dealt with summarily. One such reason was that the commander wished to make an example of a soldier or group of soldiers to deter others under his command. Executions were published in Routine Orders and circulated throughout the army. Wide circulation of sentences imposed by courts martial would achieve the aim of deterrence far better than any summary punishment, the impact of which would be more localised. Furthermore, if there was a concern about discipline in any unit a court martial could be convened as a display of remedial action, perhaps to satisfy a higher commander. Hence in many ways courts martial can be regarded as overt statements of military authority rather than judicial hearings. The trappings of legal processes merely served to put an acceptable face on what was in effect a tool of military authority.

The application of this tool was most common before and during planned offensives. There is an obvious relationship between the number of death sentences passed and British offensives. Put simply, the number of death sentences handed out by courts martial increased as zero hour approached. A marked increase in condemnations for roughly one month prior to any of the big offences can be detected.[62] This was a result of both an increased desertion rate as tension mounted close to the battle front and a general tightening of discipline as the High Command stamped its authority on the ranks in readiness for the offensive. Cecil Lewis, a pilot during the Battle of the Somme, noticed how 'the initial tension that preceded the offensive relaxed as day after day the pressure on the enemy was sustained'.[63] Whether harsher discipline at this time acted as a deterrent or not is unclear: it seems unlikely that soldiers who lost their nerve would think rationally about the consequences. Furthermore, approximately one third of those executed had been previously sentenced to death, but reprieved. Clearly, the threat of death for men who, as Sassoon put it, were 'provisionally sentenced to death'[64] did little to deter. Yet the strong belief among senior army officers that this atmosphere of fear would maintain discipline in the ranks remained a strong one.

The argument that executions were a lottery [65] is not entirely accurate. It is true that the confirmation of a death sentence did not always follow concerns about unit discipline – though some certainly did – but more immediate concerns about the general state of the British Expeditionary Force (BEF) were seemingly of greater importance to the commander-in-chief. Yet the process of confirming a sentence was a very deliberate and considered one that consumed a great amount of very senior officers' time. Many of the decisions to execute men were made on the grounds of a soldier's character and whether he remained of any value to the army. Those who were considered degenerate or were tainted hereditarily were castigated as worthless.[66] In the search for examples many of these supposedly worthless men were shot. Those who were of little further use to the army such as the shell-shocked were also in danger of facing a firing squad. It is noteworthy that the example used by Gary Sheffield to show that executions were a lottery, Private Skilton of 22 Royal Fusiliers, was quite possibly suffering from shell-shock.[67] These signs of weakness only increased the probability of execution. Executions were not entirely a lottery. However, Sheffield is correct to assert that to regard an execution as a barometer of poor discipline or morale in a particular formation is over-simplistic and unreliable.

The deterrent principle so dominant in ideas about discipline throughout the war demanded that examples were made of men at certain moments of the war – usually preceding large offensives. On the other hand too many executions could have an adverse effect on the regiments. Broadly speaking approximately one in every ten men condemned by court martial had their sentence confirmed. There are many features of this process that suggest a consistent approach. For instance, taken annually or by theatre of the war, the ratio of executions to condemnations does not vary significantly from the 10 per cent mean. Even if the regiments are broken down by country of origin a similar confirmation rate can be detected.[68] This suggests that, far from being a lottery, there was an implicit policy on the confirmation of death sentences that amounted to a form of 'bureaucratic decimation'. Ultimate judicial power rested with the commander-in-chief during the war, but the enormous burden of the task surely forced the role to be considerably delegated. Major-General Wyndham Childs claimed that Sir John French agonised over capital cases for many hours.[69] Yet this seems highly unlikely. Is it feasible that, given his other commitments, the commander-in-chief personally considered the fate of over 3000 men sentenced to be shot, not to mention the cases of another 309,511 British soldiers convicted by courts martial?[70] French considered the fate of 676 men condemned by courts martial: an average of approximately forty for each month of his tenure as commander-in-chief (for Haig the number was considerably greater, averaging more than seventy a month throughout 1916 and 1917). If we are to believe Childs' assertion then the commander-in-chief had little time for his many other duties. In reality this function was delegated – probably to Childs himself and later to the Personal Services Branch, headed by Brigadier General Wroughton, a career soldier who was also a qualified barrister.[71]

Commanders often had to account for incidents in the front line, especially those involving military reverses. Occasionally this necessitated an outline of action taken as a consequence. For example, Major-General Ivor Maxse, GOC 18th Division, submitted a report about an incident that occurred in December 1915 during which a German wiring party had entered a British trench and captured 19 men of the Northamptonshire Regiment. The report exonerated the officer in charge of the unit and laid the blame on two NCOs, Lance Sergeant Barford and Corporal Tibble, who were subsequently tried for cowardice. On 30 December 1915 Maxse wrote: 'I am therefore using the incident to illustrate to *all battalions* the necessity of never surrendering without a fight, even when caught in a hole [my italics].'[72] The wide exposure that Maxse desired from this case was only achievable by using the court as a forum and he was able to demonstrate both to those above him and to those under his command simultaneously his readiness to take positive steps to firm up discipline in his division. Summary punishment would not achieve either aim.

This case also highlights how disciplinary concerns often varied according to rank and it is interesting that the NCOs had been singled out as blameworthy. This was consistent with the general trend throughout the war: NCOs were more likely to have a death sentence against them carried out than were private soldiers. Twenty-four of the 134 NCOs sentenced to death had their sentences carried out compared to 316 out of 2938 privates[73] (15 and 11 per cent respectively) indicating that the commander-in-chief placed a greater emphasis on making examples of NCOs. There is further evidence that higher standards of discipline were expected of NCOs in Maxse's comments of 3 January 1916 in which he stated:

> By making examples of Sergeant Barford and Corporal Tibble this lesson will be further brought home to NCOs. It is thus hoped that the incident may be turned to ultimate advantage.[74]

On 11 January 1916 Corporal Tibble was sentenced to death by court martial. Curiously, Sergeant Barford was sentenced to 5 years' penal servitude.[75] However, Tibble's conviction was subsequently quashed by the commander-in-chief although the reason for this also remains obscure.

Fear of accusation of being soft on discipline caused some commanders to interfere more directly with courts martial. Writing after the war, Major Gerald Hurst, a former court-martial officer and a conservative MP, remarked how commanders would often censure officers who sat on courts martial as being unnecessarily lenient. A Brigadier, he stated, reported two officers because they were 'too kind-hearted to be efficient disciplinarians'.[76] Elsewhere, generals were prepared to challenge the findings of courts martial. Hurst cited one such example where, he alleged, the president of a court was required to 'furnish in writing a full explanation of his conduct in *allowing* the acquittals [of two men charged with plundering a shop] to take place' (my italics).[77] The court, it appears, was regarded by some as no more than an arm of the disciplinary machine and failure to arrive at the expected decision by a court could be viewed as an act of disciplinary sabotage.

When the Army Council Committee of Enquiry into the Rules and Procedures of Courts-Martial, chaired by the Right Honourable Sir Charles Darling, reported in 1919, they too raised concerns that some commanders had interfered with the independence of the courts. However, the Committee appears to have been concerned with the nature of interference rather than with the principle itself. In fact it was implicit in the report that a certain degree of interference was not only acceptable but expected. In particular the Committee recognised that the requirements of discipline often necessitated the court taking a view wider than that of the accused's own unit. Consideration, it was suggested, should be given to the prevalence of a particular offence in the brigade or division and the severity of the punishment should reflect this wider view. This clearly presented the courts martial with a problem in assessing these wider disciplinary demands. The Committee, however, recognised a *de facto* solution:

> It is, therefore, in our opinion, necessary and right that a superior officer, who alone can know the state of discipline generally in the force under his command, should be at liberty to publish in Orders notices to the effect that certain offences are becoming common, and that persons who commit them in future must expect to be dealt with more severely than in the past.[78]

The Committee did lend credence to Hurst's allegations that more direct interference had occurred when they reported that:

> We are satisfied that during the present war officers have, in one or two instances, issued circulars upon the subject of sentences in terms which cannot be justified. ... [We recommend] that the Army Council deal severely with any attempted interference with the judicial discretion of Courts which may be brought to their notice.[79]

Evidently, a fine line existed between what constituted proper concern and directives on discipline and what amounted to improper interference. Despite their recognition of the 'judicial discretion of the Courts', it is clear that the Committee acknowledged that the requirements of discipline overrode all other considerations. It was accepted that individual cases should be dealt with not according to the merits of the case but according to the wider disciplinary needs of the brigade or division. This often provided a justification for executions during the war and partly explains why some cases that resulted in execution appear to be less serious, on the basis of the evidence, than others which were commuted to lesser punishments. In most instances the decision whether to carry out an execution or not was reached on the basis of the seriousness of the individual's crime balanced against the state of discipline in the unit, brigade or division. Undoubtedly, however, there were many cases where one or other of these two criteria was considered sufficiently serious in its own right to justify the confirmation of a death sentence.

Two cases in early 1915, both in 6th Division, illustrate these differing approaches. The first was that of Private Hope, 2nd Leinster Regiment, who had deserted his unit while in trenches at L'Epiniette in December 1914. He was arrested nearby at Armentières the following February. His crime was compounded by his actions: he was wearing a stolen military police uniform and gave false particulars when challenged. He later claimed to have been captured by the enemy only to escape and return to the British lines. The court rejected his version of events and sentenced him to death. The brigade commander, Brigadier General Harper, and the divisional commander, Major-General Keir, both recommended confirmation, adding simply 'I see no reason why the sentence should not be carried out'.[80] The corps commander, Lieutenant-General Pulteney, concurred and it was referred to General Smith-Dorrien, GOC 2nd Army, who cited wider disciplinary concerns as sufficient justification for the execution:

> The Brigade discipline is second worst and the Battn [*sic*] discipline is also the second worst in the army. The case is a very bad one indeed and I recommend that the extreme penalty be carried out.[81]

This reasoning obviously impressed the commander-in-chief, John French, who duly confirmed the sentence. Hope, who also had two previous convictions for absence, was executed on 2 March 1915.

It is unclear whether Field-Marshal French was influenced most by the individual circumstances of the Hope case or whether wider disciplinary concerns were paramount in forming his decision. It is possible that either might have been sufficient to secure a confirmation of the sentence but a combination of both considerations appears to be the most likely explanation. There can be no doubt, however, in another case, also in 6th Division, which French had to consider just a few days later. Private Atkinson, 1st West Yorkshire Regiment, was convicted in March 1915 of deserting his unit in January. Atkinson's battalion commander, Major Barrington, stated that the defendant was 'a good soldier', but the brigade commander, Brigadier-General Harper, and the divisional commander, Major-General Keir, argued that it was a particularly bad case.[82] However, it was Smith-Dorrien who, on 23 February 1915, provided a broader justification for executing the man:

> The discipline of this Brigade is the worst of the army and the discipline of the 1st West Yorkshire is the worst in that Brigade this month – the seriousness of the offence of desertion to avoid duty in the trenches is not appreciated for no capital punishment has been carried out in the 6th Division [Hope was not executed until March 1915] – An example in the Division is very necessary and as this is a very bad one in itself merits the capital punishment. I recommend that it be carried out.[83]

Although Smith-Dorrien remarked that Atkinson's was a bad case this was probably to show consistency with his other generals. In any case Smith-Dorrien's reasoning hinges on his contention that the needs of discipline would be best served by an execution in the division.

In fact three men of 6th Division were executed in early March 1915: Hope, Atkinson and another man from 1st West Yorkshire Regiment, Private Kirk, who was described as an 'average Private' with a good record.[84] There was a similarity between the cases of Privates Hope and Kirk: both had presented a challenge to the authority of the army. Hope had donned none other than a military policeman's uniform and given false information. Kirk, it appeared, deserted to avoid a Field Punishment imposed by court martial for an offence of drunkenness. Such a challenge to the authority of the army and in particular the court martial was likely to have grave consequences for the individual. Significantly, the brigade commander recommended Kirk's execution on the grounds that 'it is a bad case and there is far too much crime [drunkenness and absence] in the battalion'.[85] Major-General Keir, GOC 6th Division, agreed that 'the amount of crime in this battalion is excessive'.[86] Kirk's was the third execution in the division within a few days; another followed within a month in what appears to have been a concerted effort to tighten up discipline. Eleven more executions were carried out in 6th Division during the war, a very high number when compared with other divisions.

There was little alteration in this dual approach to formulating the final decision throughout the war, with one important exception. It is evident that concerns existed from 1914 onwards about the quality of recruits. The soldier's character as well as his physique was generally thought to be the product of heredity. It was widely believed that 'degenerate' soldiers had an adverse effect on unit discipline and while these concerns were less evident whilst the army remained a Regular force issues such as eugenics became more and more important as the recruiting net was cast wider. In the minds of some the army was reaching further down towards the bottom of the barrel and from 1916 onwards 'degeneracy' became more important in the decision making process.[87] Coupled with this – and closely related to it – was an increasing concern about the effects on discipline of the condition known as shell-shock. Indeed, many believed that shell-shock was a disciplinary matter rather than a medical one and that even acknowledging the condition would undermine the fighting mettle of the army, as Lord Moran explained:

> When the name shell-shock was coined the number of men leaving the trenches with no bodily wound leapt up. The pressure of opinion in the battalion – the idea stronger than fear – was eased by giving fear a respectable name. When the social slur was removed and the military risks were abolished the weaklings may have decided in cold blood to malinger, or perhaps when an alternative was held out the suggestion of safety was too much for their feeble will.[88]

The solution for some was to combat shell-shock with tighter discipline.

Shell-shock – a matter of discipline

British soldiers, it has been argued, were especially vulnerable to shell-shock during the First World War because of their ignorance of modern war and because their idealism was constantly frustrated by incompetent generals.[89] But we should treat this view with caution. Most British troops were urban working-class volunteers or conscripts who were surprisingly well adapted for the monotony and danger of war because of their pre-war experience in industry.[90] Rather than idealistic – a trend perhaps more identifiable with First World War poetry – most workers had low expectations. According to one historian:

> Tedium, regimentation, subordination and physical hardship were the common lot of the British working man. Industrial accidents were commonplace. Those in mining could produce casualty figures almost on a military scale. During the war the British worker merely substituted one set of hardships for another.[91]

In truth, the army's perception of shell-shock and the treatment it used was most influenced by its own immediate concerns. The sole purpose of treatment, from a military point of view, was to return as many men to the fighting line as quickly as possible. This was as true of other armies as it was of the British. For example, the approach to the problem in the German army bore remarkable similarities to that of the British[92] and reflected *all* armies' preoccupation with discipline. The practice of psychology, and in particular the ideas of Freud, were to benefit enormously from the experience of the war,[93] but broadly speaking this was a development that took place despite the army's requirements and not because of them. Nevertheless, psychologists and others responsible for the treatment of men suffering from war neuroses did find some common ground with the military leadership. It has been suggested that the treatment of 'anti-military' behaviour was analogous with 'anti-social' behaviour in so far as the purpose of treatment was concerned, namely to eradicate deviance.[94] There can be little doubt that some of the treatment used was intended to act as a deterrent.

Certain individuals were subjected to particularly brutal treatment. Often this reflected pre-existing ideas about 'outsiders' who, prior to 1914, were thought to represent a danger to society. During the war a threat to military discipline was perceived. The distinction between the normal and so-called abnormal dated back to the eighteenth century, but exerted a strong influence in the diagnosis and treatment of shell-shock after 1914.[95] Especially vulnerable in this were the Irish, who, it was widely believed, were predisposed to lunacy, and those deemed degenerate. Normal men, it was thought, were capable of killing, but those who could not were deemed '"childish and infantile" and needed to regain their manhood'.[96] It has been suggested that 'so-called "emotional Irishmen" and "weak privates" were given progressively more painful electric shocks in an attempt to compel "cure"'.[97] This was not unique to the British; in other armies Jews and Gypsies were similarly singled out.[98] In the British army, though, it was the Irish and troops deemed 'degenerate' who also were most vulnerable to the death penalty.[99]

To prevent the feared shell-shock epidemic, the army employed a number of strategies. Firstly, it sought to deter through the military code and with harsh punishments. Secondly, deterrence could be achieved through the form of treatment. Finally, there was an overt reluctance to recognise the condition. Partly the result of a misunderstanding of the origins and causes of war neurosis, but increasingly to avoid legitimising what it saw as malingering, the army divided the condition into two categories: commotional and emotional shell-shock. The former was characterised by its having a physical cause such as being buried by a shell explosion and was classified as a wound, while emotional shell-shock was not. After 1918 this had profound implications for those seeking pensions.[100] During the war, though, this was a management ploy rooted in wider concerns about discipline.

Nevertheless, the relationship between discipline and shell-shock was a complex one. Some military commanders, like Lieutenant-General Goodwin, told the Southborough Committee of Enquiry into Shell-Shock that 'well trained and disciplined troops were less liable to suffer from these troubles [war neuroses]'.[101] Others such as Dr Gordon Holmes, a consultant neurologist to the BEF, agreed with Lord Moran and stated that 'the great increase in these cases [of shell-shock] coincided with the knowledge that such a condition of "shell-shock" existed'.[102] By far the greatest concern during the war was that shell-shock was infectious, causing mass hysteria, and destroying discipline in even the best units if not checked. Once again individual circumstances became less important than the wider disciplinary concerns, a view expressed to the Committee by Lord Gort:

> I think 'shell-shock,' like measles, is so infectious that you cannot afford to run risks with it at all and in war *the individual is of small account* [my italics]. If one or two go by the board it is extremely unfortunate and sad but it cannot be helped. A large proportion must be wounded or killed. It must be looked upon as a form of disgrace to the soldier. A certain class of men are alright out of the line but as soon as they know they are to go back they start getting 'shell-shock' and so forth.

It is not clear what Lord Gort meant when he used the word 'class' in this context. If he meant it as a comment on the working-class troops, who made up most of the rank and file, then we should view his opinion as yet more evidence of ascribed traits based on ideas about social status and the influence of eugenics in matters of military discipline and individual character. But it also is possible that he was referring to a 'type' of soldier rather than an identifiable social group. If so then his view was consistent with many who sat in judgment on the courts martial and indeed with those whose recommendations influenced the final outcome. After the war a memorandum was prepared by the Judge Advocate General's office based on statistics extracted from capital cases. Thirty-two cases of minors who had been executed were examined and in ten instances it was found that shell-shock had been used as a defence at trial only to be rejected by both the court and the commander-in-chief.[103] This was a very high percentage, which might suggest that shell-shock featured in approximately a third of cases tried.

In another report, written by Major Barnes, D. A. A. G., it was found that in three of the eighteen executions for cowardice, courts martial had rejected a shell-shock defence.[104] This reflected the widely held belief in the army that it was pernicious to take claims of shell-shock too seriously, to prevent what they believed would be a potential shell-shock epidemic. This was succinctly, though unwittingly, expressed by Douglas Haig when he appended the remark 'how can we ever win if this plea is allowed?' in response to a recommendation for mercy in the case of a nerve-shaken soldier during the Battle of the Somme.[105]

Throughout the war shell-shock remained a major factor in the army's preoccupation with a possible breakdown of discipline. On the other hand, as well as being considered a cause of poor discipline, shell-shock was regarded by some as a symptom of a lack of discipline brought on by a character defect, as illustrated by Lord Moran's comments:

> Good fellows in the line did not believe in shell-shock, they did not want to believe in it. Perhaps in their hearts, knowing what lay ahead, they could not altogether approve too sensitive men.[106]

Others viewed the effects of battle on the mind in a different manner. W. H. R. Rivers, best known for his treatment of the poet Siegfried Sassoon, was influenced by the ideas of Sigmund Freud. According to Rivers, shell-shock was brought on by the repression of the natural instinct to flee the battlefield. The consequent neurosis, he argued, was the result of a conflict between that instinct and a sense of duty, which weighed most heavily on officers who bore a greater burden because of the nature of public school education.[107] Rivers elaborated on his theory to the Southborough Committee:

> The explanation I give [for the causes of shell-shock] involves my special theoretical position that man's normal reaction to danger is what I call manipulative activity. Every animal has a natural reaction to danger, perhaps more than one, and man's is manipulation of such a kind to get him out of the dangerous situation.... If he cannot have that, or if it is restricted in any way, you have a prominent condition for the occurrence of neurosis in one form or another.

But this view was not as unique or as original as Rivers suggested. Nor was it radically different to the beliefs of some military theorists. Writing at the turn of the century, Colonel Henderson – military historian, theorist and instructor – remarked:

> The truth is, when bullets are whacking against tree trunks and solid shot are cracking skulls like egg shells, the consuming passion in the heart of the average man is to get out of the way. Between the physical fear of going forward, and the moral fear of turning back, there is a predicament of exceptional awkwardness, from which a hidden hole in the ground would be a wonderfully welcome outlet.[108]

This was hardly an endorsement of Freudian theory, but the recognition by some pre-war army commanders of a conflict between instinct and duty is significant. The army remained a conservative institution at this time, but care should be taken not to ignore such modernising influences as did exist.

Similar views were expressed by some former officers in their evidence to the Southborough Committee, but theirs was the minority opinion. Generally, shell-shock was seen as the result of poor discipline and it was widely held that shell-shock did not occur in the best or well-disciplined divisions – the final report was most explicit on this point.[109] Soldiers who attempted to defend their actions by citing shell-shock were, in practical terms, confessing both to the court and to the reviewing officers that they lacked discipline. In many cases the exact opposite of the desired effect was achieved. This, combined with the feeling that shell-shocked soldiers were of little further value to the army, was likely to result in the confirmation of a death sentence. This appears to have happened in the cases of Sub-Lieutenant Edwin Dyett and 2nd Lieutenant Eric Skeffington Poole – the only two officers to be executed for purely military offences – as well as in countless cases involving men of the ranks.

Dyett and Poole were both represented at their respective trials – in this respect, therefore, their cases are unusual – and both presented a sophisticated defence based on long histories of diagnosed, and therefore medically substantiated, shell-shock. Dyett, a subaltern in the Royal Naval Division, had even requested a transfer to sea duties because his nerves could not stand the strain of trench warfare. Poole, who had been promoted from the ranks, had been treated for shell-shock in July 1916 after being hit by clods of earth caused by a shell explosion near Contalmaison. Evacuated to a convalescent home, but returned to duty after a medical examination, even his comrades acknowledged that he was especially prone to shell-shock.[110] He deserted again, which confirmed in the minds of his commanders the belief that his presence in the front line had a detrimental effect on the men in his charge and on discipline in general. He was executed on 10 December 1916, the first officer to face a firing squad.[111]

Similar case histories can be found among the men of the ranks. For example, Private Harry Poole, 7th Yorkshire Regiment, had been diagnosed as suffering from shell-shock in July 1915. During the Battle of the Somme in 1916 he left the front line trench to which he had been posted. He was tried and sentenced to death for desertion. However, it was widely known in his unit that he was especially nervous under fire and this was recognised by the court and a recommendation to mercy was made 'on the grounds of his nervous condition'.[112] The brigade commander, Brigadier-General Glasgow, agreed and recommended commutation of the sentence. Major-General Robertson, GOC 17th Division, also recommended that the sentence be commuted and Poole transferred to a labour battalion because 'his fervour under fire is such as to render him quite incapable of reason or self-control'.[113] A medical examination proved inconclusive and disregarding all the recommendations Douglas Haig confirmed the sentence. It seems likely that the overriding concern of the commander-in-chief was that discipline would collapse if those who broke down under fire were transferred to less dangerous duties and this undoubtedly influenced his decision. Individuals were indeed 'of small account' when balanced against wider concerns of discipline.

Shell-shock weighed heavily on the minds of those responsible for maintaining discipline in the British Army, but rarely in a compassionate sense. It seems highly unlikely that a condemned soldier was spared the execution post because he was suffering from the condition. Indeed, as I have argued, it might even have acted as a factor in singling out some of those who were made examples. There was a clear rejection of war neuroses as an excuse for failure. What the army most needed to avoid was a general belief among those in the ranks that condemned men had been reprieved because of the state of their nerves. The treatment of shell-shock cases certainly improved as the war progressed but there is no evidence of a change in attitude towards the condition by those responsible for the implementation of military justice: they simply could not afford to be seen to allow such a plea. One witness told the Southborough Committee that increased understanding of the condition meant that one man in particular, whose case he was familiar with, who had been executed in 1915 would not have faced the same fate in 1917 or 1918.[114] The evidence simply does not bear out this interpretation. In 1917 men were sentenced to death and executed in greater numbers than at any other moment in the war – or in British military history for that matter. The reduction of death sentences passed in 1918 owed more to the altered state of the army and a growing reluctance to use the death penalty on conscripted troops than it did to increased awareness of war neuroses. In any case many of the executions of 1918 involved men who put forward defences based on shell-shock but which had been rejected by both the courts and the commander-in-chief.

Use of the death penalty on the war fronts was often the subject of debate in Britain. There was widespread unease at the thought of the execution of soldiers for military crimes such as desertion. Inevitably, concerns that executed men were suffering from shell-shock surfaced in parliament and in the newspapers. *The Times* frequently linked the condition with the army's disciplinary practices in articles that carried titles such as 'The Death Penalty in the Army' and 'Shell Shock and Desertion'.[115] Early on in the war Lord Knutsford, Chairman of the London Hospital, had identified the medical shortcomings of the army:

> There are a number of our gallant soldiers for whom at present no proper provision is obtained, but is sorely needed. They are men suffering from severe mental and nervous shock due to exposure, excessive strain and tension. They can be cured if only they can receive the proper attention. If not cured they will drift back into the world as miserable wrecks for the rest of their lives.[116]

The army, though, was more concerned with the disciplinary implications of the condition. Even Charles Myers, who resigned as consultant to the BEF in 1917 in protest at the lack of understanding of such cases, was inclined to consider shell shock in the context of discipline.[117] But as Freud observed:

> The physician himself was under military command and had his own personal dangers – loss of seniority or a charge of neglecting his duty – if he allowed himself to be led by considerations other than those prescribed for him.[118]

The home front

As the army expanded and the burden of the war impacted more on British society so too did calls for the imposition on the population of military-style discipline. This was not merely a reaction to the introduction of conscription, but can be detected during the earliest period of the war. Usually, the death penalty was omitted from such calls, but not always. Writing in 1915, Sir Martin Conway – Director-General of the Imperial War Museum in 1917 and Independent MP for the combined English Universities from 1918 to 1931 – suggested that British workers should dedicate themselves to the service of the nation. Conway further suggested that 'If he will not thus act voluntarily he must thus act under compulsion, and subject to the same penalty as awaits a deserter in the field'.[119] Not surprisingly, there appears to have been little support for this view and punishments contained in measures aimed at the civilian population such as the Defence of the Realm Act, 1914 (DORA) cannot be compared with those in the military code.

Nevertheless, military-style discipline did creep into civilian life. The organisation and control of the workforce was identified as essential to military success early in the war and legislation soon followed. The Asquith government created the Ministry of Munitions (which had its own intelligence system) in 1915, with Lloyd George as its Minister. A National Register, which contained details of everyone between the ages of 15 and 65, became law in July 1915 and formed the basis not only of military conscription, 'but conscription for all aspects of the war effort'.[120] Britain increasingly resembled a military state with 'the military in the ascendant' as the country was divided into 'special administrative areas each under the direction of an Authorised Competent Military Authority who was answerable to General Headquarters'.[121]

The realities of total war had dawned on the British and liberalism was an early victim. According to Conway:

> In former days it was impossible to co-ordinate for war purposes more than a small part of a nation; but modern conditions have altered all that. Now, by aid of developed means of communication, the complete co-ordination of all has been rendered possible, and those countries which have devoted themselves scientifically to preparation for war have learnt how to organise all of the forces of a nation to the purpose of fighting. If one combatant [Germany] is thus organised its enemy [Britain] must submit to a like discipline. If in one country individual liberty is entirely done away with, in the interests of the crowd's collective power, its opponents must submit to a like suspension of freedom, or they cannot expect to be victorious. Citizens, whose individualism is so strong that they will not submit themselves to such restraint, must either be compelled to submit to it, or should sacrifice their citizenship. This does not necessarily mean that all citizens must fight. Some are weaklings; some are cowards; some can do better work at home than at the front; these and a good many others are better suited for the various kinds of work that need to be done outside the fighting line. But all must be ready to perform the function indicated for them by the hierarchies of authority that war should install.[122]

Although the government symbolically clung to some of its liberal values it was increasingly obvious that measures such as those espoused by Conway were necessary. Lord Derby's compromise scheme for recruitment into the armed forces, which unsuccessfully sought to avoid compulsion, typified the Liberal government's dilemma. Mirroring this process was the increasing role of the State, and, in particular, the Munitions of War Act and the various amendments to the Defence of the Realm Act, which placed many factories under the control of the Admiralty and the War Office. The role of the military gradually expanded and by the end of 1917 the army was also 'responsible for monitoring and managing "industrial and revolutionary unrest in the United Kingdom" ', a role it maintained until 1920.[123] The marriage of the military and British society was hardly natural and conflict did occasionally arise. Insensitive military authorities were partly responsible for the unrest of 1917, though the main causes lay elsewhere.[124] The military for its part had little understanding of the populace and even less sympathy for workers who, it believed, had it easy by escaping military service. Consequently, it was not unusual for striking workers to be conscripted into the army, as happened in Rochdale following a dispute about illegal dilution of the workforce.[125] It is interesting that in this case, although the firm was in the wrong and was fined by the government for its actions, the response entailed handing over to the military potential ringleaders of future disputes. It appears that military punishments, including the threat of the death penalty, could be indirectly applied to troublesome workers.

Nor were such measures confined to Britain. Elsewhere in the Empire similar views prevailed in the ever-changing relationship between State and worker. In Canada, where military conscription became law on 29 August 1917, political exigencies had forced Prime Minister Borden to pledge respect for religious beliefs and to disrupt farming, family life and business as little as possible. In agrarian British Columbia objections to military service were most usually based on the impact enforced military service of the most able would have on family farms. But, following an appeal by 49 coal miners, exemption from military service was granted to 35 of them because of the essential nature of their work. In his judgment, however, Judge Thompson, warned the miners:

> These appellants must understand they are now soldiers. And where exemption is granted to them it is so granted because the Court is of the opinion they are of greater value to the nation by remaining coal miners than by becoming soldiers. And the only way they can continue to be of greater value as coal miners than as soldiers is by producing coal. ... they must work as steadily and continuously as though they had donned khaki.[126]

Judge Thompson also laid down a set of military-style rules under which the coal miners could continue to work. These included continuous employment at the mine and an obligation to ensure that no strike – including those by other workers – interfered with their work. The penalty for failure in this last instance was harsh:

> In the event of a strike or cessation of work by workmen other tha[n] exempted men whereby the latter are prevented from working, exemptions shall cease, subject however, to the provisions in rules 9 [arrest by military authorities] and 10 [future judicial orders].

This may seem a harsh ruling but it must be remembered that this appeal has been made by the United Mine Workers of America, and it will be the duty of the officials of the brotherhood to ensure that no such strikes or cessations of work occur.[127]

The relationship between the military and the civilian workforce had been realigned. Standards of discipline among the workers did not necessarily equate to those of the army and punishments were certainly less harsh, but for those who did not attain the expected standard the alternative was often conscription and, therefore, exposure to the death penalty.

For some the threat of the death penalty became a reality. After the introduction of conscription in Britain, tribunals heard applications for exemption based on grounds of conscience. Approximately 16,000 men registered their objections to military service, of whom approximately 3300 accepted service in the Non-Combatant Corps on the Western Front. Others performed additional essential work, but more than 6000 refused to assist the war effort and went to prison. About 1500 of these proved to be intractable cases, the others being employed under a Home Office scheme.[128] The challenge to authority offered by these few men baffled the military authorities, whose responsibility they had become, and resolution of the problem was sought in the traditional military manner – deterrence. Three groups of conscientious objectors were smuggled out to the Western Front and there 34 of them were convicted of the military offence of disobedience and sentenced to death by courts martial in June 1916. The death sentences were eventually commuted by the commander-in-chief to ten years' penal servitude, but only after the direct intervention of the Prime Minister. The commander-in-chief did not confirm condemnations on four more men.[129] Coming only weeks after military courts had so rigidly applied the law in Ireland following the Easter Rising, this was a clear example of how military law could be applied to the civilian populace as well as to troops.

Summation

The outcome of only a very few capital cases appears to have been decided on the basis of its own merits. Disciplinary concerns were a major feature of the decision making process in most instances and *the* major factor in many of those cases. However, a survey of all the confirmed sentences in 1914 and 1915 (58 in total) reveals that in the majority of instances unit, brigade and divisional commanders stated that discipline was good. Criticism of the state of discipline normally crept in at corps and army level.[130] There is an obvious explanation for this: commanders were unwilling to admit to poor discipline in their own units as this was tantamount to self-criticism. What this reveals is that the army placed such value on good discipline that commanders were too afraid to face the consequences of appearing to be poor disciplinarians. It also reveals that the term was sufficiently vague to be interpreted differently at various levels of command: no one appears to have been concerned with the contradictions contained in the comments attached to each case file.

Of greater concern to those in a position to influence the bureaucratic process of confirmation was the perceived effect of regular examples. Executions assumed enormous importance in the rationale that underpinned the army's disciplinary approach. This was partly because of existing traditions – the British army had carried out a surprisingly high number of executions throughout the nineteenth century – but the reformation of the military code prior to the passing of the Army Act in 1881 had also impacted on disciplinary practice. In particular, the abolition of flogging (also 1881) had significant implications for soldiers during the First World War. The army had traditionally placed such emphasis on harsh deterrent-orientated punishments that the abolition of flogging had left a vacuum. Alternatives had simply not been developed, with the result that from 1914 until 1917 the army became increasingly dependent on capital punishment, which some commanders regarded as the *only* effective measure to combat desertion in particular.

Imprisonment, it was thought, only rewarded the coward by removing him from the trenches. The Army Suspension of Sentences Act of 1915 was designed to retain men in the trenches 'with the sentence hanging over his head' rather than 'reward' offenders with prison sentences.[131] In the field, extensive use was made of the increasingly unpopular Field Punishment: 80,989 men were sentenced to field punishments by courts martial – officers were not similarly punished.[132] But the absence of traditional forms of corporal punishment and their inability to develop alternative strategies to maintain discipline increasingly forced British commanders to regard capital punishment as the solution, at least until the end of 1917. In one of the first capital cases Brigadier General Anley, commander of 12th Brigade, remarked that 'a serious example is necessary' to prevent absence from the front line.[133] Similar sentiments were expressed in other cases, but General Sir Horace Smith-Dorrien, commander of the 2nd Army, was more explicit:

> There is a serious prevalence of desertion to avoid duty in the trenches, especially in the 8th Brigade and I am sure that the *only* way to stop it is to carry out some death sentences [my italics].[134]

Identical views were expressed in another case the following year: 'there are still a few cases of this desertion and the full penalty is the only means by which it can [be] stopped.'[135]

The steady increase in the number of condemnations – 85 in 1914; 591 in 1915; 856 in 1916 and 904 in 1917 – reflected not only the enlarged size of the army, but also the increasing reliance on capital punishment in the absence of viable alternatives. In 1918, however, the number of death sentences passed by courts martial fell to a mere 515. This dramatic fall was the result of changes within the army as it modernised. Not only were conscripts, who by 1918 made up the bulk of the army, handled with greater caution than were their volunteer predecessors, but an alteration in strategic thought – resulting from the disappointments of 1916 and 1917 – brought with it a subtle shift in views about the role of individual soldiers. Fully discussed in the following chapter, the basic feature of this argument is that at the end of 1917 the British High Command abandoned as the basis for victory its reliance on the perceived moral superiority of the British soldier over his German adversary. Thereafter, the emphasis shifted away from nineteenth-century ideas of individualism.

Discipline, whether individual or collective, remained the focus of military leadership. Throughout the war the relationship between leaders and led was redefined as it increasingly absorbed men from all sections of society. As John Bourne points out: 'The new citizen army was never completely docile in the face of military authority even on first acquaintance.'[136] But the High Command clung on to ultimate control over the mechanisms of justice and discipline. Primarily concerned with defeating the enemy, the army cared little for individual soldiers. Military law merely served to legitimate this authority, which was usually handled with a surprising degree of caution, but which on occasions was applied in a most oppressive and brutal manner.

Soldiers in the German army were protected by the principle of the *Rechtsstaat,* French troops had the theoretical protection of the President of the Republic. Troops in other armies were allowed a right of appeal, but British soldiers enjoyed no such legal protection. Instead, British troops relied on the benevolence of the commander-in-chief or more likely the head of Personal Services Branch acting on his behalf. It is remarkable, therefore, that fewer British troops were executed than in the Austro-Hungarian and Russian armies where the right of appeal was preserved. Despite the lack of any clearly defined legal protection against miscarriages of justice it appears that considerable restraint was exercised during the confirmation process. But the British soldier was far more at risk than the French *poilu* and even more so than his German counterpart. Restraint there most certainly was, but in an army where traditional punishments had been so dominated by the principle of deterrent the death penalty was viewed for much of the war as the most efficient means of preserving discipline. The army's dilemma was best summed up by Childs's rhetorical question 'what alternative punishment is there, when troops are facing the enemy?'[137]

3
Military Theory and Redefining Troop Morale

The concept of 'morale' is vague. In a recent study Gary Sheffield called it 'an imprecise term',[1] echoing J. G. Fuller's 1990 evaluation that it is 'an elusive subject'.[2] Earlier commentators also struggled to define it. Even the influential military theorist, Clausewitz, whose writings were valued by European military commanders, including the British, was deliberately vague on the matter:

> We prefer, therefore, to remain here more than usually incomplete and rhapsodical [on the subject of morale], content to have drawn attention to the importance of the subject in a general way.[3]

Yet this vague term assumed an enormous importance in British military thought and during much of the war it formed an essential element of strategic planning. Napoleon and Clausewitz remained the most influential writers for those who tried to define morale. Pre-war military theorists believed that human nature and, more importantly, human character shaped the fighting qualities of their troops. Likewise, other armies relied on similar qualities among their own troops. Undermining the enemy's morale was as important as sustaining one's own. According to Colonel Henderson, an instructor at Sandhurst and the Staff College from 1890 to 1899, whose writings were widely studied in the years leading up to the First World War:

> Human nature must be the basis of every leader's calculations. To sustain the *moral*[e] of his own men; to break down the *moral*[e] of his enemy – these are the great objects which, if he be ambitious of success, he must always keep in view.[4]

In common with other theorists writing at the turn of the century, Henderson used the word moral rather than morale in his writings. This can be confusing to the modern student but, as we will see, the terms are virtually interchangeable. The initial questions then, are what was this quality, what were its origins and how was it understood by commanders during World War I?

In his evidence to the Southborough Committee inquiring into shell-shock, Colonel J. F. C. Fuller had defined morale as 'the acquired quality which in highly-trained troops counterbalances the influence of the instinct of self-preservation'.[5] This is remarkably close to Henderson's own pre-war evaluation, except that Henderson saw the suppression of this instinct as 'the moral fear of turning back', indicating that a strong sense of duty and purpose underpinned what was in effect a willingness to continue fighting.[6] It is interesting that Henderson values the moral fear – a sense of duty – more so than an actual fear of, say, the death penalty, implying, perhaps, that the consent of the troops was necessary and that it took more than mere deterrent to maintain control of an army. Despite its authoritarian nature, the British, like all other armies, had to mobilise a mixture of strategies just to keep men in the field of battle. In practice a certain degree of negotiation was essential to the process, but this was backed up by a disciplinary system that could be rigidly applied. One historian has recently observed that 'sticks' could be used if the 'carrots' appeared to fail.[7] Military theorists on the other hand regarded motivation as the key to morale. Good leadership and a belief in the justness of the cause, which to pre-war British observers usually meant the preservation of the Empire, were essential factors in building this commitment to the war effort. These ideas broadly reflected perceived Clausewitzian wisdom. According to Clausewitz there were three factors, which he termed 'The Chief Moral Powers', that impacted on troop morale: '*The Talents of the Commander; The Military Virtue of the Army; Its National Feeling.*'[8] Able generals, he argued, engendered 'a spirit of boldness' in their troops, which acted to counter 'effeminacy of feeling' and 'degeneracy in a people rising in prosperity and immersed in an extremely busy commerce'.[9] This was itself an extension of Napoleon's own ideas. In 1806 the Emperor had accused one of his generals of being 'dishonourable' by leaving his troops, with the result that 'the army is becoming effeminate'.[10] A corporate identity, or *esprit de corps,* the result of expert training, fostered the army's military virtue – Clausewitz's second determining factor. But national spirit, which resulted in 'enthusiasm, fanatical zeal, faith, opinion', was the bedrock of troop morale in the Clausewitzian sense.[11] Most of these concepts were reflected in the 1914 War Office booklet *Infantry Training*, which encouraged officers to instil in their troops 'a sense of personal honour, duty, patriotism and *esprit de corps*'.[12] It appears that less importance was placed on good leadership, the emphasis being firmly on the efficacy of British imperialism.

It was this last feature that most linked notions of morality to morale. In Britain the preservation of the Empire was often portrayed as a moral duty. Conquered peoples were referred to as savages and the British colonists portrayed as civilisers. This was particularly so in the case of India where perceptions of Indian immorality helped to define the rationale that underpinned British rule. The most potent of moralistic weaponry – sexuality and sexual degeneracy – was often used to demonstrate why India could not be trusted to rule itself.[13] This rationale, which emerged during the nineteenth century, endured until after the First World War. General Dyer told an enquiry into the massacre at Amritsar in 1919 that he had ordered troops to open fire on the crowd because 'it would be doing a jolly lot of good and they [Indians] would realise that they were not to be wicked [by resisting British rule]'. The justification, he claimed, was not 'a question of merely dispersing the crowd, but one of producing a sufficient moral effect, from a military point of view, not only on those who were present but more specially throughout the Punjab'.[14] But it was the spirit of the moral cause and the morale of British troops that were seemingly inseparable. *The Times* reported in 1912 that the 'Moral of the British Force in Egypt' was 'the same irresistible force, generated by phlegmatic, patient, obstinate British Infantry, that has built the Empire'.[15] Henderson cited 'long centuries of free government and individual liberty' as the greatest factor in sustaining British soldiers' morale, adding that:

> It was not to strict discipline, not to enterprise of war, nor even to native hardiness, that Sir William Napier [a highly regarded military theorist and historian of the Napoleonic wars] attributed the military virtues of the British soldier, but to the British constitution.[16]

This thinly veiled reference to liberalism was consistent with Henderson's stance on conscription. Despite growing calls for the introduction of compulsory military service around the turn of the century, Henderson was not convinced. Significantly, it was the commitment – the morale – of conscripts that most concerned him. Following the Boer War he had defended the principle of voluntary service, adding that 'the *moral* of conscript armies has always been their weakest point'.[17] Other commentators had also called into question the reliability of troops not fighting for a national cause. In fact this particular line of thought dates back at least as far as Machiavelli who had advised against employing foreign auxiliary or mercenary troops, whom he variously described as cowards and as being useless. Machiavelli, like Clausewitz some three centuries later, advised the use of a citizen army, bound by its very nature to be more committed to the fight.[18]

After the war it was suggested by some that there existed a relationship between a lack of patriotic spirit and war neurosis. According to Dr. E. Mapother of the Maudsley Neurological Hospital this was mostly manifested in those defective in intelligence. 'The intellectually defective', he argued, 'is incapable of endurable patriotism', which often resulted in psychosis.[19] George Mosse has argued that 'the nation reflected and supported the stereotypes of normative society'. Shell-shocked soldiers who were unable to fight, he argues, were viewed as unpatriotic. The condition was regarded as 'a mental state which mirrored a social disease and national degeneration'.[20] It was no coincidence that the same groups of men – the Irish and so-called degenerate city dwellers – who were thought to be predisposed to suffering from shell-shock, had been considered a threat to society itself before the war, especially in matters relating to crime. Patriotism, it was thought, underpinned morale and contributed to the lack of crime, especially military crime. Speaking of the Union army during the American Civil War, Henderson noted that 'the moral of the armies . . . was necessarily good. Crime was practically unknown; of insubordination there was very little'. This, he observed, was achieved in spite of low standards of discipline because of 'the presence of men of intelligence and high principle'.[21]

The suggestion that morale was the product of social and political as well as military tradition was a refinement of Clausewitz's ideas. It placed the emphasis on long-term factors and, therefore, away from Napoleon's assertion that poor morale was solely the fault of bad officers. Napoleon frequently complained of poor standards in his officer corps, and often blamed them for indiscipline or inefficiency among his troops: 'when troops are demoralised,' he told General de Wrede, 'it is for their Commanders and officers to restore their morale, or to die in the attempt.'[22] After inspecting the 37th Light Infantry in 1813, he complained to his Minister of War that 'it would be impossible to see a finer body of men – or a worse set of officers'.[23] Napoleon, it seems, rarely had poor troops, but frequently had poor officers. Despite the influence of Napoleonic thought it appears that this doctrine had limited impact on the British army during the Great War. The problem was simply that while British tactics often anticipated the collapse of German morale, little account was taken of deteriorating morale in the British army. There existed no centralised office, no uniform policy and no coordinated approach to the issue of troop-morale.[24] Consequently, commanders were able to interpret indicators in their own preferred manner, taking action as they thought fit. Needless to say, few of them viewed poor morale as the fault of inadequate generalship because that was tantamount to professional suicide. Instead, problems could be ignored by vague interpretation of the data or the fault was laid at the feet of the troops. But complaints about troops were seemingly rare before offensives: at least one British commander subsequently suggested that 'it was common talk that no Divisional Commander dared say his Infantry were unfit to attack for fear of being sent home'.[25] Travers has indicated that many British commanders focused on perceived deficiencies among their troops to account for failures in their units rather than issues of leadership and tactics, particularly following the shambles at Loos in 1915 and again during the Somme campaign.[26] Furthermore, concerns about the poor quality of troops appear to have been heightened in formations where discipline was believed to be suspect. In at least one division, a number of executions were carried out in response to criticism of the formation from senior commanders during 1916. Significantly, the executions were justified on the grounds of the generally poor quality of troops in the division – the evaluation of its commander who retained his command in spite of concerns over poor discipline in his division.[27] Generals were, however, often removed from their commands: a process known as 'degumming'.[28] It was probably through fear of this that many commanders sought to shift the blame for failure away from themselves and onto their troops. Despite the teaching of theorists such as Henderson and the intentions of the High Command it seems that Napoleon's ideas were not always adhered to by every British commander.

Clausewitz listed the talents of the commander first of his three factors that determined morale. In Britain, by the turn of the century, these immediate causes had assumed less importance and the emphasis in military thought focused on the essential role the army played in preserving the Empire. During the First World War this took a more specific form that inextricably linked it to the defeat of Prussian militarism. Both the preservation of the Empire and the defeat of Prussian militarism were invariably portrayed in moralistic terms. The increasing portrayal of the enemy as immoral was a vital ingredient in raising the morale of the country and, more specifically, of troops in the field. The main function of propaganda was to maintain the war effort of soldiers and civilians alike and the Government capitalised on incidents such as German atrocities in Belgium, the sinking of the *Lusitania* and unrestricted submarine warfare. Many of the stories concerning German atrocities committed against the civilian population of Belgium were factually correct, but others, such as the baby with severed hands, were clearly an exaggeration.[29] The importance of these stories to the army, and to British society, was that it underpinned the notion of a 'moral war' and bolstered the nation's commitment to the war effort – its morale. References to varying forms of 'divine intervention' should also be viewed in this context. It had been usual for countries at war to cite God as an ally because this tended to confirm the morality of the cause in the minds of many. Entries containing such references in Douglas Haig's diaries have been attributed to delusions on Haig's part by one historian.[30] In reality, it would be odd if the commander of an army at war did not seek to moralise the cause (if only to himself) by claiming divine support. In wartime it was common to capitalise on such views. As Jay Winter has asserted, 'consent was an essential element of mass warfare'.[31]

Brigadier General Crozier was not averse to 'doping the minds of all with propagandic poison' to inculcate 'the brute-like bestiality which is so necessary for victory'.[32] Other forms were more subtle. Troops of all armies at the front were inundated with correspondence that mixed patriotic and sacred images. The morality of one's own cause and the immorality of the enemy was a simple juxtaposition all could comprehend even if the message was differently constructed on either side of the barbed wire. Germany denounced the allies for bringing black troops to a European theatre while the allies concentrated on vilifying a militaristic culture that had inflicted 'the disease of "Prussianism"' on the world.[33] A basic ingredient of troop morale, therefore, was an enduring belief in both the cause for which men were fighting and the superiority of their national character. Morale was synonymous with morality.

This relationship between morality and troop morale was a key feature of contemporary military thought. But ideas about the nature of these qualities came from a much earlier time, and there is evidence that it was little understood by those who were expected to apply such theories in the field. Henderson suggested that:

'Moral force,' says Napoleon, 'is to the physical,' that is, to numbers, armament and training, as 'three to one.' Clausewitz, the most profound of all writers on war, says that everyone understands what this moral force is and how it is applied. But Clausewitz was a genius, and geniuses and clever men have a distressing habit of assuming that everyone understands what is perfectly clear to themselves. They often forget that they are speaking to or writing for men of average intelligence, who do not reflect deeply, and have to be told important truths instead of discovering them for themselves. Referring to my own experience, I am convinced that the young officer of average intelligence but seldom grasps the meaning of Napoleon's maxim. He accepts it, as soldiers accept the words of the greatest soldier of them all, without question. But he gets no further. His text-books repeat the maxim, but being concerned with minor tactics only, he does not discuss it; and there is no treatise, so far as I am aware, which explains what the nature of this moral force is or how it has been utilised in the field. Nothing is more difficult than to drive into men's heads the fact that the great generals took this moral force into account in all their plans of battles, that the effects they expected from their combinations were based upon moral considerations, and that it was because of this that we call them 'great'. To those, therefore, who find themselves in the same predicament as I certainly was once myself – accepting the maxim without in the least understanding it – I venture to add a few words which may enlighten them.

Such enlightenment may prove of no immediate benefit. But no general, no commander of an independent force, can hope for great and decisive success without grasping Napoleon's meaning so thoroughly that he is always trying to express it in action; and the sooner officers gain this knowledge the more familiar will it become – the more likely to be utilised when their time for command arrives. Moreover, when they read of war, when they hear of war, or when they criticise generals and operations, as young officers sometimes do, they will see things from a new point of view, listen to them with a more intelligent interest, and perhaps be more judicious in the way in which they apportion praise or blame.[34]

It appears, therefore, that even the most valued military writings available at the turn of the century, whilst they referred to the value of moral(e) qualities, were unable to provide a precise definition. Henderson, in trying to analyse Napoleon's writings, placed the emphasis on human nature and drew attention to the importance of competent leadership and the welfare of troops:

> The first thing is to realise that in war we have to do not so much with numbers, arms, and manoeuvres, as with human nature.
>
> What did Napoleon find in the history of the campaigns of Alexander the Great, Hannibal and Julius Caesar? Not merely a record of marches and manoeuvres, of the use of entrenchments, or of the general principles of attack and defence. This is the mechanical part – the elementary part – of the science of command.
>
> No; he found in those campaigns a complete study of human nature under the conditions that exist in war; human nature affected by discipline, by fear, by the need of food, by want of confidence, by over-confidence, by the weight of responsibility, by political interests, by patriotism, by distrust, and by many other things. The lessons he learned from the campaigns he studied so carefully were not mechanical movements and stereotyped combinations. He was not merely an imitator. Not one of his campaigns has its exact prototype in history – but he learned from history the immense value of the moral element in war; to utilise it to the utmost became instinctive, and he played upon the hearts of his enemies and of his own men with a skill which has never been surpassed.[35]

But the importance of the Napoleonic lessons, as seen through the eyes of Clausewitz, remained a staple for early twentieth-century military theorists. Particularly impressive to these later observers was Napoleon's grasp of the human dimension of war. Understanding human nature, and the impact of battle on human behaviour, increasingly concerned those writing about modern warfare. In his introduction to the 1908 edition of Clausewitz's *On War*, the British commander Colonel Maude cited this as an essential feature of military command:

> Death, wounds, suffering, and privation remain the same, whatever the weapons employed, and their reaction on the ultimate nature of man is the same now as in the struggle a century ago. It is this reaction that the Great Commander has to understand and prepare himself to control.[36]

Similar views can be detected during the early part of the war. Brigadier General R. J. Kentish told officers at the Third Army training course in

France in November 1915 that 'Students of human nature are the most fertile producers of Moral'. He too implied that troop welfare was of great importance:

> Provided the mind is in the proper mood, provided the individual is sat-
> isfied and contented with his lot, he will be prepared to endure and to
> face every form of hardship and danger which may from time to time
> confront him.

Kentish echoed many of Henderson's remarks concerning the kind of factors required to sustain morale:

> Moral force in modern war preponderates over physical force as greatly as
> formerly. Of the many factors which may create moral force, some of the
> most powerful – such as success in battle, a great leader, a popular cause –
> cannot form part of training in peace.

Others disagreed and placed the emphasis on more traditional ideas linking morale to firm discipline. Lord Moran, for whom morale was defined by courage, regarded them as inseparable:

> If discipline is relaxed when it has not been replaced by a high morale, you
> get a mob who will obey their own primitive instincts [self-preservation?]
> like animals.[37]

John Baynes argued that morale was defined by battlefield efficiency. He suggested that five factors were crucial to the preservation of morale. These were: regimental loyalty rooted in community; confidence in the leadership; strong discipline; a sense of duty that reduced shirking; and sound adminis-tration that ensured a steady supply of rations and ammunition.[38] This is a traditional view of morale – placing an emphasis on localised recruiting, strong rather than equitable discipline and expressing concerns about shirk-ing – fused with lessons drawn from the war experience – concerns about the quality of leadership and the importance of logistics.

Writing in eugenist tones, Lord Moran placed character, shaped by 'stock' as the most important determinant of morale. He saw in some soldiers 'a natural unfitness for war'[39] adding 'it is only bad stock that brings defeat'.[40] Morale, he argued, was produced from within rather than imposed through discipline by others: 'A man with high morale does things because in his own mind he has decided to do them without any suggestion from outside sources.'[41] Yet for both Moran and Baynes, morale entailed a purely military evaluation rooted in discipline. The former anticipated self-discipline and the latter an imposed form, but both regarded it in a purely military sense. The impact of civilian life and the home front was of little consideration here. As we shall see, however, civilian contact and the maintenance of community ties was of at least equal importance to troop morale.

However much these various accounts differ in their approach, all focus on the willingness of troops to continue fighting. This, therefore, best defines what constitutes morale – a willingness to continue fighting under whatever conditions prevail at the time. In his analysis of the subject, Gary Sheffield agrees. He also refers to the mood and spirit of the men. The mood, he argues was 'transient and subject to frequent change', but fighting spirit – a Clausewitzian concept – 'was concerned with the ultimate willingness of individuals or groups to engage in combat'.[42] It was to this willingness to fight that wartime commanders referred when they spoke of moral qualities or morale. Yet this willingness to sustain the fight, it seems, was dependent upon other factors and here there is much common ground. Factors such as confidence in the generals, belief in the justness of the cause, success in battle and loyalty to the unit or formation – what is often referred to as *esprit de corps* – were all important to contemporary commentators.

It was two of the earliest twentieth-century military thinkers who placed least emphasis on discipline, perhaps suggesting a break from traditional military thought. Henderson (1903) and Kentish (1915) focused rather on positive factors to sustain morale and did not consider how the length of the war could erode the troops' willingness to continue fighting. Furthermore, neither author appears to have envisaged a situation in which confidence in the leadership and a lack of success in battle had depleted the men's willingness to fight for a cause, which to many no longer seemed a just one. In short, those factors deemed necessary to troop morale were not in place for much of World War I and this was the situation with which British commanders had to cope. Writing after the war both Baynes and Moran appear to have recognised that morale had not been sustained throughout the war and favoured more traditional views that blamed poor morale on weak discipline. The link between morale and discipline appeared an obvious one to many. Poor performance in battle suggested 'a lack of offensive spirit', another term for poor morale, to some commanders. The remedy was often believed to be firmer discipline.

This confusion about how best to sustain the morale of the troops characterised practice during the war. In the same way that many commanders, lacking confidence in alternatives, fell back on traditional forms of punishment, so too did many apply a rigid disciplinary regime, including frequent executions, when the morale of their troops appeared suspect. The equation here was simple; some commanders believed that the best way of dealing with those who displayed little willingness to fight was the threat of brutal punishments. For example, it has been suggested that General Gough wanted to shoot two officers to restore an offensive spirit in his 5th Army during 1918.[43] Crozier believed that morale needed to be supported by deterrence:

The question of ability to 'stick it' or to do the right thing in the right way, in action, is largely one of morale; but the fact cannot be overlooked that fear of the consequences undoubtedly plays an important part in the reasoning powers of men distracted by fear, cold, hunger, thirst or complete loss of morale and staying power. I should be very sorry to command the finest army in the world without the power behind me which the fear of execution brings.[44]

But the link between morale and traditional military discipline was not always clear. According to Henderson 'the discipline of the mass is insufficient. The man must be animated by something more than the spirit of unthinking obedience'.[45] This seems to imply that a certain amount of consent was sought so that men would continue fighting. This consent also had to be retained and it was clear to many that harsh punishments could erode that consent if not handled sensitively. In a 1915 memorandum on Field Punishments, Lieutenant-Colonel S. V. Riddell – an Assistant Adjutant and Quartermaster General with Maxse's 18th Division – advised other commanders that 'the reason for these punishments should be explained . . . and thus we shall carry the public opinion of our men with us'.[46] This was certainly no rejection of harsh punishments, but advice that engendering a sense of justice would ensure that such practice could be maintained. Although military law was constructed to achieve obedience, few believed that this was possible without maintaining a sense of justice. This was also recognised in the *Instructions for the Training of Platoons for Offensive Action,* issued by the General Staff in February 1917. Platoon commanders were urged to be strict, but also to be just.[47]

The army did develop a complex alternative system to sustain the men's willingness to fight. Much of this represented a continuation of pre-war practice, but the emergence of a mass army also demanded new methods and ideas. Many of these reflected wider changes and developments in society. The emergence of mass entertainment media such as the cinema and music hall-type concerts were an important feature of this process. The army, following its own instincts based on military tradition, encouraged sports and horse trials, but the new mass army brought with it a strong demand for mass entertainment. J. G. Fuller has shown how 'British and Dominion troops in the First World War carried over from civilian life many institutions and attitudes which helped them to adjust to, and to humanize, the new world in which they found themselves'.[48] But if, as Fuller asserts, these activities were initiated not by the commanders or the officers, but by the troops themselves, then they were nevertheless sanctioned by the army, often at the expense of more traditional training. In accommodating the demands of the citizen-soldiers, the army was modernising. This casts doubt on the view of the army merely as an oppressive and authoritarian institution and of British soldiers as deferential and downtrodden. Yet oppression there certainly was; the frequency of harsh military punishments is evidence that the army could act in a most brutal manner. In truth there were great variations between units and, as we shall see, in different theatres of the war. Commanders adopted differing techniques according to their own ideas and circumstances. Some favoured a disciplinary approach, others were less severe. No doubt many were prepared to try a combination of techniques to maintain troop-morale.

There was also confusion about the state of the enemy's morale. In keeping with Napoleon's teachings, as interpreted through Clausewitz and Henderson, the British Army invested a large amount of time and energy in evaluating the morale of the German army with a view to undermining it. Brigadier General John Charteris, who was responsible for intelligence, compiled reports on German morale usually based on interrogations of prisoners. During the offensive at Vimy in 1917 Charteris was puzzled by what he took to be contradictory evidence:

> At some parts whole battalions threw their hands in with hardly any resistance, while alongside of them a group of ten or twelve would hold out with the utmost determination until the whole lot were killed. On the whole, I think there is a lowering of their [German] morale, but there were very marked exceptions, and one cannot draw any definite conclusions.[49]

Morale, whether British or German, was a complex issue that defied attempts to assess it. Charteris's reports were suspected of being unreliable and over-optimistic during the Battle of the Somme.[50] Then in October 1917 his assessment of German morale was rejected by the War Office, which believed it to be more resilient than Charteris had suggested.[51] This was partly the result of the emphasis placed on morale in contemporary military thought. Charteris merely reflected the accepted view that the war would be won by the side displaying superior morale and discipline[52] and the faintest signs of a collapse in German morale were seized upon. But the problem was not just one of military theory. Interpretation was enormously problematic, as General Robertson, Chief of the Imperial General Staff, acknowledged in a letter to General Plumer on 10 December 1917:

> The diminution of German morale has been greatly overdone [by Charteris] at General Headquarters. My opinion is that German morale will remain good until the war is over. In any case it is largely a matter of opinion and it varies from day to day and between different units. It is no sort of basis upon which to form plans so far as the Germans are concerned.[53]

Following the failure of the campaign in Flanders to bring an end to the war, strategic emphasis shifted away from traditional military doctrine that had focused on 'moral superiority' to one of technical and numerical superiority.

Charteris was among the victims as Robertson rang the changes.[54] It is not that morale ceased to be a major factor in military planning – far from it – but the emphasis shifted from the destruction of the enemy's morale onto the maintenance of one's own. The French mutinies and Russian Revolution had also brought home to the High Command the importance of troop morale and the army was no longer recognisable as the pre-war model, with conscripts filling the ranks. This development particularly concerned military leaders, who were unsure about the commitment of conscripted soldiers. In February 1918, Haig ordered that troops should be taught citizenship so that they were aware of exactly what they were fighting for. Similar developments can be detected in other armies around this time, suggesting that it was not simply a matter of concern at the worth of conscripted troops. The German army, for example, had a long tradition of compulsion but here too a programme of 'patriotic instruction' was introduced in July 1917. This, it has been argued, was to counter the negative influences of socialists and pacifists who were by this time entering the army in greater numbers than ever before.[55] An education programme was also introduced in the Italian Army in 1917 to counter anti-militarism amongst its peasant soldiers.[56] What bound these developments together, though, was the impact on military thinking of the Russian Revolution and an increasing concern about the type of recruit entering the respective armies towards the end of 1917. But fear of Bolshevism was less important to British commanders who remained preoccupied with the *quality* of recruits. According to Major-General Sir Wyndham Childs:

> The First Hundred Thousand, as they have been called, were the pick of armed manhood, but later, especially when the operations of the Military Service Act began to be felt in the form of producing recruits, crime became more prevalent, especially that of desertion.[57]

A significant reduction in the number of condemnations followed closely on the heels of the introduction of citizenship classes, changes in strategy and heightened concerns about recruits. For the British at least, morale – the determination to fight – had ceased to be regarded in purely individualist terms. That it occurred at the same moment as the effective end of coercion in the army was no coincidence. The British army had entered a new phase. John Bourne has correctly identified this as 'a significant moment in the history of the British army'.[58] It is, therefore, not surprising that wholesale changes should occur, including a certain shift in the army's approach to discipline: the death penalty ceased to be applied with such regularity after 1917.[59]

Assessing morale

Given that there was considerable confusion about what was meant by the term troop morale, how was it assessed? Problems in assessing German morale had focused attention on a strategy which itself had depended on an unreliable methodology. Likewise, the method of assessing the morale of British troops had been revised in an attempt to cope with the exigencies of modern warfare. The traditional method of assessing morale in the British army was by a loose, unofficial method known as 'grousing'. Grousing allowed the men to vent their displeasure about senior officers, food, accommodation, the weather or the war. During the war the men's grousing was not limited to the spoken word, and the proliferation of trench magazines and songs performed the same function.[60] Rudyard Kipling noticed this traditional system take an instant hold in the New Armies, accurately describing it as an unofficial network whereby soldiers could air their grievances.[61] Senior officers usually took a keen interest in the nature of the men's grousing and by monitoring the complaints of the men the army was able to gauge their mood, but it is questionable whether this was sufficient to form a realistic assessment of morale.

Clausewitz had warned about mistaking the mood of the men for an indicator of their spirit: 'Beware then of confusing the *spirit* of an Army with its temper', he informed his readers.[62] The army's fighting spirit – its morale – might be influenced by the mood of the troops, but they remained separate concepts. As Gary Sheffield has shown, 'it was perfectly possible for a soldier's mood to be poor but his military spirit [morale] to be sound'.[63] Mood was subject to wild shifts dependent on weather, food and other mundane factors. Morale on the other hand was more resilient. According to Sheffield, 'the BEF's mood fluctuated [throughout the war] but its spirit remained unbroken'.[64] Sheffield notes that unlike the US and French armies, the British did not plan any system to sustain men's morale, preferring instead to concentrate on the destruction of that of the enemy.[65] This, though, was largely the result of a continuing faith in traditional methods. However flawed it now appears, the army's continuing reliance on complaints being passed up from the ranks via subalterns is suggestive of its perceived ongoing value. Monitoring men's grousing might have provided an informal network by which the army could assess the mood of its troops, but as an indicator of morale it was wholly unreliable. Yet its eventual replacement – by reports and assessments of troop morale based on mail censorship – amounted to little more than a formalisation of the existing system.

Success in battle was considered an essential element in improving and sustaining troop morale. Clausewitz cited 'a succession of campaigns and great victories' as invaluable to an army.[66] Little attention, though, was paid to how an army's morale could be retrieved following defeat. Travers has argued that in the British army 'the cult of the offensive' predominated. This, he suggests, was based on a pessimistic evaluation of society whereby the quality of troops was thought to be poor and the only way to sustain both discipline and morale was through offensive action, capturing ground from the enemy and interpreting that as success in battle.[67] Older precedents suggest a more doctrinaire explanation for this practice. Close engagement of the enemy, a relic of pre-modern warfare, remained a powerful symbol of what pundits understood as fighting spirit. In his account of the Boer War, Winston Churchill stated:

> Battles now-a-days are fought mainly with firearms, but no troops, however brave, however well directed, can enjoy the full advantage of their successes if they exclude the possibilities of cold steel and are not prepared to maintain what they have won, if necessary with their fists. The moral strength of an army which welcomes the closest personal encounter must exceed that of an army which depends for its victories only on being able to kill its foes at a distance. The bayonet is the most powerful weapon we possess out here. Firearms kill many of the enemy, but it is the white weapon that makes them run away. Rifles can inflict the loss, but victory depends, for us at least, on the bayonets.[68]

The impact of a weapon of terror, as Churchill regarded the bayonet, could have a devastating effect on morale. Gas was the terror-weapon of the First World War and the fear it caused among troops subject to gas attacks certainly lowered morale, at least temporarily, whenever it was used; so too did the tank, at least initially. But this new weapon did not always have the same appeal as weapons with a more romantic history. The association of morale with the chivalric ideals of an earlier age remained a potent one during the war. The reluctance of many senior commanders to abandon cavalry as well as close engagement with the enemy owes more to the expected effect such action would have on the enemy's morale than it does to pessimistic assumptions about society as Travers would have us believe.

Success in battle was also taken as an indicator of good morale and, therefore, failure was regarded as a symptom of poor morale. This has proved to be an enduring assumption. In a recent article Gary Sheffield suggested that 'the ultimate test of morale is combat effectiveness', adding that a good combat record was evidence of good morale in a unit.[69] This line of argument ignores the impact of other factors such as the action and effectiveness of the enemy, but it was common among officers such as Baynes during and immediately after the war. Nor was this unique to the British army. In his evidence to the Southborough Committee, Professor G. Roussy, who had acted as Consultant Neurologist to the French Army, stated that: 'When a certain regiment was found to have a greater number of "shellshock" cases than another it was considered that they were inferior troops.'[70]

Another barometer of unit morale was the sick parade. Medical Officers played a key role in the construction of this and Captain J. C. Dunn for one viewed it as a test of the MO's prestige.[71] This, though, was essentially a logistical issue unlike perceived poor performance in battle by a particular unit, which was often cited as a justification for carrying out executions.[72]

Some conditions such as shell-shock and 'trench-foot' presented a serious threat to manpower if left unchecked. Accordingly, they were often regarded as matters of discipline and not purely medical problems. The Director General Medical Services of 3rd Army noted in December 1915 how trench-foot cases occurred less when the temperature fell below freezing. In 3rd Army, he noted, there were as many as 43 new cases in a single day (1 December 1915) and no day had passed throughout November without at least one new case being reported. There had been 426 new cases diagnosed in the month 3 November to 4 December 1915 in 3rd Army alone.[73] The link between the condition and troop morale was an obvious one for many. Crozier recalled how:

> The fight against the condition known as 'trench-feet' had been incessant and an uphill game. However, science and discipline had conquered, and now we seldom have a case, and if we do there is trouble.[74]

What is interesting here is that, rather like shell-shock cases, the solution was regarded as being not only a medical one, but also one of discipline. Crozier himself linked the incidence of trench-foot with self-inflicted wounds by comparing his unit with others where 'men have taken to blowing off their fingers to escape service in the line', implying that the condition was not usually a genuine one. This reference to an incident during 1915 suggests that morale was fragile early on in the war. Robert Graves also saw the link between the condition, morale and discipline. '"Trench feet"', he stated, 'seemed to be almost entirely a matter of morale, in spite of the lecture formula that NCOs and officers used to repeat time after time to the men.'[75]

In the absence of any coordinated approach, the improvement of morale, like the maintenance of discipline, remained the responsibility of unit commanders. Nor was it generally believed that either was achieved from the ranks: rather that it was manufactured from the top downwards. In his pamphlet on training, Maxse told commanders that they 'cannot pay too much attention to raising *esprit de corps* and morale of the troops serving under them to the highest standard'. This, he suggested, could be achieved by 'encouraging healthy rivalry between units under their Command'.[76] The assumption that morale could not be maintained or improved by those in the ranks was based on pre-war beliefs about leadership, paternalism, the working class and social hierarchy. Yet the majority of the most beneficial morale-boosting measures adopted by the army were actually responses to grousing in the ranks or initiatives by the men themselves.[77]

Trench magazines, of which there were many, were usually the initiatives of subalterns. Humorous and popular, they could hardly be considered subversive and the High Command tolerated them. They often conveyed messages from the unit's own commanders. The magazine produced by

1/5th Battalion, Gloucestershire Regiment, for example, published a series of articles entitled 'The Battle Honours of the Gloucestershire Regiment' in the December 1916, February 1917 and April 1917 issues.[78] The timing of this initiative was most significant, coming as it did immediately after the battalion had seen action in the Battle of the Somme. As if to emphasise the point, photographs of members of the battalion killed in the battle were included in the February 1917 issue on pages adjoining the article. This was obviously intended to bolster the unit's morale after it had suffered considerable casualties in the fighting by reminding the men of their martial ancestry.

The magazines could also perpetuate the image of the 'cheerful tommy'. This view of soldiering, which is mostly found in accounts by officers, reinforced the value of 'moral force . . . military discipline and example, and the impersonal acceptance of casualties as part of the job'.[79] But accounts and cartoons mocking these views were quite common. In the November 1917 edition of the magazine of 1/5th Gloucesters a cartoon entitled 'Our "Tommies" are always cheerful' and said to be 'From the "Daily Liar"' showed a disgruntled soldier gazing scornfully at the reader.[80] However, the enemy was invariably shown to be even worse off. For example, in the April 1917 edition the same magazine featured a cartoon purporting to show an 'Enemy ration party seen on the skyline at 5-15 p.m.' which showed German troops carrying off three rats and a cat.[81] Such images, although humorous, carried an important message to the men and formed an essential function in the maintenance of morale.

On the other hand, what was actually understood by the term morale often reflected the concerns of the senior officers – usually tactical considerations – rather than those of the men whose main objectives were survival and a more bearable existence in the trenches. The rivalry to which the usually forward-thinking Maxse referred actually centred on existing military, and therefore disciplinary, necessities. For instance, he suggested that individual troops should be encouraged to 'compare his unit's guard with the guard of the next unit'.[82] Furthermore, he urged competitiveness and rewards for snipers, adding that 'it must be considered an honour to be picked as a company sniper. Sniper's badges may be used and fatigues may be excused'.[83] Although all portrayed as measures to improve morale, it is clear that each has its origins in discipline; the assumed relationship between the two could not be more plainly stated.

Awarding medals to the troops was another method employed by the army to maintain their morale. The names of medal recipients were widely disseminated through official and unofficial means. Citations appeared in the press and in army orders, but awards and promotions were a regular feature of trench magazines such as *The Fifth Glo'ster Gazette*.[84] This was not confined to British troops. In May 1918 Douglas Haig sent a note to Field-Marshal Sir Henry Wilson, Chief of the Imperial

General Staff, requesting him to 'send me *as soon as possible* the following [100 DSOs, 200 Military Crosses and 500 Military Medals] for the French Troops fighting under Plumer *to encourage them* [*sic*]'.[85] It was usual for the French army to make similar awards to troops in British, Belgian and American armies.

Medals, like sniper's badges, encouraged competition between units. In many ways this was a logical progression from the prestige building identified with the county regiment system, itself intended to build *esprit de corps*. The inculcation of regimental pride by association with its history and traditions was highly valued, and when the Kitchener 'New Army' recruits arrived they were absorbed into this system as 'service' battalions rather than forming new units of their own. Comparisons of guards, marksmanship or marching, as recommended by Maxse, were one way of building on unit rivalry. Another was sport. But J. G. Fuller has shown that the development of sport as a recreational pursuit behind the front line owed more to those in the ranks than it did to their officers. This was reflected, he has argued, in the preference for football over rugby or cricket.[86] Other diversions focused on entertainment and commanders certainly recognised the importance of keeping their troops amused. Maxse advised others to organise sports and theatre to improve the morale of the men in their charge. Perhaps reflecting ideas of paternalism towards his troops, Maxse believed that the theatre 'can also be used for educating the men and elevating the men in the ranks, as well as for amusing them and counter-acting the strain of war'.[87] But here too Fuller has identified the predominance of the music-hall style over supposedly higher forms of entertainment. The cinema in particular proved to be popular.[88]

Troop morale relied on much more than unit rivalry. The strains of modern warfare required that greater attention be paid to the more basic considerations such as leave and supplies. Much has been written on the effects of grievances felt by French troops and the resulting mutinies in 1917.[89] The British army did not escape the disturbances that swept through the armies in 1917. War weariness played a part in the serious disturbances at Etaples and a general increase in disobedience during 1917. It is most significant that principal among the grievances raised by the mutinous French divisions were leave and rations. In the British army, however, leave was a much scarcer commodity than it was for the French and iniquities in its allocation was the source of much complaint. The mail censor for Third Army commented in November 1916:

> The most frequent complaint, or plaint more often than complaint, is in regard to LEAVE; its frequency and uneven distribution. . . . leave is the commonest topic of correspondence: mention of leave, past or future, occurs in almost every letter.[90]

This is clear evidence of a continued attachment between the home and war fronts. Contact with family dominated soldiers' thoughts. Most significant is the importance attached to reminiscing about previous leave. If the pre-eminence of leave as *the* major topic had been limited to the prospect of future leave, then it could be argued that this represented a simple desire to escape the fighting, but the importance attached to past leave suggests that there was little sense of isolation from a home front that continued to form a part of the mental landscape of those in the trenches.

The importance for morale of a good supply of food to the troops cannot be overstated. The experiences of other armies suggests that without it morale would undoubtedly have collapsed. For example, Ernst Jünger, in his memoirs published in 1929, recalled his astonishment at the abandoned supplies of food in a captured British trench in 1918:

> Against the walls were stacks of tinned meat, cases of priceless thick jam, bottles of coffee essence as well, and quantities of tomatoes and onions; in short all that a gourmet could desire. This sight I often remembered later when we [the Germany army] spent weeks together in the trenches on a rigid allowance of bread, washy soup, and thin jam [. . .] It is much to face death and die in the moment of enthusiasm. To hunger and starve for one's cause is more . . .

But the British army proved to be more able to feed its men sufficiently than many others. Bully beef might not have been popular – next to leave, it was probably the largest single cause of complaint according to the mail censor of Third Army[91] – but at least it arrived regularly. Furthermore, army rations were regularly supplemented by food parcels sent from Britain. This fulfilled two roles: as well as providing some much needed variety for the troops it was also a vital link with family and communities left behind. The mail censor for Third Army commented in his report of November 1916:

> Complaints of food are remarkably rare. . . . There is a large clamour for parcels of food from home, resulting in a large import of tomatoes, cheese, kippers, cake, pork-pies, 'sausages and mash', 'fish and chips', and other commodities. . . . Continual Bully Beef and Jam, however good and sustaining, tend to become monotonous.[92]

Two months later the censor was able to report that complaints 'have an ulterior purpose, as a preface to a request for a parcel'.[93] Although this indicates that some of the complaints regarding food might not have been entirely genuine, there can be little doubt that contact with those at home was vital to sustaining the morale of the troops. In a letter sent from France to his family in October 1915, Private E. C. Perham, a pre-war Territorial, described his involvement in the fighting: 'we have seen some fighting my rifle was that hot that I could not hold it all the wood was steaming with the heat.' Yet the majority of space is taken up by concerns about the well-being of those at home, a shopping list and most importantly news from his native St Albans.[94] In another letter, written during the Battle of the Somme, there is barely a mention of the fighting, but the arrival of a food parcel is the first item mentioned.[95] Contact with those at home was crucial to the morale of the troops, but also it was the nature of that contact that was so important. Food parcels provided tangible evidence to the troops that they were not isolated from their families. Significantly, in early 1918 news of food shortages at home had a seriously adverse effect on morale, according to Captain Hardie.[96]

The problems of food production, transportation and supply were most severe on the Eastern Front and were a major factor in the disintegration of the Austrian army and the mass disaffection of Russian soldiers. Germany too experienced severe problems in feeding its army, and morale suffered partly as a consequence.[97] Rather as the British economy proved to be more adaptable than that of many of the other belligerents, so too did British army logistics. The building of railways and roads was crucial both to the movement of troops and to keeping them adequately supplied. Clearly, the further from Britain soldiers were the less likely they were to receive the eagerly awaited food supplements from home and there is evidence that food shortages caused a downturn in troop morale in the Italian Expeditionary Force during late 1917 and early 1918.[98] Generally speaking though, the time and effort expended by the army to ensure that this aspect of the war was not overlooked was invested well, a view shared by Niall Ferguson who has remarked that 'morale was heavily dependent on good rations'.[99] Regular food supplies ensured that morale in the British Army remained comparatively solid, at least until the end of hostilities.

Concerns about conditions at home were often the final straw for soldiers in the trenches, causing some to desert. For example, Private William Nelson, 14th Durham Light Infantry, the sole provider for his family, received news of the termination of the arrangements made for the care of his nine-year-old sister immediately before his desertion from the front line in the summer of 1916.[100] A soldier of the Somerset Light Infantry, Private Phillips, told a court martial in August 1915 that he had 'lost my head through worry having not heard from home for some time'.[101] In another case Private Albert Ingham, who had joined the Salford Pals (18th Manchester) in 1914, told a court martial 'I was worrying at the time [of his desertion] through the loss of my chums [in the Battle of the Somme]'.[102] Like Privates Nelson and Phillips, thoughts about the home front were uppermost in Ingham's mind and he told the court that he was worried 'about my mother at home, being upset, through hearing bad news of two of my comrades'.[103] We shall return to this case when the Battle of the Somme is subjected to a closer scrutiny in a later chapter.

Cases such as those of Privates Nelson, Phillips and Ingham and the impact that news of food shortages had on morale are clear evidence of a solid and continued attachment between the trenches and home. Few things were as likely to heighten a soldier's desire to return home than a deepening concern that all was not well at home. The absence of news or contact with home played on the minds of the men in the trenches, often causing an irrational supposition that something was wrong. For some the fear that something was amiss at home overwhelmed the fear engendered by the threat of the death penalty and excited an instinct to return home.

The impact on local communities of huge losses in one single action was a major factor in the abandonment of the regional system of recruitment,[104] but its impact on the army itself is less obvious. Certainly the army continued to execute soldiers, paying greater attention to disciplinary needs than to morale, and the details of those executed continued to be widely promulgated. Objections to the executions as expressed by soldiers who witnessed or carried out the task were based on the unpleasantness of their role rather than any ethical stance. This is hardly surprising given that officers censored their mail. The effects on morale of an execution within a unit are, therefore, scarcely documented. Even the army overlooked this aspect of the application of harsh discipline, which is surprising given that unit pride was considered so important a feature of morale. That stated, there were fewer executions carried out in elite regiments such as the guards than in the infantry of the line, and none in the cavalry. Baynes justified executions on the grounds that they were essential to the maintenance of discipline and that strong discipline was one of the five factors essential for preserving morale in a unit:

> However barbaric the firing squad may have been it brought home to those who had knowledge of its existence a realisation of the lengths to which their superiors would go to ensure their orders were obeyed. One will never know how many men were frightened into or out of various courses of action by the threat of execution, but it was certainly a threat that was not trifled with.[105]

Executions could, however, have a negative impact on unit loyalty and there is evidence to suggest that troop morale was badly affected by either witnessing or carrying out an execution. Lord Moran expressed regret at some of the 'poor wretches' who as a medical officer he had effectively condemned.[106] He was equally troubled by the case of a man who was examined by a fellow medical officer prior to being shot, describing such verdicts as 'guesses with a bullet behind one of them'.[107] His own morale was clearly shaken by such thoughts and he recognised that 'a sense of injustice eats away the soldier's purpose'.[108] Given the emphasis placed on morality this had serious implications. Unfortunately, the scarcity of records allows us only limited analysis of this important issue.

Although there appears to have been no official response at all an idea of the impact an execution had on unit morale can be pieced together from diary entries and letters home. Accounts of executions vary little. One diarist described the execution of Rifleman Bellamy (Kings Royal Rifle Corps) in July 1915 as 'a pathetic incident'.[109] Another barely literate diarist recorded the last moments of Private Briggs of the Border Regiment:

> We fell in at 6-50 a.m. and marched up to Regt. HQ Depond [Depot?] were one of our men paid the penilty of his life for cowdice when on A.S. [active service] The Regt. fell in to see him shot by 12 of his own Regt. *This is a sad sight to see but it must be done* [author's italics]. I must say he mote have been a coward but he marched to his death with soldier hart.[110]

Executions, it seems, were accepted by most but with considerable reluctance, and allocating men to firing squad duty proved particularly problematic for the unfortunate subalterns upon whom the task fell. Furthermore, the high incidence of officers having to administer a *coup de grâce* suggests that many firing squads, perhaps formed from the condemned man's own unit, deliberately shot wide of the target.

After the war the nature of criticism altered. Of course it was difficult for soldiers to express themselves during the war when their mail was censored, and the keeping of diaries was discouraged. That notwithstanding it has been noted that criticism of military justice took on a much harsher tone in the 1920s in both Britain and France.[111] In Britain witnesses vented their anger through the Labour MP Ernest Thurtle, who reproduced some of their accounts in his pamphlet *Shootings at Dawn*. Although anecdotal in character there can be no mistaking the angry tone in these statements, a stark contrast to surviving wartime versions. One of Thurtle's witnesses recalled the execution of a private of the Royal Berkshire Regiment in 1914 who can now be identified as Private Ward. The witness claimed to be 'the only man that saw what happened, and yet I was never called'.[112] There was also a profound sense of injustice felt by troops who were increasingly aware that executions were carried out against rankers only. In an unpublished diary Leading Seaman MacMillan, a clerk in the Royal Naval Division, described the reaction when the papers arrived confirming that Sub-Lieutenant Dyett was to be shot. Dyett was in fact the second officer to be shot. Second Lieutenant Eric Poole had been executed approximately three weeks earlier, but this was unknown to MacMillan, who wrote:

> was he, I wondered, to be the first martyr to the clamour from the ranks for an example to be made of an officer for desertion or cowardice? 'How is it', the men were asking and rightly so, 'that only rankers are being shot for cowardice? How many officers have been guilty of this offence and why have they not been made to answer for it with their lives, as we

have to do?' The Higher Command must have heard this grouse grow louder and could not fail to admit the justness of it. If however, they were forced to act, why did they select a mere boy for their first victim?[113]

This is evidence that a strong sense of injustice about executions existed in the ranks. It is also clear that the impact of Dyett's execution on his unit was a negative one. Another of Thurtle's witnesses recalled how men fainted at the sight of an execution, and other executions were invariably described by witnesses as horrible and shameful experiences.[114]

A memoir, written by Private John McCauley of the Border Regiment and published in a local newspaper in 1920, gives a grim account of the execution of Private Briggs immediately prior to the Battle of Neuve Chapelle. The author, so it seems, was one of fifteen ordered to make up the firing squad but was not one of the twelve who carried out the task. There was considerable unease in the battalion, all of whom were paraded to witness the execution. Worse still, men from the condemned soldier's own town were among those ordered to fire the fatal shots. The author's description of the execution as 'cold-blooded murder' is consistent with other accounts. The impact on the witnesses was obviously harrowing:

> Many of those who stood on this strange parade on that cold morning in March [1915] were men who had seen death in a hundred hideous forms since the days of Mons. They had faced death a hundred times, too, laughing, cheering, shouting and cursing as they leaped to meet it. But this was something different. They just stood in solemn silence.[115]

Although it seems the prisoner was killed outright by the volley – thereby avoiding the need for a *coup de grâce* – some of the firing squad apparently hesitated before firing. During the build-up to the execution many of the witnesses were openly weeping and afterwards:

> It was a mournful body of men that tramped silently back to billets. Even the birds seem to be stilled that morning. We were all unnerved and disconsolate. The firing party filed back into the barn where we were quartered, and several flung themselves down and cried openly and bitterly. We could thoroughly understand their feelings. Very little food was eaten in our billet that day. It was not easy to shake off the thoughts of the early morning death parade.[116]

The oppressive nature of military authority and discipline could indeed have a devastating effect on morale.

There is also evidence that the harshness of military discipline drove some men to violent protest. Men of the 10th (Irish) Division in Salonika were said to have rioted after the execution of Private Downey, who was shot for disobedience in December 1915.[117] At Blargies prison on the Western Front, general disturbances during August 1916, themselves a result of grievances about military punishments, escalated when a large crowd overpowered a Provost Staff Sergeant in order to release a man sentenced to Field Punishment.[118] The incident resulted in six death sentences being handed out by court martial, although only one was carried out.[119] Such incidents were an indication of how in extreme cases men were prepared to challenge military authority and acted as a constant reminder to the High Command that discipline needed to be handled with a degree of care.

Troop morale and mail censorship

The army's main source of information on morale later in the war was the regular reports of the mail censors. Unfortunately, little of this has survived but what remains provides the historian with an invaluable insight into how troop morale was assessed. Much of this refers to the army in Italy and is the subject of detailed analysis in a later chapter, but we need to make some general observations about the army's assessment of morale here. The main source of this information comes from the reports based on mail censorship compiled by Captain Hardie of Third Army. Other reports do exist but not in any great quantity.

The reports based on mail censorship were an attempt to interpret morale in a subjective manner. This of course relied on the censor's own ability to read the men's mail and to communicate his interpretations to the High Command. There was also a quantitative evaluation of morale based on an examination of the green envelopes, which had not previously been subject to censorship. In September 1917 the Director of Intelligence Services reported that 4552 letters in green envelopes from troops in France had been examined and was able to conclude that there was a negligible amount of war weariness in the BEF.

> A report has now been received showing that of these 4552 letters only 28 or 0.62% contained any expression of complaint or war-weariness. Since 7 of these 28 letters contained specific complaints that had no relation to war-weariness, the total number of letters showing weakening of morale is less than 21 or 0.5%.[120]

At roughly the same time Captain Hardie reported that morale in the Third Army, which was still in France, was beginning to be a cause of some concern:

> In regard to morale it must be frankly admitted that the letters show an increasing amount of war-weariness. There is a large despondency that

has never been apparent before, together with a large amount of unsettled feeling about the continuation and conclusion and after-effects of the war. The trouble is undoubtedly a mental one, which does not affect the discipline of the Army, but its presence must be noted.[121]

What is most surprising about these two reports is that while morale in the BEF was thought to be good, despite the impact of the Third Battle of Ypres, in the Third Army, posted to a relatively quieter sector of the front, the assessment of morale was far less optimistic.

However, this should not be interpreted as evidence of morale crumbling when troops were not engaged in battle. Another examination of mail contained in green envelopes was carried out, this time involving some 17,000 letters. The report, completed in December 1917 after the full impact of the Passchendaele offensive had been felt, showed the effects of battle on troop morale.

> There is a very striking difference between the results of the examination of the Second Army, which at the time was bearing the brunt of the fighting, and that of the other Armies, and it must be admitted that in the former the favourable and unfavourable letters were almost evenly balanced: but taking into consideration the stress both mental and physical under which letters were written by men who were in the thick of the struggle, it would be an injustice to the men to suggest that no mental reaction will take place under less strenuous circumstances anymore than that the high morale of troops in the quieter sectors would die away when they are moved to more lively positions. In the other Armies the favourable extracts greatly exceeded the adverse.[122]

Once again the report on troop-morale written by Captain Hardie, now posted to the Italian Front, appears to contradict this sentiment. There, morale was said to be much the same as in France despite the general feeling that the Italian Front was something of a 'picnic' in comparison.[123]

The relationship between the progress of the war and the state of morale was a complex one. At the end of the Battle of the Somme Captain Hardie was able to report that morale in the Third Army 'has never been higher than at the present moment'.[124] Granted, the Third Army had seen relatively little action in the battle, being positioned just north of the most serious fighting, but surely the reality of the situation could not have been hidden from troops in such close proximity.

These contradictions, however, allowed the army to interpret morale in a positive manner under most conditions. On the one hand there was the well-established military concept that idleness was not good for morale and that troops needed to be kept occupied: by that was meant fighting. Duty was also the preferred treatment of regimental medical officers for many a medical condition. Siegfried Sassoon, in his poem 'A Footnote on the War', referred to Captain J. C. Dunn's 'medicine and duty' approach, especially to minor ailments.[125] One of the root causes of shell-shock, many believed, was the inactivity of the men leading to excessive imagination. Generally, the reports of Captain Hardie fall into this category. For example, in his report for the period February to July 1918 he clearly states that the spirit of the men was enhanced by the Austrian attack, which, he said, gave them a sense of purpose.[126] Hardie had also gauged morale to be particularly high during the latter stages of the Somme offensive in November 1916 and again he noted that news of the German offensive during the Spring of 1918 'had a stiffening effect on men who were in comparative idleness'.[127] Hardie's subjective interpretation of morale, therefore, reflected traditional military values, which partly explains some of the contradictions contained in his reports. For example, in January 1917 he praised the stoicism of the British soldiers, who he said were 'prepared to "carry on" without comment or discussion'.[128] Four months later in May 1917 he reported that morale remained good, but then added:

> The men are still 'fed-up'. 'I cordially detest military life and wish I might see the end of all this futile and reckless sacrifice of human lives' is not an uncommon sentiment.[129]

It seems that Hardie didn't regard this as evidence of war-weariness, for in August 1917 he reported noticing 'a large despondency that has never been apparent before'.[130]

The statistical approach of the green envelope censorship might have resulted in a somewhat different analysis, but the censor was still at pains to present his findings in a positive light. No matter how the information was gathered, interpretation was still necessary. In the report of December 1917, for instance, the censor drew attention to evidence of war-weariness, but qualified it, saying that most mail examined was 'merely cheery ordinary letters which taken as a whole may be regarded as a favourable sign'.[131]

It is impossible to say which method produced the most accurate report, but occasionally the contradictions are striking. The report of the British armies in France, dated December 1917, concluded:

> War-weariness there is, and an almost universal longing for peace but there is a strong current of feeling that only one kind of peace is possible and that the time is not yet come.[132]

In his final report from the Western Front, dated 25 August 1917, Hardie interpreted similar data rather differently, noting that 'furtive suggestions of a patched-up peace and vague mutterings of "trouble" are beginning to make their appearance for the first time'.[133]

Despite their rather differing interpretations, however, there can be no doubt that there was a significant amount of evidence of deteriorating morale in the British Army towards the end of 1917. Yet there is no corresponding rise in the number of death sentences meted out by courts martial for offences such as mutiny, disobedience or insubordination during this period. There were only two condemnations for mutiny in 1917, 15 for disobedience and five for insubordination, compared with 11, 35 (not including the Non-Combatant Corps) and four respectively for 1916.[134] If the army was at all concerned about the 'trouble' to which Hardie referred then the courts martial certainly did not respond by ordering more executions. The truth was that, generally, there was no upsurge in military crime even though troop morale appeared shaky. As I have argued, disciplinary concerns had a small but significant influence on the final outcome of death sentences, but it appears from this evidence that the state of morale was far less influential.

Morale in the British Army appears to have survived the ravages of the big offensives and rumours of food shortages at home alike. However, it suffered something of a collapse after the armistice and discipline crumbled along with it. Once victory had been achieved many troops withdrew their consent: they were unwilling to continue fighting when there was obviously no necessity. A similar trend has been detected in the German army in the autumn of 1918 when troops could no longer see the need to continue fighting in a war that was obviously lost, and desertions increased dramatically.[135] In the British army, mutiny, previously a rare charge, became quite common after November 1918. Most of the incidents were simply the result of frustration at the slow pace of demobilisation, but there is evidence of a growing resentment prior to the armistice. In 1917 Captain Hardie had commented:

> In reading the letters on this subject [peace] one cannot help feeling impressed by the fact that the British Army – a heterogeneous collection of men who before the war had the wide freedom of thought, speech and action that are their national birthright – should submit without a murmur to guidance and authority, and be prepared to simply 'carry on' without comment or discussion. In Germans one expects a submissiveness that has been bred in them and enforced by pains, penalties and fear through their whole national training before the war.[136]

Only eighteen months later in July 1918 Hardie's assessment had dramatically altered:

> Demobilisation and his [unfavourable] feelings towards the Italians practically monopolise the attention of the soldier on general subjects to the exclusion of political or other home affairs. . . . Considered as a whole,

this branch of the correspondence indicates that many men take far too short-sighted a view of the question, and it is thought the imperfect comprehension of the aims, difficulties and machinery of the Scheme for Demobilisation and resettlement creates in the minds of many men, who would otherwise be much more patient, a feeling of personal victimisation, which, coupled with a sense of revolt against uncongenial surroundings, gives rise to a condition of increasing discontent and general weariness.[137]

This is further evidence that the British soldier's consent was becoming increasingly fragile towards the end of the war, even though victory was by no means guaranteed at this point. Following that victory much of it would be withdrawn. This coincided with increasing concern in the higher command following the Russian Revolution, the British Army's metamorphosis into a conscript army and the abandonment of undermining German morale as the keystone of military strategy. The introduction of citizenship classes and the reduction in the number of condemnations meted out by courts martial were but two outcomes of these concerns.

Summation

Ideas about morale were shaped from pre-war teachings, some of which, including Napoleon and the commanders of ancient Greece and Rome, were very old. Clausewitz, though, remained the most important writer to British generals and interpretations of his work formed the basis of military thought throughout the second half of the nineteenth century and in the years immediately prior to the First World War. These ideas focused on individual qualities of personal character – of both the generals and their men. A lingering faith in the character and superior 'moral qualities' of British troops fighting for King and Empire was further bolstered by a stubborn belief that the morale of the enemy could be broken and victory achieved. There was no one central body or even policy on troop morale and, accordingly, it was left to individual commanders to administer to the 'fighting spirit' of their men. Some adopted a progressive approach, encouraging initiatives from the ranks. The nature of entertainments and sports competitions often reflected this process. Others favoured the traditional method of tightening discipline to shore-up flagging morale. No doubt many of the executions were a direct result of this process. But most commanders followed a mixture of the two approaches, embracing new ideas while at the same time exacting harsh discipline if they thought it was necessary.

As the war drew on it became apparent that victory depended more on bringing sufficient *matériel* to bear on the enemy. This became most apparent after the failure of the 1917 offensive in Flanders, when Robertson noted that too much emphasis had been placed on dubious assessments of crumbling German morale. This coincided with the transition of the British Army from a volunteer to a conscript force and increasing evidence that the consent of British troops could not be taken for granted. There followed a significant shift in strategic thought, which had profound implications for army discipline and less use was made of the death penalty. The emphasis was no longer on individual qualities such as 'moral superiority', and while troop morale remained important to the army, it was increasingly obvious that victory could not depend solely on breaking the enemy's morale.

Confusion about what constituted morale was reflected in the attempts at assessing it. Initially, the army was more concerned with the state of German morale than it was with its own. However, a formalisation of the existing system of monitoring men's grouses, in 1916, indicated a realisation of the importance of maintaining the spirits of the troops. Whether this achieved anything beyond gauging the mood of the army is debatable, but its real significance is as evidence of the army modernising itself and learning to cope with its massive enlargement.

Certain issues dominated men's morale. Much has been written about the importance of good food, but it is my contention that not sufficient emphasis has been placed on the maintenance of links with the home front. This continued link was vital to troop morale. Leave – past, present and future – was the thread that linked home life to the trenches. Food parcels were tangible evidence of its perpetuation. While complaints about the weather, food and conditions tended to affect the men's mood, only concerns about the progress of the war itself could impact on their spirit in the way that worries about the home front could. A significant number of men who were executed for desertion committed their fatal act upon hearing bad news from home. Others cited concerns about their family and communities in defence of their actions. It is important also to note that the mail censor detected a downturn in morale following news of food shortages at home.

Few memoirs mention the impact of executions on the units concerned. It is clear, though, from those available that executions left behind a deep sense of shame. There is evidence to suggest that most men resented the army for acts they saw as vindictive. In an army where a belief in the justness of the cause was encouraged, such resentment was likely to undermine the morale of the men. Yet many commanders regarded executions as vital to inculcating fighting spirit as well as maintaining discipline. This was partly because discipline and morale were inexorably linked in the minds of many. Theorists such as Henderson had separated the two concepts, but this was not necessarily accepted by those commanding troops in the field. Baynes, Crozier and Moran, for instance, all considered morale only within the scope of wider issues of discipline.

The relationship between morale and discipline is a complex one and it was continually redefined during the war. The progress of the war itself was probably the most influential factor. The failures of the first three years prompted a new approach. So too did the altered state of the army. Discipline was gradually relaxed in 1918 as signs of war-weariness were detected, but the High Command, which remained authoritarian in nature, never relinquished its control: the last two executions for desertion were carried out just four days before the armistice took effect.

4

Pour encourager les autres: Morale, Discipline and the Death Penalty on the Front Line

Having examined how military law was structured, and analysed attitudes towards morale and discipline, we must now consider how British commanders used the death penalty, or at least the threat of it, during the war. Two broad questions will be explored. First, what general trends can be discerned? To what extent do these reflect pre-existing structures? And was any military formation more vulnerable to capital sentences than any other? Second, how were the sentences applied in individual units? What variations from any detected general trends were there?

Broadly this chapter will demonstrate that there were general trends. There were three 'types' of divisions in the British army during the war; the approach to discipline often reflected this and important individual differences existed. The use of the death penalty as a means to enforce discipline was a contentious issue which was viewed differently by individual army commanders. Even some who expressed faith in its deterrent value remained reluctant to employ it; but some were less reluctant than others. The number of death sentences passed by courts martial largely reflected the divisional commanders' approach to discipline and the court was itself an extension of his authority rather than an instrument of general army policy. Executions were, however, largely out of the hands of the divisional commander. In theory this was the commander-in-chief's domain, but matters were often left to the Personal Services Branch. Divisional commanders' recommendations were no doubt valued, but the final decision to confirm a sentence, or otherwise, was taken elsewhere and it is at this stage of the proceedings where a general army-wide policy can be detected.

The importance of the divisional commanders in the disciplinary process needs to be reassessed. The popular public view of a callous commander-in-chief, epitomised by Haig's reputation as the 'butcher of the Somme', has infiltrated what few writings there are on the subject. While the commander-in-chief's *office* was responsible for confirming death sentences the evidence suggests that the nature of discipline *in the field* was largely the result of a number of other factors. Not least among these were the character,

100

personality and attitude of the divisional commander. Battalion and brigade commanders also played a part in shaping disciplinary policy, but theirs was a lesser role in this regard. Furthermore, commanders at levels higher than division could exert a considerable influence on events although they relied heavily on the divisional commander to implement their decisions. Divisional commanders appear to have retained a surprisingly high degree of autonomy resulting in quite diverse disciplinary records in similar divisions. Consequently, in many cases the record of death sentences and executions in each division can be said to have reflected its commander's own approach rather than that of the High Command.

When dealing with records concerning crime, whether military or civil, it is important to keep in mind that we must qualify our conclusions with the proviso that we are dealing with *recorded* crime only. This is especially true of punishments and convictions. Most courts martial were assembled in the field, many of them hurriedly so, and the records are incomplete. For example, we have no records whatsoever of summary executions (and there is other evidence that many were carried out[1]) and at least two capital courts martial files are missing from records at the Public Record Office.[2] This, however, is not a problem for our purpose here, which is to explore the manner in which the threat of execution was deployed as a disciplinary tool. Paradoxically, capital convictions and executions carried out by authority of courts martial were of greater use to the army in this respect than summary executions since they were more widely promulgated, spreading the fear factor far wider than localised summary shootings.

It was also on the basis of statistical reports, including crime, that the state of morale and discipline in individual units was initially assessed, but this method was hardly an accurate gauge of the level of offending in any unit. Such figures were merely a measure of the number of convictions for a given period. Criminologists are familiar with the problems associated with this type of data-driven analysis. Rather than providing an accurate indicator of the level of crime in a particular army formation, these reports might be no more than a reflection of the willingness of the commanders to bring prosecutions, indicating that what these figures most accurately reflect is the divisional commander's approach to discipline and the death penalty.

One further problem remains. The army kept detailed records, but their accuracy can occasionally be called into question. The divisional reports on crime sent to the commander-in-chief are a case in point. Until 1917 these reports provided the basis for the army's assessment of morale in battle formations. However, now with the benefit of a computer, serious omissions – or at least contradictions – become evident. Some reports showed that there were no convictions in divisions in which capital convictions (not to mention convictions for minor offences) can be traced in other registers. A minor headache for the researcher, this calls into question the whole manner by which the British army assessed the state of morale among its own troops.

The three armies

Gary Sheffield has shown that the army's approach to discipline varied from one unit to another, and that the type of unit was significant.[3] Sheffield argued that Regular divisions maintained a traditional style of discipline which tended to be harsher, authoritarian, and reminiscent of the pre-war army. Territorial divisions also retained their pre-war style of discipline, but this was characterised by a more negotiated and, therefore, less severe regime by which, in some degree, the consent of the men was sought. This was itself a product of the nature of the pre-war Territorial Force where men were unlikely to remain if they regarded discipline as excessive, harsh or overly authoritarian. The Territorials had also retained something of a community spirit and hierarchy in their ranks and men were likely to know their officers and NCOs in their normal civilian lives. Despite the losses inflicted on the first formations sent overseas in 1915 and the topping up of units with volunteers or conscripts, the disparate approaches to discipline in the Regular and Territorial divisions proved to be remarkably resilient and to a large degree the ethos of each survived.

Added to these formations were the New Armies largely associated with Lord Kitchener. Without the traditions of the Territorial Force, which proved so resilient, these formations were more prone to Regular-style discipline creeping in. Although discipline in the New Armies was rarely as harsh as that in the Regular army, senior commanders' concerns about the reliability of these citizen-soldiers ensured that severe punishments were often meted out in an attempt to ensure obedience. Broadly, in terms of discipline the New Armies fitted somewhere between the Regular and Territorial divisions.

This assertion can be tested and quantified by reference to the number of condemnations and executions in each formation. While this might not be a perfect method of assessing the different approach to discipline in the 'three armies' it is, nevertheless, a convenient one and is in any case probably the best one available to the historian as being readily quantifiable. Furthermore, it is perfectly reasonable to assert that, if there was a marked difference in the manner of maintaining discipline in the various formations of the British army, then this would manifest itself in the most extreme from of authority available to divisional commanders, the death penalty. What then can we learn from a comparison of condemnations in the various formations of the British Army?

The Regular divisions

There were twelve Regular infantry divisions in the army, not including those British units serving with the Indian Army, and three cavalry divisions. For reasons that remain obscure there were only ten condemnations on men serving in the cavalry divisions and no executions were carried out. The temptation to attribute this to a bias that favoured men in these divisions (the two commanders of the British Expeditionary Force were both cavalrymen) should be avoided in the absence of any real evidence. We should note also that the first British soldier to be sentenced to death during the war was a cavalryman.[4] However, as the death penalty was not a significant feature of discipline in the cavalry divisions the following analysis is confined to the infantry divisions.

There were a total of 908 condemnations in the Regular infantry divisions with 114 executions. On average then there were 76 condemnations and ten executions for every Regular division. The rate of confirmation was, therefore, approximately 13 per cent. Needless to say there was a great variation within these units and to talk of typicality can be a little misleading. Some units saw much more action than others, but only two formations – the Guards and 27th Division – experienced fewer than 60 condemnations within their ranks. The highest was 3rd Division where 121 men were sentenced to death by court martial and 22 were executed. Interestingly, this division had been singled out by General Douglas Haig in 1914 for its lack of military efficiency. In an implied criticism of Smith-Dorrien, who had ordered the stand at Le Cateau, Haig recorded in his diary for 7 November 1914:

> A very anxious day on account of the steady and determined advance of the Germans so close to our communications, and also because of the want of fighting spirit in the 3rd Division. This Division has never been in an efficient state since Le Cateau.[5]

Significantly, 23 death sentences were passed on men in this division during the following four months – a high proportion compared to other divisions at this time – with three men being executed in February 1915. There had been only two condemnations in this division prior to Haig's remarks – one in September and another in October 1914. This is suggestive of a close relationship between beliefs about the military efficiency and the frequency of condemnations in army formations, with a corresponding increase in condemnations following poor assessments of either discipline or morale – the two main criteria of military efficiency.

There were other reasons why 3rd Division might have suffered poor morale. The original commander of the division, Major-General H. Hamilton, was killed in action on 14 October 1914. He was replaced by Major-General C. J. Mackenzie whose command lasted a mere 14 days, being himself invalided on 29 October 1914, whereupon Major-General F. D. V. Wing assumed command. Without continuity of command it is no wonder that 3rd Division's fighting spirit was suspect. Haig's comments on 7 November were swiftly followed by yet another change in divisional commander. On 21 November 1914 Major-General Aylmer Haldane was appointed

to the command of 3rd Division.[6] It was after this appointment that condemnations rapidly increased. It is unclear whether Haldane was appointed
to this particular command because of his reputation as a strict disciplinarian or whether he was merely asserting his authority through the courts. The
case of 3rd Division in 1914 demonstrates how death sentences could reflect
particular concerns about a unit.

In most Regular divisions the number of condemnations was in the seventies
or eighties. The average can, therefore, be safely regarded as a good reflection of
a typical Regular division. Most Regular divisions – though not all – arrived on
the Western Front in 1914 and were involved in the fiercest battles throughout
the war. Most underwent at least one change at the top, but the rapid turnover
of commanders of 3rd Division in 1914 was highly unusual.

Figure 4.1 shows that the greatest number of condemnations in 3rd
Division occurred during the early part of 1915, the period of the battle of
Neuve Chapelle, though the division had not been deployed in that particular action. Executions too were most frequent in 1915, this time in July.
The later battles of the Somme in 1916 and Ypres in 1917 are less obviously
represented even though the division was deployed at both. This is surprising because it was during these latter battles that British courts martial
passed most death sentences and more executions were carried out.[7]
However, during these later battles, after the considerable enlargement of
the army in France with the arrival of New Army divisions, the Regular divisions bore less of a burden. In 1915 the Regular divisions performed the main
offensive tasks of the British army. To a certain extent, then, 3rd Division's
record of condemnations and executions was a reflection of its own battle
experience combined with the experience of the BEF as a whole and analyses of the division's military efficiency.

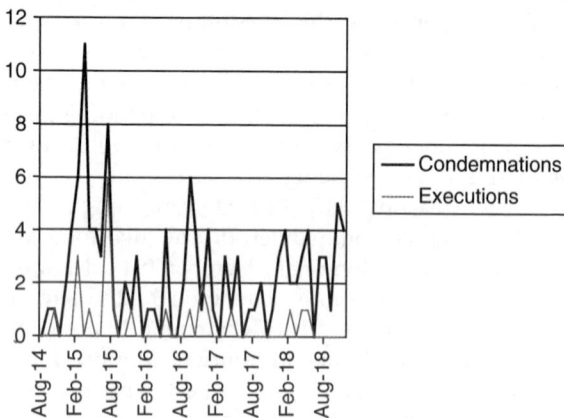

Figure 4.1   Condemnations and executions in 3rd Division

Similar observations can be made for 6th Division, again represented in a graph: see Figure 4.2.

Once again there was a high incidence of condemnations in early 1915. However, not all of the capital sentences in 6th Division can be attributed to its experience in battle. There was a noticeable increase in the number of death sentences handed out by courts martial in January 1916, after which the pattern settles down to fairly high numbers of death sentences in the division, but only the occasional execution. This pattern was seemingly unaffected by the division's involvement in the Battle of the Somme. It was not until August 1917 that the number of capital sentences once again declined, and this reduction can be explained because the division was not deployed in the Third Battle of Ypres.

The problem with the statistics for 6th Division is that the pattern of death sentences during 1916 does not obviously coincide with battle experience. There was a slight rise in the number of capital sentences during the battle of the Somme, but this was not particularly high in contrast with those in the preceding months. The first few months of 1916 are most intriguing, for it was then that courts martial passed the highest number of capital sentences in 6th Division for that year. The explanation is probably to be found in a change of commanders. On 14 November 1915 Major-General C. Ross replaced Major-General Congreve as commander of 6th Division. Ross remained in command until 21 August 1917 when he was replaced by Major-General T. O. Marden. It was during the period of Ross's command that high numbers of death sentences were most consistently passed by courts martial.

Death sentences were common in this division, as they were in other Regular divisions, but the period of Ross's command is synonymous with a

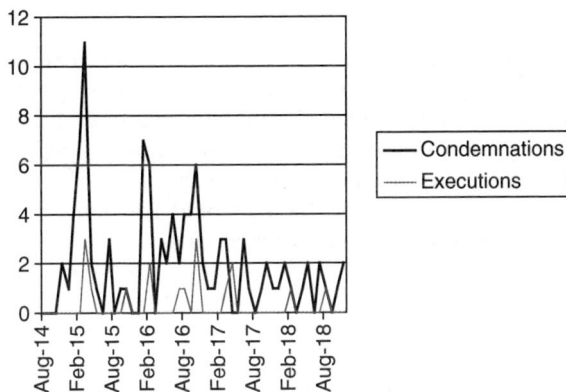

Figure 4.2   Condemnation and executions in 6th Division

greater frequency of capital sentences. What is so remarkable about this period is how the numbers of condemnations was sustained over a number of months and not merely subject to sudden increases at times of battle. Does this suggest that Ross adopted a consistently harsher approach to discipline than other commanders of the division? It would appear logical to argue the case, particularly since the high numbers of capital sentences passed in January and February 1916, all for desertion, came shortly after Ross had taken command – a time when he was seeking to assert his authority. There could be no clearer demonstration of authority than the use of capital punishment as a disciplinary weapon.

The Territorial Force

In the 14 divisions of the first-line Territorial Force there were just 283 condemnations and 31 executions. Typically then the divisional average was 20 condemnations and two executions, little more than half the rate of the Regular divisions. Again, however, there was a wide variation with some formations such as 43rd and 44th Divisions, which were posted to garrison duties in India, not experiencing any condemnations at all, while at the other end of the scale there were 39 condemnations and four executions in 55th Division.[8] Yet the overall average remains a good benchmark of death sentences in a 'typical' Territorial Force formation, with condemnations in most divisions somewhere in the twenties and thirties. This appears to confirm the existence of a less severe approach to discipline than that of the Regular divisions. The confirmation rate in the Territorial divisions was also less than that of the Regulars. Only 11 per cent of those 'Territorials' condemned by courts martial were executed. This is less than might have been expected, suggesting that the Territorial Force's reputed leniency extended somehow beyond courts martial.

A second line of Territorial divisions was raised in August 1915; six of the 14 divisions never left the United Kingdom and there were 33 condemnations and two executions in the others. As the period of service was relatively short and the numbers involved so small a statistical analysis here would be pointless. Nevertheless it should be noted that based on this evidence the death penalty does not appear to have featured highly in the disciplinary ethos of the second-line Territorial Force.

Most references to divisions of the Territorial Force are, therefore, concerned with those first-line formations that went overseas from May 1915 onwards and were numbered in the order they were sent. The first such division to arrive in a foreign theatre was 42nd Division, which was posted to Gallipoli, arriving there, via Egypt, on 9 May 1915. It was immediately moved into the reserve positions and although it did not take part in any major offensive action until early June, two men, both serving with the 1/10th Manchester Regiment, were convicted of cowardice by a court martial on 29 May. Both had their death sentences commuted to five years' penal servitude. Intriguingly, there had been a problem landing two companies of the 1/10th Manchesters at Cape Helles at the same time as the rest of the division: the navy had inexplicably carried the two companies off, eventually landing them five days later. There is nothing other than speculation to connect the incident with the capital courts martial, but clearly the division had seized on some incident early on and shown its determination to impose strict discipline. Its timing was significant: intense fighting had preceded 9 May, the day of the landing of most of the division, the reserves were used up and the commander-in-chief, Sir Ian Hamiliton – still unable to get his headquarters ashore – had been forced to cable Kitchener to plead for more divisions.[9] Indiscipline, it appears, could not be tolerated at such a moment.

A further thirteen soldiers of 42nd Division were sentenced to death before the peninsula was evacuated in January 1916, but none was executed. The division sailed to Egypt and eventually arrived on the Western Front in March 1917. Again it was not long after arriving at the front that a capital sentence was passed on one of the men in the division. Private Walton, a Lancashire Fusilier, had his capital sentence for quitting his post reduced to seven years' penal servitude by Field Marshal Haig. However, a number of other men were sentenced to death in the final months of 1917, during the Third Battle of Ypres, three of whom were executed. It appears that condemnations in this division followed a discernible pattern and were apparently used to tighten up discipline whenever deemed salutary – when first arriving at a battle zone, for example. The executions, all on the Western Front, also came at key moments in the division's active service. Three men were shot following offences committed during the Ypres offensive in 1917 and a further two following the German offensive in the spring of 1918.

This pattern – death sentences following specific battles – was typical of most Territorial Force divisions. Unlike the Regular divisions, the death sentence does not appear to have formed a major part of discipline in Territorial formations in the periods of relative calm between engaging with the enemy. This is supported by a survey of death sentences in the 14 first-line Territorial Force divisions, as shown in Figure 4.3.

The big battles can be easily identified in Figure 4.3: the Gallipoli landings (May 1915), Loos (September 1915), Somme (July – November 1916), Messines Ridge (June 1917), Third Ypres (September – November 1917), German offensive (April/May 1918), and the Allied advance (August 1918) are all denoted by an increase in the number of condemnations in the Territorial Force. Moreover, although the total numbers are fewer than in the Regular divisions, the differences between battles and times of relative inactivity are far more marked in the Territorial formations. Indeed, Figure 4.3 shows that death sentences were extremely rare in between these big battles. The death penalty might not have formed a fundamental role in the routine discipline

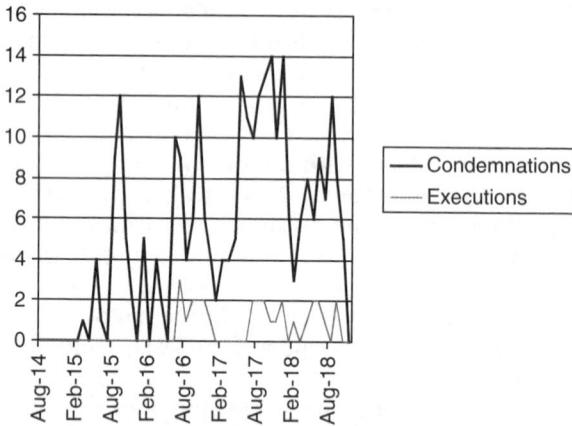

Figure 4.3 Condemnations in the First-Line Territorial Force

of the Territorial Force, but its commanders were willing to resort to it in times of battle, albeit in a relatively muted form.

The New Army

Thirty New Army divisions were raised and served in most theatres of the war.[10] 1049 death sentences were passed on men serving in these units and 135 executions carried out – a confirmation rate of 13 per cent, identical to that of the Regular divisions. With so many divisions it is no surprise that there should be a large variation in the number of condemnations in these units. In no New Army division were there no condemnations at all. The overall average per division is 35 condemnations and five executions. However, it is wholly erroneous to refer to a *typical* New Army division: such a thing did not exist. Accordingly, it is difficult to sustain an argument that an average figure can be regarded as a true reflection of the New Army divisions' brush with the death penalty because of the broadly differing experiences of so many units. Three divisions (13th, which was not deployed on the Western Front, 15th and 17th) experienced more than sixty condemnations and six others (22nd, 26th, 38th, 39th, 40th and Royal Naval Division) fewer than twenty. As the rest fit within that broad span between 20 and 60 condemnations the average of 35 per division is not a bad benchmark by which to measure the New Army, but the word *typical* has to be avoided wherever possible when referring to the New Army divisions.

Paradoxically, the absence of tradition in the New Army was at once liberating yet potentially enslaving for men of the 'service' battalions of the New Army. Commanders of these divisions were not snared by tradition: they had a blank canvas on which to paint. This partly explains why there is such diversity in the approach to the death penalty in New Army divisions when compared to other types of formations. More so than in other units, the commanders of New Army divisions could impose their own character on their charges. We will deal with this in more detail when we come to examine specific units and commanders, but some important observations need to be made at this point.

Some commanders of New Army divisions clearly appreciated the enthusiasm and general quality of the volunteers in their charge. Maxse regarded the troops in his 18th Division as potentially better than those of the Regular army.[11] However, not all commanding officers held the volunteers in the same high regard. Moreover, for those who doubted the abilities of the New Army it was their discipline that was of greatest concern, hence the surprise expressed by General Rawlinson at the achievements of his New Army divisions after the Battle of the Somme.[12] Some commanders appear to have resented their commands – perhaps preferring command of a Regular formation – and set about imposing an especially harsh form of discipline on their divisions, with the death penalty a vital component. Most vulnerable in this regard were the unpopular commands such as 35th Division, a formation composed entirely of so-called 'bantam' units, battalions of men who did not reach the normal height requirement of the army, but who had volunteered to serve in specially constituted units. The men in 35th Division had to endure a tirade of abuse from the press, from other soldiers and finally from their own commanders who imposed a particularly harsh disciplinary regime on their unwanted charges. Eventually, the division found itself a scapegoat following the Somme offensive and 37 men were sentenced to death during the second half of 1916 alone, seven of whom were executed.[13] In such cases the absence of tradition acted to enslave these units in a pre-war style of discipline based on fear and deterrence. Tradition served to protect Territorial Force divisions from such excesses, but there was no such check in the New Armies which were at the mercy of their commanders.

Most commanders of the New Armies appear to have taken a traditional view of discipline such as Brigadier General F. P. Crozier, commander of a brigade in 36th (Ulster) Division. Crozier's belief in the deterrent value of the death penalty is best known from his own publication, *A Brass Hat in No Man's Land*. Indeed, Crozier appears to have been fond of his reputation as a hard disciplinarian; he had no qualms about ordering the summary shooting of fleeing Portuguese troops in 1918[14] and he certainly considered the discipline of the New Armies to be generally deficient.[15] It is impossible to say to what extent his views reflected those of the divisional commander or whether he was able to shape the approach to discipline in this division, but discipline in the 36th Division had much in common with that of Regular formations. The death penalty was used more frequently than in most New Army divisions, but not overly so: there were 32 condemnations and five executions.[16] However, they were not restricted to times when the division was engaged in battle and condemnations during the relatively quiet times were common. During the early months of 1916 a number of men were sentenced to death, mostly for desertion, and three were executed. There were 14 condemnations in the division before the end of 1916, all but one in Crozier's 107th Brigade where the only three executions of this period also occurred. Six of the nine condemnations in 36th Division during 1917 were also in Crozier's brigade, but the two executions carried out that year were against troops serving with other brigades. Condemnations in 107th Brigade reduced following Crozier's departure in November 1916. Interestingly, discipline in 119th Brigade, 40th Division – Crozier's new command – appears more reliant on the death penalty after that date: the five condemnations recorded in Crozier's new brigade amount to half the total for the entire division.

It appears, therefore, that reference to the frequency of death sentences provides a quantifiable means by which to measure discipline in various units. This is in keeping with Gary Sheffield's thesis. Discipline appears to have been imposed with the most severity in the Regular divisions. The Territorial Force seems to have retained a less harsh form of discipline with fewer condemnations, while the New Army divisions usually fit roughly halfway between the two. Condemnations were more common in the New Armies during times of relative inaction than in the Territorial Force. Accordingly, capital sentences in the New Armies were not so much a response to battle experience as an intrinsic part of the process adopted by some commanders for instilling discipline in these 'citizen-soldiers'. The death penalty formed a vital part of the disciplinary process during major battles, but its use in New Army divisions at other times should not be overlooked. In terms of the death penalty it is true to say that the New Army units were something of a hybrid between their two more established army ancestors, reflecting a limited form of both traditions, but they increasingly leant towards those of the Regular army rather than the Territorial Force.

Nowhere is the encroachment of Regular-style discipline into the New Army more apparent than in the number of condemnations. Discipline in the New Armies was also a major concern for the High Command.[17] In spite of reports by some commanders such as Maxse, the view still persisted in the higher echelons of the British army that the volunteers could not be trusted and needed firm handling. This is reflected in the rate by which death sentences were confirmed. Indeed, the New Army experienced an identical rate of confirmations to that of the Regular divisions. When it came to the death penalty the citizen-soldiers were not spared or given any special allowance by the commander-in-chief.

The rate of confirmations in the Territorial Force was lower than in the Regular or New Armies. This is curious because the decision whether or not to confirm a death sentence was made by the commander-in-chief rather than a division's own commander. Pre-war traditions could have little impact on decisions taken at a level of command higher than division, so how was it that this less severe form of discipline appears to have been carried over into the confirmation process? It is possible that more lenient recommendations by the unit, brigade and divisional commanders served to mitigate here. This seems to be the most likely explanation, but in the absence of each and every court-martial file it is impossible to be absolutely certain. In any case it should be noted that the variation is only slight.

The impact of the big offensives

A number of factors could have played a significant part in determining how many condemnations courts martial were likely to pass. First among these is the big offensive scenario. In the build-up to a large-scale offensive such as the Somme in 1916 or Ypres in 1917 tension increased. The intensification of the preliminary bombardment although directed at the enemy also played on the minds of those awaiting orders to advance. This might have resulted in an increase in desertion. Furthermore, charges of cowardice in the face of the enemy were most likely to be brought during battle itself rather than at times when most units were out of the line. The enormous number of casualties experienced in these battles might also have acted as the catalyst for more desertions. Add to this the increased determination of commanders, up to and including the commander-in-chief, to ensure tight discipline at such times and it appears perfectly reasonable to expect more death sentences to be passed during or as a result of the large offensives. This can be tested by comparing the number of condemnations in divisions deployed in these battles with those others on the Western Front which were not deployed and then with those in other theatres of the war. The total number of death sentences and executions for British divisions during the period July to December 1916 is shown in Table 4.1 below. The month

Table 4.1 Condemnations and executions during the period of the Battle of the Somme (executions are shown in brackets)

Date	Divisions deployed in Somme battle	Other divisions on the Western Front	Divisions in other theatres
July 1916	45 (5)	3	1
August 1916	49 (9)	4	5
September 1916	44 (8)	1	6
October 1916	59 (10)	2	2
November 1916	61 (13)	2	3
December 1916	60 (6)	0	3
Total	318 (51)	12 (0)	20 (0)

of December has been included as part of the period covering the battle to account for cases arising from the action but dealt with later.

A striking feature of this comparison is that executions were only carried out in those divisions engaged in the battle. The 51 executions were a measure of the resolve of the commander-in-chief, Douglas Haig, to assert his authority during the offensive. This represented a far higher rate of confirmation than for the war as a whole: 16 as opposed to 11 per cent. Significantly, no executions were carried out in other divisions on the Western Front or elsewhere during the same period.

The relatively low number of divisions in other theatres, and the still fewer divisions on the Western Front which were not deployed in the battle, render direct comparisons with those engaged in the Somme offensive difficult. However, what can be stated with confidence is that, in addition to there being no executions, even allowing for their smaller numbers, there were also far fewer condemnations in divisions away from the Somme offensive. For example, in the other theatres there were two and a half condemnations for every division during this period. This is comparable to the divisions on the Western Front not deployed in the Somme offensive, for whom there were just under three condemnations for every division. However, there is a major difference in the divisions involved in the battle. Soldiers in these divisions were more than twice as likely to be condemned by a court martial: there were more than seven death sentences for every division deployed in the battle.

Of course, none of this is particularly surprising. The stakes were significantly raised in those divisions employed in the titanic struggle in Picardy and this has understandably affected the nature of discipline in those divisions as well. What though of the three types of division involved in the battle – how do they compare with the analysis (above) of condemnations during the war as a whole?

Eighty-seven of the condemnations arising from the Battle of the Somme were passed on soldiers in Regular divisions, roughly ten for every Regular division. Eleven, or 13 per cent, of these were executed, a rate comparable to the Regular divisions' experience throughout the war. The same can be said of the New Army divisions where there were 191 condemnations arising from the battle and 31 executions, or approximately seven condemnations for every New Army division and a confirmation rate of 16 per cent.

However, the Territorial divisions' experience of discipline appears to have differed remarkably during the Battle of the Somme. The number of condemnations per division is lower than in the other types of division: there were 40 death sentences, or five for every Territorial division. This is consistent with the overall picture – more condemnations in the Regular divisions, slightly less in those of the New Army and fewer still in the Territorial Force. Yet the nine executions represent a substantial increase (from 11 to 23 per cent) in the likelihood of a condemnation in the Territorial Force being confirmed.

This is suggestive of a harsher line being adopted with Territorial Force units during the Somme offensive. It is interesting that the commander-in-chief did not confirm death sentences in the Regular divisions – where discipline was reputedly more severe – at an increased rate during the months of the Somme offensive, but slightly increased the number of confirmations in New Army units. The only major increase was in the Territorial Force, indicating a heightened concern about discipline in these units during a major battle.

Similar conclusions can be drawn from an analysis of condemnations and executions for the period July to December 1917: the Third Battle of Ypres. During this period there were 311 condemnations in British divisions and 45 executions. As we might expect, most of these concerned divisions engaged in the action at Ypres where the numbers were 264 and 43 respectively, or approximately six condemnations per division with roughly 16 per cent confirmed. This can be contrasted with the three condemnations per division both on the Western Front and in other theatres of the war during the same period. Again executions were virtually non-existent away from the major battle: just two executions were carried out in France in a division not deployed in the Flanders campaign.

There were approximately six and a quarter condemnations per Regular division, a figure remarkably similar to the six and a half per New Army division. However the number of condemnations per Territorial Force division was less than five.[18] Once again though, the proportion of confirmations was much lower in the Regular units (10 per cent) than in Territorial (17 per cent) or New Army (18 per cent) divisions. That the rate of confirmations in Regular divisions did not appreciably increase during either the Somme or Passchendaele offensives yet rose substantially in the Territorial Force during these large-scale battles, and in the New Armies during Third Ypres, suggests that concerns about the discipline of civilian-soldiers not only persisted, but might even have increased.

There is other evidence that commanders were more concerned about the discipline of New Army and Territorial Force units than they were of that in the Regular army. Lieutenant-Colonel F. P. Crozier's comments that 'the discipline of the 9th R.I. Rifles is good for a service [i.e. New Army] battalion',[19] implied that good discipline was the exception in the case of New Army battalions. This is supported by Travers, who has observed that the state of discipline (and, therefore, the reliability) of their own troops, particularly those of the New Armies, preoccupied 4th Army commanders during their preparations for the Somme offensive in 1916. More attention was paid to discipline in the plans for the battle than was afforded the enemy about whom concerns were less obvious.[20]

Other commanders, however, saw different qualities in the men of the New Army. In his *Notes on the New Armies by a DIVISIONAL Commander,* dated November 1914 and circulated to Lord Kitchener and Lieutenant-General

Murray (Chief of Staff of the BEF), Major-General Ivor Maxse said of the citizen-soldiers:

> The distinguishing features of the infantry of the New Armies appear to be:-
> (I)   The excellent physical and moral qualities of the Subaltern Officers. They have tackled the job of commanding war strength platoons with a zest and a fearlessness which augers well. . . .
> (II) The quality of the men is undoubtedly of a higher standard than that of the average men we usually recruited in the old Army. Every one I have spoken to holds the same opinion. Having discussed the matter with ex N.C. Officers who have re-enlisted, I find they hold the opinion that they never had better men in their old Regiments.[21]

Maxse's opinion did not alter in the following few months and he restated it in a second report on the New Armies in February 1915. However, he did raise concerns about the experience of the officers and he believed that a limited exchange of personnel between Regular and New Army officers would be beneficial to all concerned.[22]

If, however, the fault lay in the inexperience of the officers of the New Armies the solution to most disciplinary worries was held to be the occasional shooting of men in the ranks to set an example. Or to put it another way, perceived deficiencies in the management of the men was compensated for by the coercion of the rank and file through a regime of fear. Execution was widely held to be the *only* way to restore discipline where it was thought to be suspect. Furthermore, the use of the death penalty was frequently believed to be the most effective way of maintaining discipline and it might be recalled that General Horace Smith-Dorrien had considered that 'the only way to stop it [desertion] is to carry out some death penalties'.[23] Smith-Dorrien also insisted on another execution later in 1915 because he did not want the resolve of the High Command to appear weak by reducing the fear of execution in the ranks:

> only yesterday a man in this very battalion [1st Battalion King's Own Royal Lancaster] was shot for a similar offence and it is not yet possible to see that an example is necessary – I think though it will have a bad effect if it is not carried out and therefore recommend it.[24]

In many other cases executions were carried out even though discipline in the unit was regarded as either very good or excellent.

Similarly, recognition was given to those commanders whose disciplinary methods met with the approval of the High Command. In recommending the execution of a Scots Guardsman, Major-General Capper, commander of 7th Division in 1915, wrote:

> The battalion [2nd Scots Guards] has good discipline but it has been put into this state by a C.O. who has taken severe measures against those who have attempted to desert their comrades in action.[25]

The Major-General was not explicit about what these severe measures entailed. Not only was this the first case resulting in execution in 2nd Battalion Scots Guards, it was also the first condemnation. In the absence of any evidence to the contrary it can only be assumed that summary executions were not being practised in this unit and, therefore, the 'severe measures' must refer to field punishments. However, what is interesting is that the mere threat of an execution was not considered sufficient deterrent in itself, and this in a unit said to have good discipline.

This might indicate an over-reliance on the death penalty as a means to maintain discipline, which as such marks a degree of continuity with concerns raised by politicians of the Left during the pre-war debate about army punishments.[26] It might be recalled that during the debate about the abolition of flogging many senior commanders appeared unable to see an effective alternative. In the absence of corporal punishment many of those in senior posts of the British Army during the First World War fell back on the ultimate punishment rather than exploring other methods of managing discipline. This doctrine was applied every bit as much in units where even by their own standards no example was necessary, as it was in those where they perceived a problem.

In his study of discipline and morale in the British Expeditionary Force, James Brent Wilson, argued that there was a relationship between experience in battle and the rate of crime in any particular unit, contending that crime tended to rise most in units which experienced setbacks in action. This, according to Wilson, was the result of a collapse in morale.[27] To this we might add that it could just as easily be a reflection of increased coercion on the part of commanders. This assertion can also be tested by a more detailed analysis of divisions deployed in specific actions. The first day of the Somme offensive, perhaps the most controversial of all actions during World War I, is an ideal case in point. I have shown elsewhere how the number of condemnations increased roughly in line with the rate of casualties sustained – indicating that the threat of the death penalty was most often deployed at times of the greatest action on the battlefield.[28] Was the experience of those units engaged on the first day of the Somme offensive consistent with this general trend?

The Battle of the Somme

A total of thirteen divisions were deployed on the morning of 1 July 1916: four Regular formations (4th, 7th, 8th, 29th); seven New Army divisions (18th, 21st, 30th, 31st, 32nd, 34th, 36th); and two from the Territorial Force (46th, 56th). Close scrutiny of these divisions highlights the problem with relying exclusively on generalised conclusions. However helpful these general conclusions are there will always be exceptions which can only be revealed by close study of individual units at a given time. Viewed along with the general trends already identified, these more individualised cases facilitate a more complete analysis of how the death penalty was operated at the time of a major battle.

The two Territorial divisions had similar battle experiences. Involved in the same pincer movement, 46th from the north and 56th from the south, the two divisions suffered similar disappointments on 1 July. 46th Division had suffered from the start of their attack; many were lost in the smoke and the attack became bogged down in the mud. On reaching the uncut enemy wire some men made it as far as the German second line, but the division was repulsed with considerable casualties. Although initially enjoying more success, largely thanks to the enemy's wire being cut, 56th Division was also repulsed after heavy fighting with a high number of casualties.[29]

There were also some similarities in the discipline approach in the divisions. In each division a mere five death sentences were passed throughout 1916, one prior to the attack on the Somme and four afterwards. However, the similarities end there. While there were three condemnations in 46th Division in July there were none in 56th. One of the condemnations in 46th Division was carried out – the division's only execution throughout the war. The individual, Private Hawthorne, was convicted of an act of cowardice on the first morning of the battle.[30] It appears, therefore, that although their experiences were similar, the reaction in each division, at least in terms of the death penalty as a means of reinforcing discipline and maintaining fighting spirit, was quite different.

Interestingly, the three condemnations in 46th Division were evenly distributed across each of its three infantry brigades with the executed soldier belonging to 137th Brigade which had made the initial assault on the German lines. Condemnations in 46th Division were rare and three in one month was unprecedented. This, therefore, appears to be a case of *pour encourager les autres*. That the same did not occur in the other Territorial Force division, which had endured a similar experience that morning, is further evidence that sentencing by court martial more often than not was the outcome of different approaches to the same problem by the respective divisional commanders. Throughout the whole war there were 21 and 22 condemnations in these two divisions – a relatively low number typical of Territorial Force formations – but on this occasion one commander had differed, perhaps under pressure from elsewhere, and sought examples from the ranks to firm up divisional discipline.

The crime statistics quoted by Wilson for these two divisions are incorrect. His table shows there to have been no convictions at court martial for either division in the month of October.[31] There were, however, two death sentences passed on men in 56th Division on 14 October.[32] The two men concerned, serving with 1/13 (Kensington) London Regiment, were spared the firing squad by the commander-in-chief. This raises doubts about the accuracy of Wilson's figures and, therefore, those contained in the reports in the division's war diary – Wilson's source. If indeed there was a genuine rise in *recorded* convictions in the two Territorial Force divisions during August 1916 following their involvement in the first day of the Somme battle, as Wilson argues, it was certainly not matched by an increase in the number of *recorded* condemnations. This suggests that the nature of that crime was not thought to be a threat to discipline and only the commander of 46th Division deemed it necessary to deploy the firing squad in an attempt to bolster discipline.

The number of condemnations and executions in the four Regular divisions show some remarkable similarities. Each division experienced a slight rise in the number of capital sentences during the Somme battle – hardly surprising. Furthermore, the total number of condemnations in each division for the whole of 1916 varied little from the mean of ten. However, in the period prior to the start of the battle in July condemnations were far more common in these divisions than in the Territorial formations. This was particularly so in 4th and 7th rather than in 8th and 29th, which differed slightly from the other Regular divisions in that originally they had been assembled from various units serving across the Empire in 1914. Despite there being something of a rise in the number of soldiers in Regular divisions condemned by courts martial during the Battle of the Somme, this was far less than can be discerned in other types of division. In short the approach to capital punishment in these divisions varied surprisingly little over the twelve months despite the considerable impact of the Battle of the Somme.

A number of executions were carried out in 4th and 7th divisions. Two men from the 4th Division were executed in August. The first, a soldier from the Hampshire Regiment, was shot for cowardice, then a few days later a Highlander was executed for desertion. The men served in different brigades and their crimes were unrelated. Their treatment was entirely consistent with the division's record since arriving in France in 1914. Discipline in 4th Division had been strictly enforced since the beginning of the war. Condemnations were common and five executions had already been carried out before these two on the Somme. Nor were these men the last to be shot, underlining the fact that while recourse to the death penalty during the Somme offensive might have marked a change of direction for Territorial formations, for those in Regular divisions it represented continuity.

Other Regular divisions might not have been subject to quite such a harsh approach as 4th Division, but their experience remained different to that of the Territorials. Condemnations were not as common in 7th Division throughout 1916, but it was rare for a month to pass without at least one.

Again this was consistent with the division's record; as with 4th Division, condemnations had been a feature of the division's disciplinary approach since 1914 and, also like 4th Division, five men had already been executed. However, unlike in 4th Division no executions were thought to be necessary in 7th Division during the Battle of the Somme. There was much commonality of experience of discipline within Regular divisions, but subtle differences did indeed exist.

Variations in the New Army divisions are even more marked. In some units such as 30th Division there was a long history of condemnations. Throughout 1916 there were only three months when no soldiers in this division were sentenced to death by court martial: April, December and, paradoxically, July. Nor was this merely a question of single condemnations. Again, surprisingly, the only month when there were fewer than two condemnations was August; there were four in February and nine in November. However, no sentence was carried out until November when a total of three soldiers were executed. Was this a response to a particular incident or, given the frequency of condemnations in this division during 1916, did it signify an attempt to demonstrate a more general determination on the part of Major-General Shea, the division's commander, to enforce discipline?

Interestingly, although arising from two separate incidents, all three executions were carried out against men serving with the same unit: 18th Manchester Regiment. Four of the five soldiers whose death sentences had been commuted to lesser punishments also belonged to a single unit – 19th Manchesters – while the one remaining, a Green Howard, was serving in the same brigade. The executions were carried out, it appears, at the insistence of the divisional commander, following setbacks in action, despite some opposition from his own junior commanders.

On 1 July 30th Division had achieved all its objectives, but successes in the following months eluded them. In mid-October the division had taken part in the Battle of the Transloy Ridges, but despite the use of tanks had been unable to hold onto its gains. The attack by 21st Brigade on 18 October had been chaotic. It was probably as a result of this that the four men of 19th Manchesters had been condemned to death by court martial on 13 November (the day that the Battle of the Ancre opened) for the offence of cowardice. All had their sentences commuted to 10 years' penal servitude.

The three men whose sentences were carried out had been convicted of desertion. The first case was a direct result of the battle, the second – involving two men – was more an indirect consequence. Together these cases clearly demonstrate how battle could differently affect the men involved. The first case was that of Private William Hunt, who was tried for desertion during the battle of Flers on 12 October 1916. Hunt had absented himself during an attack on an enemy trench and made his way to a First Aid Post where he was seen by the battalion Medical Officer. The Medical Officer told the court:

I saw him standing outside the First Aid Post. I asked him what he was doing. He made no reply. I ordered him to return to his company. Shortly after I again saw him helping a man to the First Aid Post. He made no complaint about being ill or wounded. He had no rifle. I again ordered him to rejoin his company.

However, Hunt only temporarily rejoined his unit and was, some two days later, discovered to have attached himself to another battalion, repairing trenches.[33]

Hunt's defence was that he had lost control of his limbs and had made his way to the First Aid Post. After he was sent away by the Medical Officer he had assisted a wounded corporal to the same First Aid Post. Then, having become detached from his unit he had joined another. This was corroborated by two defence witnesses, but the court decided that Hunt had deliberately absented himself from his unit with the intention of avoiding duty in the front line and found him guilty. His previous convictions for absence and disobedience, both in August 1916,[34] might have been a factor in the decision to sentence Hunt to death. But the decision to carry out the sentence was probably more a question of timing: his was the nineteenth condemnation in the division during 1916 and at the height of a major battle it was likely that an example was deemed necessary.

Despite Hunt's claim that he had been unable to control his limbs, he was never medically examined. It seems likely that Hunt's nerve had cracked during the attack and his attempt to perform other duties had been to no avail. Nevertheless, he was not immediately singled out as an example to deter others. The brigade commander, Brigadier General Lloyd, recommended that the sentence be commuted. Lloyd's comments are interesting: he clearly had little regard for Hunt's qualities, but appears to have been one of only a few generals to record their disapproval of the death penalty:

There is *no circumstance* which requires the extreme penalty to be inflicted [my italics]. The man is young, but his presence in the ranks of new reinforcements is not at all desirable.[35]

Others were less inhibited. Lloyd was overruled by the divisional commander, Major-General J. S. M. Shea, who justified the execution on the grounds that 'the accused deliberately absented himself from the firing line'.[36]

The unambiguous rejection of the death penalty as a means to enforce discipline by the brigade commander sheds some light on the commutation of so many condemnations in 90th Brigade; Hunt's was the eighth condemnation in the brigade, but the first to be carried out. Interference in the independence of courts martial, especially from divisional commanders was quite common, as we shall see.

The second case in 30th Division involved two pre-war friends, Albert Ingham and Alfred Longshaw, who had tried to flee the battlefront and return to England. I have briefly alluded to this case in an earlier chapter, but here we must consider the case in the context of the Battle of the Somme, the nature of the offensive and the consequences of the huge loss of life. The co-defendants' testimonies are clear evidence of the effects a major action such as the Battle of the Somme could have on both unit and troop morale, in particular the impact of large numbers of casualties. Unlike the case of Private Hunt, who had seemingly cracked as a consequence of a single action, Ingham and Longshaw's decisions to desert were the outcome of an accumulation of factors, not all of them related to events on the battlefield.

Privates Albert Ingham and Alfred Longshaw were both employed as clerks at the Salford Goods Yard of the Lancashire and Yorkshire Railway before enlisting together at the outbreak of war.[37] Although not deployed on the first day of the Somme offensive their unit had seen much action in the following weeks: the battalion war diary records how the commanding officer, Lieutenant-Colonel W. A. Smith, was killed on 7 July. They had also been involved in the unsuccessful attack on Guillemont on 30 July.[38] It was when the unit was returning to the front-line trenches on 5 October that Ingham and Longshaw absconded. They successfully negotiated their way to the coast where, dressed in civilian clothes, they boarded an England-bound ship at Dieppe. But there good fortune deserted them. Their attempts to pass as American tourists did not deceive the military police; both were apprehended and immediately admitted their crime. The prosecution case was not a difficult one – the facts of their capture alone were sufficient evidence to prove desertion. It must be acknowledged that this was a *prime facie* case which was likely to result in death sentences for both men regardless of unit history or commander's character. The evidence presented by the two defendants, recorded in the transcript of the trial, indicates that the soldiers were aware of the implications of their actions and that they were on trial for their lives.

A clerk recorded Longshaw's statement in which he told the court that he had absented himself from his unit, adding:

> I was prompted to act thus by the state of mind caused by the wish to visit my people at home, about whom I was greatly worried; also my service at the Somme front had reacted on my state of mind, which had become morbid and irrational, also the fact that practically all my comrades were gone induced me further to this act. Also all immediate prospect of leave was denied.[39]

Longshaw's account raises a number of important considerations. Firstly, it is clear that concerns for his 'people at home' were paramount and it is significant that he put this first. This suggests that the link between home and battle fronts was an important one. When the link came under threat, as appears to be the case here, it could induce men to react without regard for the consequences of their actions. The link with home was crucial to the morale of the troops and should not be underestimated. That so much mail, parcels and the like were received by men at the front even at times of fierce engagements with the enemy suggests that the importance of this was not lost on the army at the time.

Another important feature of army discipline and morale was the so-called *esprit de corps*, which was so enthusiastically encouraged by commanders. The impact then to troop morale of huge losses within tightly knit units could be devastating. Perhaps it was this effect that Wilson has noticed with the increased incidence of crime after units had seen action. Longshaw's concern about the loss of so many of his comrades should be viewed within the context of the inculcation of *esprit de corps*. Thought to be a valuable adjunct to fighting spirit, *esprit de corps* was a remarkably fragile concept on the modern battlefield, especially in a 'Pals' unit such as this, enlisted *en masse* from work colleagues, sporting clubs or other tightly-bound groups, their mutual sense of loyalty often transcending military training.

Longshaw's complaint regarding leave might seem a minor one under the circumstances. However, this issue had also concerned the mail censor, Captain Hardie, who had identified leave as the single greatest complaint affecting the morale of the troops in Third Army around the same time.[40] Indeed, leave appears to have been a universal concern among troops at the front: Pétain had to make significant concessions to French troops following the mutinies of 1917. Although the prospect of no leave was in itself unlikely to have induced Longshaw and others like him to desert, it had an enormous compounding effect on other concerns in soldiers' minds. Most notable among these was worry about family and friends at home. For a soldier many miles away from his family the solution to such concerns would in all likelihood appear to be leave. Its denial, or the prospect of its denial, was probably powerful enough to make some act irrationally.

For good measure Longshaw also appealed to the better nature of the court in which he unwittingly re-stated this desire for familial contact:

My motive was *first to visit home* and then to join in the same unit of the Naval Forces as my *brother* [my italics]. I regret this act. I have served with my battn in France for twelve months and hope that this service and my character will aid in my plea for a chance to make full reparation in service to condone my offence.[41]

Not surprisingly Private Ingham, the co-defendant, made a similar plea:

I was worrying at the time through the loss of my chums. Also about my mother at home, being upset, through hearing bad news of two of my comrades. I plead for leniency on account of my previous good conduct. I beg for a chance to make atonement. I left with my chum firstly to see those at home and then to try to get into the Navy along with his [Longshaw's] other brother, who is serving there.[42]

Concerns like these, most particularly the longing for home, became especially heightened during battle. This is hardly surprising. Battle would have made soldiers most aware of their own mortality and thoughts about home took on a morbid tone, with some wondering whether they would ever see home or family again. Then there was the lingering concern about how one's family would cope financially should the worst happen. It seems likely that these two defendants had discussed their respective defences and the similarities probably owe something to this. However, the mail censor for Third Army had noted identical concerns about home amongst troops in his formation. The clamour for parcels and the like from home, he stated, had been duly met,[43] which suggests that the desire for a continued link between home and war fronts was a mutual one. In assessing the state of morale of men, especially, those involved in a battle as fierce as the Somme, we should not overlook the importance of the home front.

Paradoxically, there appears to have been no disciplinary necessity to carry out the executions of Longshaw and Ingham. The brigade commander, Brigadier General Lloyd, accepted that a well-thought-out plan to desert such as theirs was likely to attract the extreme penalty, but added, 'There is however no other reason either for the sake of discipline or example in the units concerned that it should be carried out.'[44] The circumstances of their desertion, however, were such that again Lloyd's opinion was discarded by Major-General Shea, the divisional commander, whose view that 'this is a clear case of desertion' met with the agreement of corps and army commanders.[45] The near success of their desertion was probably the undoing of Longshaw and Ingham. Theirs was the kind of desertion for which the Army Act had been designed to punish in the most extreme manner. Clearly the divisional commander was not prepared to allow the culprits to escape with their lives despite the protestations of the brigade commander. To have done otherwise would probably have met with disapproval from the High Command, but there is nothing in the division's record to suggest an alternative outcome.

Other divisions' experience differed. In 18th Division, a New Army formation commanded by Major-General Maxse, condemnations were rare and executions rarer still. Throughout 1916 there were only five condemnations in 18th Division and no executions; of the New Army divisions only 34th Division had fewer condemnations during 1916. This contrasts with most other divisions where condemnations were far more common, and highlights the problems associated with general conclusions, especially those concerning the New Armies. Maxse had stated how he decided to use the trial of two soldiers of the Northamptonshire Regiment in January 1916 'to illustrate to all battalions the necessity of never surrendering without a fight'.[46] However, he did not specifically call for the death penalty and the one death sentence passed in that case was later commuted. Unfortunately, Maxse's recommendations have not survived, nor is anything known of his attitude towards capital punishment, but the rarity of condemnations in 18th Division suggests that he might not have been a supporter of the death penalty as a means to enforce discipline.

Significantly, it was during the first two months of the Somme offensive that four of the five condemnations in 18th Division were passed. On 1 July the division had achieved its first and second objectives despite encountering some stiff opposition and being held up at significant points. Enemy counter-attacks were beaten off and further progress made the following morning. They were also involved in the dawn attack on 14 July, capturing Trônes Wood. Casualties had been high, yet it was in the battalion held back in reserve on 1 July, 12th Middlesex, that two condemnations followed rather than in those deployed in the battle. This must cast some doubt on Wilson's argument that increased levels of crime cannot be separated from reverses in battle. The circumstances of the offences are unknown, but it appears likely that the two men, convicted of desertion on 12 July, had absconded while the battalion was being moved forward to captured enemy trenches.[47]

The key issue here is whether the comparatively low number of condemnations in 18th Division were attributable to its relative success in battle or whether it should be viewed in the context of Maxse's more progressive approach to discipline. Certainly, the five condemnations during 1916 were the only ones in 18th Division during the entire period of Maxse's command and there were no executions. Furthermore, the division's record was markedly different under another commander. After Maxse's promotion and departure to XVIII Corps in 1917 the number of condemnations in the division increased massively: there were 18 condemnations in 1917 and a further five in 1918 with a total of four executions carried out. In this case at least it appears that the character of its commander had a profound effect on the division's approach to the death penalty.

Maxse's views of discipline in his troops was closer to the concept of 'intelligent bayonets' more usually associated with the French army than with the British. It is also, at this point, worth, reconsidering another case – from 1917 – related by the Courts-Martial Officer, Gerald Hurst. Two soldiers had been acquitted of the offence of plundering by a Field General Court Martial. The president of the court was, according to Hurst, an experienced barrister. However, as Hurst stated: 'The 42nd *Divisional* Staff required the President to furnish forthwith in writing a full explanation of his conduct in *allowing* the acquittals to take place [my italics].'[48]

The important point here is that it was the divisional commander who sought to extend his authority in an attempt to influence the findings of the court and not some higher office such as the commander-in-chief, as is far too often assumed by historians and public alike. Hurst, who was support- ive of the courts-martial system as the most efficient and fair means to administer military law, gave details of other incidents of interference with judicial process. Invariably, it was divisional commanders who were guilty of these 'gross tamperings with the course of justice'.[49]

Of course divisional commanders could be cajoled or bullied into following certain courses of action. Some were simply afraid of being branded poor disciplinarians. An obvious case concerned 35th Division, already discussed, above. The 29 death sentences passed on men in this 'bantam' division followed prejudicial remarks made at an inspection by the corps commander, General Aylmer Haldane. This prompted a purging of so-called 'degenerates' from the division and four executions were carried out. However, these 'worthless men' had endured a torrid time long before Haldane's inspection; more prosecutions were brought against men in this division than in any other in the corps.[50] The divisional commander, Major-General Landon, had blamed the poor quality of the troops for this and justified a number of executions on the grounds of the 'mental and physical degeneracy' of his men.[51]

An analysis of 35th Division demonstrates how the British army assessed discipline and how it sought to address concerns. On 26 November 1916 Corps Headquarters took a close interest in 35th Division, focusing on their high crime rate – as represented by the number of prosecutions. This accord- ing to the corps commander was a sign that discipline was 'not what it should be'.[52] However, the timing is interesting – one week after the end of the offensive. The bantams, it was said, had 'not done well in the fighting line',[53] but in reality they had achieved as much as many other units: they repelled three enemy attacks on 18 July and captured a section of enemy trench two days later despite heavy losses.[54] Discipline was believed to be suspect, but the only means of assessment appears to be the crime rate recorded in the division and it was this that corps focused on. The divisional commander, Major-General Landon, had every reason to fear for his own professional reputation. In 1914 Landon had been the commander of 1st Brigade at the First Battle of Ypres when, owing to an injury to Major- General Lomax, he became *de facto* commander of the 1st Division. Despite the division capturing the village of Gheluvelt, General Haig was not overly impressed with Landon, who was then returned to England to assume his unwanted command of 35th Division. Haig recorded in his diary for 17 November 1914:

> I saw General Landon today. Although he has done well as a Brigade Commander [*sic*], and had my confidence as such, I have not felt the same feeling in his judgement since he took over the 1st Division after Lomax was wounded. I have therefore recommended him to be transferred to England to help to train the New Army for which he is well

qualified and because the strain and hard work has begun to tell on him. He quite agreed when I told him of my decision and said he did not feel the same. He has certainly had a very hard time, nerve-racking to a degree, being for many weeks constantly under shell-fire.[55]

This was clearly a retrograde step for Landon, but there was yet another reason why Landon might have resented his appointment to 35th Division. Landon had been an inspector of gymnasia in India before the war, only to find himself commanding a division of men whose physical fitness was openly questioned. The supposed degeneracy of the 'bantams' provided an acceptable explanation of the high crime in the division. This explanation by Landon prompted the inspection by Haldane and the subsequent dismissal as 'unfit for infantry duty' of 2784 men.[56]

Such liberal use of the death penalty in conjunction with the medical discharges suggests that Landon was eager to dispel any lingering concerns about his approach to discipline. Examples were hardly necessary in a division that had virtually been broken up. Degeneracy and the poor quality of recruits was little more than a convenient excuse for Landon. But in this he was supported by other commanders in the division including the divisional historian who, some years after the war, wrote:

the men who were sent to take their [casualties] places were, in most cases, not 'Bantams' at all, as the term was originally understood, but undeveloped men, who had been previously rejected by the commanders and who were unfitted, both morally and physically, to take their places in the fighting ranks of the British Army.[57]

This merely justified the expulsion of unfit men and does not explain the necessity of carrying out executions. Surprisingly, Wilson, in his thesis, also blames the breakdown in discipline on 'lower quality troops'.[58] However, neither Davson nor Wilson appear to realise that the executed men had originally been sent overseas with the division in February 1916 and were not part of a later top-up.

The death penalty had been used in the division before the Somme battle: there had been three condemnations and one execution in May and June 1916. But condemnations and executions on the scale that followed the Battle of the Somme amounted to an overt demonstration of military authority. The timing was important coming as it did at the end of the battle. This appears to have been common in other divisions where more death sentences were passed as commanders' attention shifted from fighting to discipline. The measures taken clearly became more extreme in the last months of 1916. In taking stock of the battle divisional commanders and the High Command alike were more prepared to take extreme measures to rectify perceived problems.

It was during November that the greatest number of condemnations and executions occurred amongst those divisions involved in the first day of the Somme offensive. There were 27 condemnations during November in the 13 divisions compared with only 14 in July itself, 18 in August, eight in September and six each in October and December. In short it was as the battle was coming to a halt rather than at its height that discipline appears to have been most ruthlessly enforced. The evidence of Ingham and Longshaw suggests that, towards the latter part of 1916, troop morale was suffering the effects of the offensive. This was especially the case in units where casualties had been heaviest – a phenomenon less obvious in divisions not so heavily engaged in the fighting on the Somme. For example, Captain Hardie was able to report in November that, in Third Army at least, 'the spirit of the men, their conception of duty, their Moral [*sic*], has never been higher than at the present moment'.[59] The reaction in those divisions suffering a crisis of morale was to pass more death sentences as a demonstration of the command's resolve to enforce discipline. It was only in the Territorial divisions and in Maxse's 18th Division that there were no condemnations in November. There were condemnations in all the other divisions engaged on 1 July, with the greatest numbers occurring in the very divisions which had previously been most liberal with capital sentences – the 30th and 36th. These were the divisions whose commanders were less willing to explore alternatives to the deterrent approach to discipline. However, in what appears to be acts of desperation most other commanders did likewise.

Assessments of discipline based on achievements in battle were as unsatisfactory as those based on crime rates. A division's success in any given engagement depended not only on its own abilities, but also on those of other units. Most important was the artillery bombardment. Invariably wherever the wire was uncut the attack became bogged down as the forward units struggled to overcome the first line of defence. Once objectives had been gained they could only be held with the arrival of reserves. Each division also relied on those divisions on either side making similar progress to avoid becoming isolated or exposing its flank to the enemy. In the post-mortem that followed the Battle of the Somme, however, commanders appear to have taken little account of factors outside the ranks of their own divisions.

The effects of battle on morale and discipline were even more numerous and complex. It appears, however, that the modern battlefield had a tendency to erode the very foundations on which good morale and discipline was based, at least in the British army. The local identity, so keenly fostered in the county regiments, was something of a double-edged sword. *Esprit de corps* might have been easier to engender in a locally recruited unit. but the price was a high one and was cruelly exposed by the Battle of the Somme. The huge casualties, concentrated in the first units to be sent into action, had the dual effect of destroying the fighting potential of certain battalions while at the same time focusing the concerns of the survivors on how the news would be received at home. This, fused with the despair felt at the loss of comrades, was a powerful cocktail which destroyed the ability of men such as Longshaw and Ingham to endure any more.

Concerns about leave, or the lack of it, were paramount in men's minds. This was a key issue in men's mail and frequently emerged in defences at courts martial. In *The Pity of War*, Niall Ferguson cites leave as one of the seven 'carrots' that, according to him, kept men in the fighting line.[60] Surprisingly he places it last in his list, arguing that the 'sense of alienation' was resented by those fortunate enough to be granted leave. The problem for Ferguson, like Fussell before him, is that he placed too great an emphasis on accounts by officers such as Robert Graves and Siegfried Sassoon.[61] As the evidence contained in the mail censor's reports and the testimonies of Ingham, Longshaw and a host of others who stood trial for their lives shows, the men saw things rather differently. Concerns about rations and other creature comforts, placed higher in Ferguson's list of 'carrots', were of less importance when it came to men's motives to desert, but they were nevertheless important underlying issues. The army did much to counter these: the reports of Captain Hardie show that the army was aware of the problems and constantly monitored them. Yet so long as it maintained an offensive policy on the battlefront the army was powerless to prevent the sudden erosion of troop morale. Instead it sought to deter with overt threats of certain death inflicted by one's own comrades those who would not face possible death inflicted by the enemy. Not all divisional commanders pursued this policy with alacrity. They, though, were the exceptions rather than the rule. But did executions deter others as was no doubt intended?

An execution in a division was often followed by a period during which further condemnations were rare. For example in 31st Division three men were executed from a total of five condemnations during August 1916. There then followed a period of three months before another was condemned. In 4th Division two executions were also carried out in August. Again it was three months until another condemnation. A similar period without condemnations followed the execution of a soldier in 21st Division and there were also significant pauses following executions in 29th and 46th Divisions. There are a number of possible explanations for this. First, it is possible that the executions did indeed have a deterrent effect on the troops. On the other hand it could be the case that commanders felt they had demonstrated their resolve sufficiently and that further condemnations were not necessary. The answer remains elusive. However, increased unwillingness on the part of courts martial to pass further death sentences cannot be discounted. Court-martial duty was unpopular at the best of times and most courts appear to have had no great desire to have their condemnations carried out – in most cases the court, in passing a sentence of death, made a recommendation to mercy.

The effectiveness of the death penalty as an instrument of discipline is difficult to measure. We have discussed the deterrent effect on the individual in an earlier chapter, but we must also consider it in the wider context of its effect on divisions. The executed individuals were in most cases unfortunate men who simply could go on no longer, which meant that their usefulness to the army was over. As such they were the ideal candidates for examples to others. But how far this policy succeeded remains open to debate and the relationship between military effectiveness and the death penalty – essentially an extension of Wilson's thesis – is a dubious one. Failure in battle often led to an increase in condemnations, but this was most marked in those divisions where the death penalty was already a common feature of discipline – 30th Division for example. Furthermore, condemnations tended to remain a constant feature of discipline, save the usual one-or two-month pause following an execution. There is no evidence to suggest a greater military effectiveness in any divisions during these periods. However much commanders justified the death penalty *pour encourager les autres* the truth was that in most cases it was no more than a signal to those senior in rank as much as those below, that the divisional commander was a tough disciplinarian.

Summation

The manner in which the death sentence was applied clearly varied from one division to another and a number of factors were influential in this. First, the type of division appears to have made a considerable difference. Even allowing for the different lengths of time spent on the Western Front, soldiers in Regular formations were more vulnerable than those in Territorial units. Divisional commanders, it appears, followed long-established traditions of discipline whereby Territorials were not treated in as harsh a manner as their Regular counterparts. This was reflected in the relatively low number of condemnations in the Territorial divisions. These traditions proved to be fairly resilient to change and were only slightly diluted by the topping-up process that invariably followed the huge losses inflicted in battle.

Men serving with New Army formations were subject to something of a hybrid version of these two approaches. As Gary Sheffield has shown, without the long-standing traditions of the Territorial Force the New Army divisions were more vulnerable to a 'Regular' style of discipline creeping in.[62] This trend can certainly be detected in the approach to capital punishments. Maxse's 18th Division is a good case in point: capital punishments were unheard of in the early years, but after Maxse's departure in 1917 the threat of the firing squad became commonplace. Although it should be noted that this reflected an army-wide development whereby the frequency of condemnation and executions peaked in the autumn of 1917 before decreasing once again in 1918, the period of Maxse's command of 18th Division was synonymous with an extremely low incidence of capital sentences. Such variation, however, was mostly restricted to the New Armies and is less obvious among the other types of divisions, which appear to have followed their established traditions in this regard.

Unit traditions, and even structures for that matter, exerted a heavy influence on divisional commanders. Few were able, like Maxse, to act with apparent total autonomy when it came to the use of capital punishment in their formations, but most nevertheless stamped their own identity on their divisions. Accordingly, condemnations usually follow a pattern that can be regarded as an outcome of unit tradition coupled with the commanders' own approach. Yet both these factors were very much in the shadow of the pre-war structures, in particular the very nature of military law. Few commanders were able to pursue a disciplinary policy that compromised the principles of the 1881 Army Act. Accordingly, most fell back on the Regular-style discipline – even the Territorial Force frequently resorted to the death penalty when discipline was at its most vulnerable during big battles. The discernible difference between the three types of division was a reflection of their respective traditions – or in the case of the New Army divisions the absence of tradition – but these were compromised by the expectations of a High Command that required the compliance of the divisional commander. In most cases his compliance was forthcoming. This was certainly the case in 35th Division where the commander responded directly to criticism from his superiors, resulting in the death by firing squad of three of the troops under his command on a single day. When it came to generals' reputations the lives of the men were extremely cheap and most divisional commanders could be easily bullied by those at corps, army or higher level. Disciplinary policy within each division was formulated by its commanding officer, but this could only be achieved within the confines of the structures of command and military law. The law placed a responsibility on all commanders to put discipline ahead of concerns for justice and the High Command expected divisional commanders to comply. Tradition, it seems, could only mitigate the effects of battle on disciplinary policy within divisions.

The involvement of commanders below divisional level was apparently restricted to implementing decisions made elsewhere. Battalion commanders frequently recommended commutation of death sentences, only to be overruled. Indeed, it was rare for a battalion commander to sanction an execution and some gave evidence to the courts martial in defence of their troops. Of course this could have been motivated by a desire to avoid criticism of poor discipline in their unit, but if so it was a risky policy to pursue. Undoubtedly, general discipline was diluted as it descended the chain of command until it reached company commanders, but rarely did this impact on capital punishments. It is unlikely that commanders below the level of division were able to influence official discipline policy in the most severe cases. Even a brigade commander who opposed capital punishment could be overruled by his immediate superior.

The role of the officers commanding divisions was, therefore, most crucial. Nowhere does this become more apparent than when we analyse the differences between individual formations. The number of condemnations and executions in many divisions was often a reflection of the personality of its commanding officer. The cases of Generals Maxse, Landon, and Shea have been discussed at length, but the same was equally true of many other formations. Most conformed to a style of discipline based on fear and deterrent, but exceptions such as Maxse are evident, albeit rare.

The evidence suggests that we should dispense with the notion that capital punishments were carried out merely at some implicit insistence of Douglas Haig. The reality was far more complex than that. Tradition played a significant role. So too did the personalities of many commanders junior to Haig. The divisional commanders had a large professional stake in the discipline of their formations and sought to impose their will by utilising the methods they were most comfortable with. In most cases this entailed maintaining a tight grip on courts martial and ensuring not only the desired verdict but the sentence too. In this they were well served by military law, which ensured that their power to control army discipline was not compromised by civil servants, appeals or an overriding concern for justice. The law had also preserved the role of the commander-in-chief, again protecting it from outside interference. Confirmation of sentences was a matter for the commander-in-chief, but divisional commanders' recommendations carried great weight in the process. As we have already seen, Haig's office carried out the task with surprising leniency given the circumstances and beliefs prevalent in the army at the time. Clearly the execution of one in ten was regarded as a 'safe' level politically speaking, satisfying both military and judicial considerations.

Commanders-in-chief were granted wide powers by Parliament. In most cases this was interpreted as a confirmation of pre-war style military discipline of which the death penalty was considered a vital component.

5
Discipline and Morale in the Three Armies[1]: Case Studies of Three British Infantry Divisions

The British Expeditionary Force that landed in France in August 1914 was a very different organisation from that which fought the later phases of the war. Over the course of four years the changing nature of modern battle led to the composition and organisation of infantry divisions being gradually altered. The number of horses declined from 5594 in 1914 to 3838 in 1918; the number of machine guns increased from 24 in 1914 to 400 in 1918. The allocation of artillery pieces to infantry divisions also decreased from 76 to 48, but trench mortars were added in 1916. The personnel of divisions also fluctuated between 1914 and 1917: there was a total of 18,179 all ranks in 1914; 18,122 in 1915; 19,372 in 1916; and 18,825 in 1917. But the most significant change in manpower came in 1918 when the strength of an infantry division was reduced to 16,035 all ranks.[2]

Hidden behind these figures were the most important changes of all: the enlargement of the Regular army by deploying the Territorial Force overseas followed by the addition of the New Armies and finally the introduction of conscription. As we have already discussed, the three armies – Regular, Territorial and New Army formations – retained differing approaches to discipline, which were reflected in the numbers of condemnations and executions in the divisions. In this chapter we will analyse three infantry divisions, one from each type of formation, and assess the experiences of each over the course of the entire war. Although it is impossible to disentangle conscripted men from volunteers, we will also consider the impact of conscription on the morale and discipline of the divisions selected. What changes can be detected in disciplinary practices and how are these affected by the type of formation, by assessments of morale, the theatre in which the divisions were deployed and the progress of the war?

The three divisions selected – 7th Division, a Regular formation; 48th (South Midland) Division from the Territorial Force; and 23rd Division of the New Army – represent an ideal cross-section of the British Army in the war. There are a number of advantages in analysing these particular divisions. Each served on the Western Front, being deployed in the major battles. There were condemnations and executions in each division, which broadly conform to what we have already identified as typical for the type of formation. Finally, in November 1918 all three divisions were posted to the Italian front. Although little use was made of the death penalty in Italy, this remains a major advantage because it allows us to compare the divisions' experience in two different theatres of the war and also enables us to make ample use of the assessments of troop morale by Captain Hardie, the mail censor.

This chapter is divided into three sections. The first deals with the three divisions in general terms and examines how they fit within the broader model for the British Army, discussed earlier. In the second section a detailed analysis is made of each division on the Western Front. Finally, the experiences of the Italian front are considered in detail with particular reference to Captain Hardie's reports on morale and the impact of the influenza epidemic in the winter of 1917–18. It is also possible – because of the lower numbers involved – to consider convictions for other, non-capital, offences on the Italian Front.

7th, 23rd and 48th Divisions in France and Italy: an overview

Despite their differing origins, the three divisions shared similarities in battle experience that went beyond merely forming the backbone of the Italian Expeditionary Force. During their respective times on the Western Front the divisions were deployed in the large offensives of 1916 and 1917, often fighting in the same battles (both the Somme and Third Ypres campaigns can be divided into a series of separate battles). Furthermore, the divisions often shared the same front. Accordingly many place-names crop up in the history of each division: names such as High Wood, Bazentin-le-Petit, Langemarck and Poelcapelle appear frequently. It would be wrong to assert that the divisions had identical experiences of battle. Variations in terrain, the manner of defence and innumerable other factors affected the deployment of these divisions and, equally important, their fortunes. Similarities there were, though, and the comparisons are revealing.

There were 101 death sentences passed in these three divisions on the Western Front. Fifteen condemnations resulted in execution and included the case of Second-Lieutenant Eric Poole, who, as noted earlier, was the first officer to be executed. This rate of 15 per cent of death sentences confirmed does not exactly match the 11 per cent for the British Army as a whole, but is consistent with practice on the Western Front where 307 out of 2247 condemnations resulted in execution, a rate of approximately 14 per cent.

A further ten condemnations can be detected in the divisions in Italy – all but one for the offence of desertion. Although less use was made of the death penalty in the British army as a whole during 1918, this is nevertheless considerably fewer than the number of condemnations experienced by most divisions on the Western Front at this time. No soldiers from the British Isles were executed in Italy which, together with the significant fall in the number of condemnations in each of the divisions following their arrival in Italy, is suggestive of a different approach to the death penalty. This might reflect the differing battle experiences – in particular the changing fortune of the British army in 1918 – but, as we will discuss later, there is evidence that by being posted to Italy the three divisions enjoyed a far more relaxed disciplinary regime.

These divisions are also representative of the British Army for a number of other reasons. In common with the rest of the army, desertion was the most prevalent capital conviction: there were 86 death sentences for desertion, nine for cowardice, seven for sleeping on post and four for quitting post. Although one might expect the number of condemnations for sleeping on post to be higher if this was a true reflection of the rest of the army, the essential features are nevertheless in place.[3] Desertion and cowardice were the most important military offences and in spite of the huge number of condemnations for sleeping on post it was not an offence that the army took particularly seriously.[4] Of course, the army could not afford to recognise this and was often at pains to give the opposite impression with severe warnings about the consequences of sleeping on post posted in Routine Orders.[5] Fourteen executions in the three divisions were carried out for desertion, the other for cowardice. Again, this is an accurate reflection of the general trend in the army as a whole. In short, for our purposes this small selection from just three divisions, when considered together, represents a reasonably precise microcosm of condemnations in the British army.[6] Each type of unit is represented; there is a typical spread of death sentences; a confirmation rate consistent with the rest of the BEF; and the execution of one single officer and fourteen other ranks.

Broadly speaking, there is much here to support the view that the approach to capital punishment conformed to more general disciplinary trends identified in Sheffield's thesis.[7] It appears that a harsher form of discipline – characterised by more frequent use of the death penalty – was practised in the Regular 7th Division than in 48th (Territorial Force) Division. Furthermore, the different approaches to discipline proved to be remarkably resilient, suggesting that the character of the officer–men relationship and the nature of discipline outlasted the original members of the unit. In terms of discipline, subsequent drafts appear to have experienced something akin to those whom they replaced. 23rd Division, in common with most other service units, fitted somewhere between the two, being heavily influenced by practices in the Territorial Force, but with Regular style discipline increasingly creeping in.

The 7th Division was formed from four Regular battalions in Britain and eight from overseas in September 1914 and transferred to the Western Front soon afterwards. During the period spent in France there were a total of 57 death sentences passed on men in the division, eight of which were carried out. 48th Division, a South Midland Territorial Division which existed at the outbreak of war, was transferred to the Western Front some months later, landing at Le Havre on 13 May 1915. In stark contrast to 7th Division only 12 men serving with 48th in France were sentenced to death, with three executions being carried out. Even allowing for the different amount of time spent in the war zone (which was, in any case, negligible given the duration of the war) the variation is quite staggering.

On the face of it, then, the numbers of death sentences appear to reflect the differing attitudes to discipline adopted in the Regular and Territorial divisions. There is further evidence to support Sheffield's argument if we examine the death sentences passed in 23rd (Service) Division, a New Army formation created during the rush to the colours in August 1914, which landed at Le Havre in August 1915. Thirty-two death sentences were passed on men in 23rd Division with six executions being carried out. On the basis of death sentences, then, this particular service division does indeed fit somewhere between the Regular 7th Division and the Territorial 48th Division.

In general terms, therefore, it can be stated with confidence that our three divisions outwardly displayed the sort of approach to discipline one might expect given the type of divisions concerned. If discipline was applied on an ascending scale of severity in 'Territorial', 'Service' and 'Regular' divisions it is likely that this would be reflected in the approach taken towards capital punishment, with less tolerance to crime exhibited in the Regular formations. This, however, presupposes that each division had a comparable experience of the battlefield. If, for example, 7th Division saw more action, suffered greater casualties and, therefore, experienced a greater turnover of personnel than the other two divisions then it might raise questions about its *esprit de corps* and morale. Furthermore, to be consistent with Sheffield's thesis, the vital officer–men relationship might have been adversely affected if there was a high wastage among officers of the division. We must, therefore, examine in some detail the war experience of each division and, at the same time, contextualize each condemnation.

The Divisions

7th Division

In common with most Regular formations, 7th Division was thrown into the action shortly after its arrival on the Western Front. Its first engagement came at Antwerp on 9–10 October 1914, only three days after landing at Zeebrugge. This was followed by the First Battle of Ypres between 19 October and 5 November 1914, where the division experienced heavy fighting during the battles of Langemarck (21–24 October) and Gheluvelt (29–31

October). Some units in the division appear to have suffered heavily in these early exchanges: the war diary for 2nd Royal Warwickshire Regiment records heavy casualties suffered during the battalion's first experience of heavy artillery fire from the Germans on 24 October, many officers being among the dead. By the end of the month things were desperate in the division and cooks and officers' servants were put into the firing line. A large contingent of 2nd Royal Warwickshires were cut off by the enemy on 31 October resulting in the effective strength of the battalion being temporarily reduced to little more than 100 all ranks.[8]

The first death sentences passed in the division, not surprisingly, occurred in 2nd Royal Warwickshires. On 8 December 1914 the battalion was moved back into the front line in readiness for an attack on the enemy lines near Bas Maisnil. On 14 December three men from 2nd Royal Warwickshires were tried for desertion and sentenced by the court to be executed. The sentences were commuted to two years' hard labour. The following day two men of the Bedfordshire Regiment, also in 7th Division, were condemned for quitting their posts. They too had their sentences reduced to two years' hard labour.[9] The subsequent attack on 18 December was a disaster, with 363 casualties in the ranks of 2nd Royal Warwickshires and several officers, including the battalion commander, Lieutenant-Colonel Brewis, among the dead.[10] The 2nd Bedfordshires, being in a different brigade, were spared the experience.

The most likely explanation behind these condemnations is that the commander of the division was eager to firm-up discipline in the formation following its uncomfortable early experiences on the Western Front. The divisional commander, Major-General T. Capper, had also toured his units in an attempt to improve morale. On 4 December he had inspected 2nd Bedfordshires, telling them that they had endured a 'severe test' in the opening months of the war.[11] In this their experience was similar to the other divisions of the BEF in 1914.

The first execution in 7th Division came in February 1915. Private A. Pitts, 2nd Royal Warwickshire Regiment, had been found guilty of desertion and sentenced to death by a court martial on 30 January 1915. Pitts had actually absconded on 24 October 1914 during the fighting around Ypres – the day the battalion suffered heavy casualties from artillery fire. The unit had also made an attack to recapture lost trenches near Zonnebeke that day. Pitts had successfully negotiated his way to the coast and was captured by the military police at Boulogne on 12 January whereupon he had compounded his crime by giving false particulars.[12] Given the circumstances it is hardly surprising that Pitts was shown little mercy by the court or by the commander-in-chief.

Interestingly, Pitts' was the twentieth death sentence to be passed in the division and the twelfth in 2nd Royal Warwickshires. It was likely, therefore, that it would have been carried out regardless of the extreme nature of the case, which probably only made the court's task far simpler. There was clearly a perceived discipline problem in this unit during the end of 1914, which continued into early 1915 – another four men of 2nd Royal Warwickshires were condemned in February[13] – and if its commanders desired to rectify it by setting an example, Pitts was an obvious choice. However, it seems likely that the battalion did not recover from the high number of casualties suffered in the early engagements with the enemy and in particular the loss of its commanding officer.

The second execution followed approximately a month later. The case contains evidence that makes explicit the true purpose of the imposition of the death penalty. Private James Briggs of 2nd Battalion Border Regiment had also managed to escape from the battle zone – this time whilst his unit was resting on 20 January 1915. He too had made it as far as the coast and was actually stowed away aboard an England-bound ship at Le Havre when he was apprehended.[14] Briggs was only the second man from his battalion to be condemned by court martial, but owing to the circumstances of his offence he was an ideal candidate *pour encourager les autres* and many of his comrades were forced to witness his execution on 6 March 1915. A graphic account of the execution can be found in the diary of an unknown British soldier.[15]

2nd Border Regiment had also endured a torrid time during the early exchanges and had fought with conspicuous bravery during November 1914 when it had been surrounded by the enemy at Veldhoek but, despite heavy losses, had held its line. This action had brought commendation from Major-General Capper, the divisional commander, who informed Corps headquarters:

The devoted and firm conduct of this Battalion repeatedly called forth the admiration of the Brigadier and of other officers in other battalions in the same brigade; and I, myself, can testify to its fortitude and determination to maintain its position at all costs; a spirit which saved a difficult and critical situation. It is impossible to praise this Battalion too highly for its firmness and battle discipline.[16]

By the middle of November 1914 2nd Battalion Border Regiment had suffered enormous casualties: nine officers and 79 other ranks killed; 6 officers and 259 other ranks wounded, and five officers and 253 other ranks missing.[17] The battalion, however, remained an effective fighting unit and was again involved in fierce fighting, this time at Rouge Bancs during December 1914 where two of the battalion's other ranks won Victoria Crosses.[18]

It is unclear whether it was 2nd Battalion Border Regiment that was forced to witness the execution of Briggs, but it seems likely; the battalion was in the area where the execution took place and the firing squad was obviously made up from his unit. In the light of the commendation of the commander of the division and the decorations won by this battalion there cannot possibly have been a question mark over the discipline and fighting abilities of the battalion. Yet it appears that it was still felt necessary to parade the entire unit in the early hours to witness Briggs's execution. It is highly improbable that unit discipline could have deteriorated in the two months intervening. This graphically demonstrates the army's unquestioning commitment to the principle of deterrence.

Four days after Briggs's execution the division was deployed at the battle of Neuve Chapelle, but the deterrent value of the public execution remains suspect. Private Isaac Reid of 2nd Scots Guards, a unit attached to the same brigade (20th) as Briggs's battalion, deserted during an attack on 11 March 1915. Reid was later tried, and executed on 9 April 1915.[19] There is nothing to suggest why two executions were deemed necessary in such a short space of time in 20th Brigade, and Reid's crime does not appear to have been particularly unusual: there were literally thousands of similar desertions during battle. Morale in the formation appeared to be good even though the brigade had undergone a number of changes in leadership. The original commander, Brigadier General Ruggles-Brise, had been wounded in the particularly fierce fighting during the previous November. He was temporarily replaced by Major Cator who himself was replaced by Brigadier General F. J. Heyworth on 14 November 1914.[20] Reid's commanding officer and his brigade commander both recommended commutation of the sentence. Reid's character was regarded as 'very good' and it was generally acknowledged that 'The battalion is in an excellent state of discipline'. The divisional commander, Major-General Capper, agreed but indicated that he was not prepared to tolerate desertion from the battlefield itself and recommended the death sentence be carried out.[21] It seems likely that Capper regarded this case as an opportunity to demonstrate that the high standards of discipline already achieved would be maintained, by extreme measures if necessary.

Major-General Capper was himself wounded on 1 April 1915 and Brigadier General Lawford, previously commander of 22nd Brigade, assumed command of the division. One day after the start of Lawford's command two men of 1st Battalion Royal Welsh Fusiliers were condemned by court martial for desertion. Both men had been absent from their unit for some months and it was generally accepted to be a serious case. Given the standards already set in the division, it seems likely that the sentences would have been carried out in any case. However, both men had originally been serving with Lawford's brigade and he was familiar with the state of discipline in the formation. Lawford recommended that even though it was a serious case the sentences should be commuted because 'there has already been one example in the brigade since which there has been no case of desertion'. Both the corps commander, Lieutenant-General Rawlinson, and the army commander, General Haig, disagreed and Privates Penn and Troughton were executed on 22 April 1915.[22]

The original divisional commander, Capper, returned to his command on 19 July 1915, but was mortally wounded little more than two months later whereupon the commander of 21st Brigade, Brigadier General H. E. Watts, was promoted and assumed command. It is unclear whether Lawford's recommendations to mercy in the case of the two Welsh Fusiliers had been a factor in his being overlooked for the command vacated by the death of Capper. In September 1915 Lawford took command of 41st Division. The figure of 22 condemnations in 41st Division is relatively low for a New Army formation, but the four executions carried out – all for desertion – is higher than most. The divisional commander could exercise considerable control over condemnations, but could only hope to influence the final decision.

The new commander of 7th Division – Watts was promoted to Major-General on 27 September 1915 – appears to have adopted a relatively lenient line with the division during the entire period of his command, which lasted until January 1917. The division consistently saw action in all the major battles over this period yet few condemnations occurred and no executions were carried out.[23] The division was deployed at the battle of Loos in the autumn of 1915 but it is the battle of the Somme, where the division was involved in some of the most intense fighting, that is of particular interest.

The 7th Division's experience in the battle of the Somme was a mixture of successes and failures. Overall, the division appears to have demonstrated a level of efficiency akin to that shown during 1914. On 1 July 22nd Brigade had been involved in the attack on Fricourt under heavy machine-gun fire. They were able to hold on to their gains and consolidate them during the night. Four days later the same brigade mounted further attacks in the Mametz Wood area, but they were driven back by German counter-attacks. The brigade obviously maintained its fighting spirit because it was able to mount two more attempts to regain the lost ground before being forced to abandon the attack, again due to heavy machine-gun fire. The only death sentence to originate from this period was passed on a man serving with a brigade not directly involved in the attack. Private Albert Holloway of 2nd Battalion Royal West Surrey Regiment (91st Brigade) was charged with cowardice in the face of the enemy, indicating that his offence had been committed on the field of battle.[24] His sentence was not confirmed, which means that it is unfortunately not possible to obtain further details of the case.

The whole division was involved in the highly successful night-time attack of 14 July 1916. The German first and second lines were captured with comparative ease and the division pushed on to Bazentin-le-Petit, which it captured and then held against persistent counter-attacks by the enemy. Attempts to capture High Wood the following day met with less success and after sustaining heavy casualties from enemy machine-gun fire the attack was called off. A German counter-attack forced a retirement, but again the division's discipline remained good and the lost ground was recaptured. Douglas Haig recognised the ferocity of the fighting in his despatch: '[the 7th Division] entered High Wood at about 8.0 p.m., and, after some hand-to-hand fighting, cleared the whole of the wood with the exception of the northern apex.'[25] Further attempts by the division to capture High Wood – presumably the northern apex – were repulsed by the Germans on 20 July. Private William Carden's unit, 22nd Battalion Manchester Regiment (91st Brigade), had been involved in this phase of the fighting and had sustained heavy casualties, especially in the attempts to clear High Wood. Carden was convicted of desertion and sentenced to death on 3 August. His sentence was commuted to three years' penal servitude.[26] Again, there are no other details available, but the timing of the trial suggests that Carden had deserted during the fighting at High Wood; the new divisional commander appears to have been more tolerant of such an offence than his predecessor.

The division saw less action during August, but was deployed once more on 1 September when its attack on Delville Wood was repulsed, again by machine-gun fire. The attack was renewed some four days later. Again it was unsuccessful, but a further attack on 5 September resulted in some limited gains. Attempts to improve on those gains during the following afternoon failed. The division remained in the Somme area for some months, but saw relatively little action. It was during this period of comparative inactivity that two more death sentences were passed on men in the division, one for desertion the other for sleeping on post[27] – perhaps a symptom of the tedium of the less active phases of trench warfare.

The 7th Division, then, had been involved in some of the best-known battles of the Somme offensive, yet, unlike most other divisions, it had not seen any executions and little in the way of the threat of the firing-squad. The division had maintained an aggressive role during the offensive despite heavy casualties. It seems that its morale remained high and the division's proven military efficiency rendered the threat of the death penalty unnecessary. It also appears that Major-General Watts relied less on the death penalty to maintain discipline than had Capper before him – and less so than most other British commanders for that matter.

Watts was replaced as commander of the division by Major-General G. de S. Barrow on 7 January 1917.[28] This was followed by an increase in the number of condemnations: four in March alone, when the division was deployed in operations in the Ancre area. There were, however, no executions during this period. Barrow was replaced by Major-General Shoubridge on 1 April 1917, who remained in command of the division until the end of the war except for a brief period in February 1918 when he was sick.[29] This final command was punctuated by a number of executions.

The first execution involved a soldier who had first arrived in France with the division in 1914. Private Samuel Cunnington was a member of 2nd Royal Warwickshires, the unit that had endured a spate of condemnations in 1914. Cunnington had deserted during the fighting on the Somme the previous year and had remained free, largely because of assistance from a French couple, until his capture in December 1916. To compound matters Cunnington also had previous convictions for desertion.[30] Given the circumstances, his execution, in May 1917, was hardly unusual, but the timing is interesting coming as it did the day after the division was relieved in the battle of Bullecourt. It seems likely that the command used this relatively serious case to reinforce discipline in the division.

Operations early in 1917 had won the praise of the commander-in-chief and the division was mentioned in his despatches for its action during the German retreat to the Hindenburg Line on 2 April and again during the battle of Arras on 7 May 1917.[31] But while the Battle of the Somme had been a relatively successful campaign for the division, the Third Battle of Ypres was not. The 7th Division was deployed in Flanders throughout most of October 1917 and after some involvement in the battle for Polygon Wood the division moved on to Broodseinde where, on 4 October, all three brigades were involved in a successful attack. Objectives were swiftly taken and casualties were light. On 9 October the 22nd Brigade attacked again as part of the offensive on the village of Poelcapelle. After some preliminary difficulties the brigade was able to take and consolidate its objective – to 'straighten' the British line in the area known as Judge Copse. Not all had gone according to plan though, and a few days later three men were condemned by courts martial for deserting the battle. Two of the men came from 2nd Battalion Royal Warwickshire Regiment – the unit which had experienced most difficulties during the attack. The other came from 21st Battalion Manchester Regiment. All three sentences were commuted to ten years' penal servitude.[32]

The division was relieved on 21 October, but five days later went into action once again, this time in the battle for Passchendaele. Units from all three brigades took part in some of the fiercest fighting of the offensive. Some objectives were taken, but most were lost to German counter-attacks. The 2nd Battalion Queen's (Royal West Surrey) Regiment and 21st Battalion Manchester Regiment (both 91st Brigade) were pinned down by machine-gun fire and were unable to make any headway. The 2nd Battalion Border Regiment (20th Brigade) saw some initial success but became literally bogged down in marshes around Krommebeck where most became casualties to sweeping machine-gun fire. The survivors unsuccessfully attacked the pill-boxes around Gheluvelt. The attack was continued by 8th and 9th Battalions Devonshire Regiment which seized a defensive position in a railway-cutting north of the village, but they were driven back by German counter-attacks. By midday 7th Division had been convincingly repulsed, losing all the ground it had taken during the morning.

Two men who deserted the fighting were tried in the days following the battle. Significantly, both came from units that had suffered badly in the attack at Gheluvelt. A man from 9th Battalion Devonshire Regiment was condemned for desertion, but had his sentence commuted to five years' penal servitude[33] – a remarkably light sentence by the standards applied by the commander-in-chief during the battle for Passchendaele. The other, a private from 2nd Battalion Queen's Regiment, was executed for his offence.[34] It is unclear why these two cases received such radically different treatment from the High Command. Putkowski and Sykes suggest that Private Thomas Hawkins – who was executed – was a persistent offender with an earlier suspended death sentence to his name.[35] A search of the courts-martial register reveals that a Private T. Hawkins of 7th Battalion Queen's Regiment had been sentenced to death by courts martial on no fewer than two previous occasions – on 3 January 1917 and 12 June 1917 – but had escaped with 10 years' penal servitude (suspended) each time.[36] Although not an uncommon name it seems likely that this was the same person – transfers to other battalions were not unusual – which explains the final decision to carry out the sentence. The only execution in the division to be carried out during the Flanders offensive, therefore, was not a reflection of the division's performance in battle and had more to do with the soldier's own disciplinary record.

Two other men who deserted during the disastrous attack at Gheluvelt were able to escape the military authorities for some months. In fact the division had been posted to Italy (from 17 November 1917) by the time Privates Johnson and McClair, both of 2nd Battalion Border Regiment, were tried. On 8 July 1918 a court martial convened on the Western Front sentenced the two soldiers to death for desertion. The decision to execute them was based on the seriousness of their crime rather than any disciplinary shortcomings in their unit.[37] Men who had been absent for eight months were unlikely to receive mercy regardless of the type of unit they belonged to or how it had performed in battle.

The relationship between battle experience and the death penalty in a division such as 7th is a tenuous one and not at all obvious. In fact 7th Division experienced fewer death sentences in its ranks during the third battle of Ypres than it had during the Somme offensive. This was despite there being more condemnations in the British army as a whole during the Flanders campaign than at any other point in the war. The acts of desertion that resulted in death sentences during these large battles had their origins in the experience of battle, occurring most often in the units worst affected by the fighting. Yet the decision to carry out an execution was invariably based on the seriousness of the individual crimes, long periods of absence being the most normal reason given.

Was this also the experience of the Territorial Force?

48th (South Midland Territorial Force) Division

The 48th (South Midland) Division was a pre-war Territorial Force formation. A change in commander in late July 1914 was swiftly followed by another the day after war was declared. The original composition of the infantry remained unchanged for the duration of the war, but in common with other divisions of all types, trench mortar batteries were added and modest alterations were made to the artillery. The original three infantry brigades, the Warwickshire, the Gloucester and Worcester, and the South Midland brigades, eventually became known as 143rd, 144th and 145th brigades respectively. The division arrived on the Western Front on 1 April 1915 where it remained until moving to the Italian front in November 1917. The commander, Major-General Heath, retired sick little more than a month after its arrival in France. A temporary commander was immediately installed, but was soon succeeded by Major-General R. Fanshawe who took command of the division on 31 May 1915 and remained in charge until the middle of 1918.[38] Despite the rapid turnover in command at the beginning of its war the division enjoyed continuity of command at the times when it mattered most. This might explain why the approach to the death penalty in the division throughout its time on the Western Front is characterised by consistency.

In keeping with its Territorial Force traditions few men serving with 48th Division were condemned by courts martial. However, a high proportion of those who were condemned had their sentences carried out: three executions were carried out from a total of just nine condemnations. This is consistent with trends already identified in the Territorial Force and discussed in the previous chapter. Although there were condemnations in all three brigades, the distribution was not even: there were four condemnations and two executions in 143rd (Warwickshire) Brigade; three condemnations and one execution in 145th (South Midland) Brigade; and two condemnations with no executions in 144th (Gloucester and Worcester) Brigade. This might suggest that discipline was more problematic in 143rd Brigade than in 145th and more so still than in 144th.

Concerns about the physique of troops in the division had been raised as early as December 1915. The Director General Medical Services (DGMS) for Third Army noted that a sanitary report had singled out 48th Division, which was said to be in poor physique with 'signs of overstrain among the older and younger men'. The DGMS recommended maximum rest and observed that one possible cause was overcrowding of the billets. 48th Division was compared unfavourably with all other divisions, especially 18th (commanded by Maxse).[39] Despite this the commander did not seek to bolster discipline through liberal use of the death penalty, although this appraisal of the division might cast some light on the high ratio of condemnations confirmed by the commander-in-chief.

The division's first experience of battle came during the Somme offensive in 1916. Initial experiences of the battle were confined to acting as comparatively small units in support of other divisions. One battalion, 1/6 Royal Warwickshires, was deployed on 1 July in the fighting around the village of

Serre, sustaining casualties from machine-gun fire and enemy bombing attacks. On 14 July another unit, 1/7 Royal Warwickshires, took part in the daytime attack on the Bazentin Ridge with little success. The involvement of larger forces from 48th Division began on 16 July with a successful attack on Ovillers village by 144th Brigade with one battalion from 143rd Brigade and, a little later that day, the rest of the division. This action attracted the attention of the commander-in-chief who wrote of the division in his despatches:

> On the 16th July a large body of the garrison of Ovillers surrendered, and that night and during the following day, by a direct advance from the west across No Man's Land, our troops (48th Division, Major-General R, Fanshawe) carried the remainder of the village and pushed out along the spur to the north and eastwards towards Pozières.[40]

The first execution in the division was a result of this opening phase of the Somme offensive. Private A. Earp, 1/5 Royal Warwickshire Regiment, actually committed his offence prior to the start of the battle. His unit was holding the line near Hébuterne during the preliminary bombardment, but had been unnerved by the enemy's counter-barrage. He was found guilty of desertion by a court martial convened on 10 July and sentenced to death. The court recommended mercy and Earp's commanders agreed that the sentence should be commuted.[41] This suggests that the divisional commander believed that the mere knowledge among the men in the division of a death sentence on one of their own was a sufficient deterrent to maintain discipline. However, General Hubert Gough, the army commander, viewed matters in broader terms and recommended confirmation of the sentence. Douglas Haig concurred and Earp was executed on 22 July 1916.

The timing of this execution is crucial to understanding its true purpose. It came immediately after the division's first experience of battle. Although there was no suggestion of poor discipline or morale in the division, the execution was no doubt designed to reinforce the army's determination to impose its authority. Furthermore, the execution was carried out on the eve of the division's next deployment – the battle of Pozières.

The battle of Pozières can be divided into two phases. The 48th Division was deployed in both. The first phase started with an unsuccessful attack on 23 July. Another attack in the Mash Valley area resulted in sections of enemy trenches being captured and a counter-attack beaten off, but some units, particularly 1/6th Glosters (144th Brigade) suffered severe casualties. Attempts to advance further the following day were unsuccessful. During the following few days, 143rd Brigade in particular were involved in further attacks in the same area, often in conjunction with Australian units, with some limited successes.

The division returned to the attack on 14 August and continued fighting for the following few days. All three brigades were involved in action around the so-called Leipzig Salient, although fortunes were mixed: 143rd and 144th Brigades suffered heavy casualties during the first day and were forced to give up most of their gains, but four days later the division made good progress despite determined resistance from the enemy. In the following week the division repulsed a number of German counter-attacks. Attempts to make further gains between 23 and 27 August resulted in heavy casualties.

Two capital trials resulted from the battle of Pozières, both held on 2 September when the division was resting. The first, a man serving with 1/1st Oxford and Buckinghamshire Light Infantry, was condemned by court-martial for cowardice. Fortunately for the individual concerned, Private B. Schulman, the sentence was not confirmed.[42] A soldier who deserted on 14 August, the first day of the battle, was less fortunate. On 13 September 1916, Private Charles Depper, 1/4th Royal Berkshire Regiment, was executed for desertion.[43] The battalion war diary recorded that 'the execution was witnessed by 40 men of the battalion under the command of Lieutenant Hampshire'.[44] This was a sufficient number of men to ensure that the deterrent effect was achieved in the unit.

The battle of the Somme had been a hard introduction to the war for 48th Division. They had suffered considerable casualties and two men had paid the capital penalty for moments of temporary indiscipline. A number of other death sentences had not been confirmed but, interestingly, all can be directly attributed to specific incidents in battle.

In 1917 48th Division, in common with other divisions on the Western Front, enjoyed an early advance as the Germans retreated to the Hindenburg Line. On 17 March the division occupied Pérrone and then took up positions at Mont St Quentin.[45] The next major deployment for the division was during the Flanders offensive in the following Autumn, and in particular the battle of Langemarck from 16 to 18 August 1917.

The fighting during this part of the offensive was particularly difficult for the advancing British divisions as they confronted a chain of concrete bunkers and pill-boxes. According to Haig's despatches:

These field forts, distributed in depth all along the front of our advance, offered a serious obstacle to progress. They were heavily armed with machine guns and manned by men determined to hold on at all costs. Many were reduced as our troops advanced, but others held out throughout the day, and delayed the arrival of our supports. In addition, weather conditions made aeroplane observation practically impossible, with the result that no warning was received of the enemy's counter-attacks and our infantry obtained little artillery help against them. When, therefore, later in the morning [of 16 August] a heavy counter-attack developed in the neighbourhood of the Wieltje–Passchendaele Road, our troops, who had reached their final objectives at many points in this area also, were gradually compelled to fall back.[46]

Elements of 48th Division had reached its objective on 16 August, but had not been able to hold onto it. The attack had started at 4.45 am, spearheaded by 145th Brigade (1/5th Glosters, 1/1st and 1/4th Oxford and Bucks Light Infantry, with 1/4th Royal Berkshire in reserve) which captured the village of St Julien. The attack then pressed on towards the objective, Springfield Farm, which men from the Oxford and Bucks Light Infantry were seen to reach. The rest of the brigade were unable to join them and the objective was lost, together with the men who had made it thus far. By mid-morning a new line was established approximately halfway between the starting point and the objective, and in the evening a number of determined German counter-attacks were repulsed. The importance of holding this line was recognised by Haig who commented: '[48th Division] established themselves on a line running north from St Julien to the old German third line due east of Langemarck. This line they maintained against the enemy's attacks, and thereby secured the flank of our gains further north.'[47] Losses, however, had been substantial and a further attempt to advance the following day failed.

Greater success followed for the division on 19 August when, supported by a number of tanks, the line was advanced closer still to the original objective, the divisional diarist recording a number of strong points overrun and many enemy defenders killed.[48] The division extended its gains on 22 August with 1/5th Royal Warwickshire Regiment capturing strong points along the line of the original objective. The gains were lost to a German counter-attack, but recaptured later. Other units of the Gloucestershire Regiment encountered a similar ferocious defence, gaining, and then losing to enemy counter-attacks, a number of pill-boxes. Further gains were made on 25 August, but the division still had not reached its original objective for the opening day of the offensive, such was the ferocity of the fighting around Langemarck.

Following this intense fighting, the division was able to pause for a while and a number of capital trials were convened. On 31 August Private Charles Britton, 1/5th Royal Warwickshire Regiment, was found guilty of desertion and sentenced to death. He had absented himself from the original attack on 16 August. His offence was not especially unusual or serious, but Britton was executed on 12 September 1917.[49] There can be little doubt that the execution was designed to bolster discipline for the remainder of the offensive: General Hubert Gough, the Army commander, ordered that details should be read out on parade immediately after the execution.[50]

As usual timing was the crucial factor. Britton's was the first condemnation in the division during the Flanders campaign, therefore giving the commanders an early opportunity to demonstrate their resolve. Subsequent condemnations were treated less harshly. On 3 September Private Bullas, 1/7th Worcestershire Regiment, was convicted of cowardice – arguably a more serious offence than desertion – and Private Collins, 1/4th Gloucestershire Regiment, of desertion. Neither sentence was carried out.[51] Both offences probably originated from the attack on 22 August when the men's respective units were most heavily affected by the action.

There were no further capital trials in 48th Division during the remainder of its time on the Western Front. The division continued to be involved in the Flanders campaign, taking part in the battles of Polygon Wood, Broodseinde and Poelcapelle between 28 September and 9 October 1917. It even suffered the potentially morale-sapping experience of being shelled by British guns during an attack at Poelcapelle on 9 October, which was otherwise marked by some success. Unit discipline had never been called into question, with the commander-in-chief commenting favourably about the division in his despatches. Casualties, like those of other British divisions at Third Ypres, were heavy, but the division had maintained its offensive spirit, displaying the tenacity that characterised the British offensive during the autumn of 1917. The division left for Italy on 21 November.[52]

Condemnations in the 48th Division during its time on the Western Front, although few in number, can be directly attributed to specific battles. Executions were often the outcome of disciplinary considerations, although not necessarily because of a lack of fighting spirit or unit discipline. Moreover, executions were seen as a method of reminding the men that indiscipline would not be tolerated. In this, timing was often the most important factor, with men being executed at moments when commanders deemed it appropriate rather than on the basis of the gravity of their crimes. This trend was a consistent feature of discipline in 48th Division and can be detected during the formation's involvement in both the Somme and Flanders offensives.

23rd (New Army) Division

Unusually, 23rd Division enjoyed continuity of command for almost the entire war. Major-General J. M. Babington commanded the division from the date of its formation on 18 September 1914 until 15 October 1918 – less than one month from the end of the war. That aside, there was little else to distinguish the division from others of the New Army. The usual problems of New Army divisions – lack of officers, uniforms and equipment – were eventually overcome, and the formation arrived on the Western Front on 29 August 1915 where it remained until its transfer to the Italian Front in November 1917.[53]

The death penalty was relatively common in this division. A total of 40 death sentences were passed by courts martial while the division was on the Western Front. Six executions were carried out in this period – a high proportion. Among those executed was Second-Lieutenant Eric Skeffington Poole. In terms of the death sentence, therefore, 23rd Division could be considered atypical. The formation appears to have maintained a good fighting spirit in both the battles of the Somme and Third Ypres, but the death penalty was frequently applied. This might suggest that the commander adopted a style of discipline that resembled a Regular formation rather than a Territorial one. Indeed, little more than a month after arriving on the Western Front, two men of the division were condemned by court martial for sleeping at their posts.[54] Although neither sentence was carried out it was nevertheless an indication of the nature of discipline to come.

23rd Division was heavily involved in the battle of the Somme, its first deployment in action. Initially, the division was used to support attacks by other formations, but major deployments soon followed. On 5 July 1916 the division made an attack on German strongholds just south-east of La Boiselle. Early gains were gradually lost to enemy counter-attacks, which continued most of the day, before the division rallied, made further gains and consolidated its position in the region of Contalmaison – an action that earned the division and its commander, Major-General Babington, a mention in despatches.[55] The division attacked enemy positions in the village of Contalmaison three days later, but was beaten off by intense machine-gun fire, although some ground was taken unopposed the following day. Among the many casualties from the early encounters was Second-Lieutenant Eric Skeffington Poole, serving with 11th Battalion West Yorkshire Regiment. Knocked out by a shell explosion and evacuated to hospital via a Field Ambulance on 7 July suffering from shell-shock, Poole was prematurely returned to his unit only to desert at a later date. This act of desertion was the incident which resulted in his execution.[56]

Meanwhile, the division spent the next few days trying to improve the newly gained position by mounting bombing raids and generally harassing the Germans opposite them. Unfortunately, one such raiding party was shelled by British artillery on 9 July forcing the party to abandon its position, in the so-called Bailiff Wood (south of Contalmaison), which the division recaptured later that day. The new position in Bailiff Wood provided the platform for a highly successful, if costly, attack on 10 July. A frontal attack by 69th Brigade resulted in the capture of Contalmaison and retreating enemy troops were cut off by units attacking their flank from Bailiff Wood. Determined enemy counter-attacks were beaten off in the evening. However, casualties were extremely high and the battalion war diary records that the strength of 8th Battalion Yorkshire Regiment (69th Brigade) was reduced to five officers and 150 men by the end of the fighting.[57]

On 17 July the division went into action once again. This time 68th Brigade spearheaded an attack near Pozières, which was stopped by German machine-gunners. The division then spent a period of relative inactivity during which time the first capital trial occurred. Private

Robinson, 12th Battalion Durham Light Infantry, was found guilty of desertion by court martial on 24 July 1916 and sentenced to death.[58] Robinson's unit was one of those involved in the attack of 17 July and it seems likely that his offence was committed that day. Fortunately for him the sentence was not carried out. Once again, however, the timing was significant and 23rd Division went back into action just two days later – long enough for word of the condemnation to have circulated. The attack by the division, on 26 July, was again spearheaded by 68th Brigade (including 12th Durhams), but failed.

There then followed a period of consolidation. Again bombing parties raided the German trenches, but the division did not undertake any major frontal assault for a number of weeks. Relatively small sections of trench were captured from the enemy by these operations, often at night. On 28 August a court martial passed another capital sentence for desertion. The sentence on Private Clee, a soldier serving with the Pioneer Battalion, was commuted to ten years' penal servitude and suspended.[59] Around the same time (16 August) Private James Grampton, 9th Battalion York and Lancaster Regiment, had been detailed to carry out pioneer work, this time assisting the Royal Engineers. Grampton deserted and managed to stay free until long after the battle of the Somme was over. He was tried in January 1917 and shot on 4 February – the length of his absence sufficient justification for his commanding officers.[60] These two cases highlight the nature of the work being undertaken by the Pioneers, which became increasingly hazardous during this period of consolidation – digging trenches and carrying out repairs, often under enemy fire.

The division was again deployed as the battle entered another phase in mid-September. On 15 September units of 70th Brigade acted in support of 15th Division in the attack on the village of Martinpuich near Thiepval, but by the evening the Brigade held the forwardmost position, just west of the village. A few days later the whole division was deployed on newly captured ground to the north and east of the village, which had fallen to the British advance. The division gradually extended the line during the following days. An attack by 70th Brigade on the morning of 29 September succeeded in seizing German strong-points at Destremont Farm and further gains were made by the Brigade in the region of Le Sars during the following days. A more ambitious attack by the whole division on 1 October was unsuccessful. Curiously, a court martial was convened that same day. On trial was another Pioneer – Private Botfield. The case originated from an incident during the night of 21 September when Botfield, with others from the Pioneer Battalion, was sent out to dig new trenches in open ground. The working party had come under enemy fire and Botfield had fled when a German shell exploded nearby. Botfield was condemned for cowardice and shot a little more than two weeks later.[61] Again the timing of the trial was important, coming on the day of a failed attack by the division and just before another attack was to go ahead. The village of Le Sars eventually fell to the division after a determined and steady attack on 7 October. The position was improved further by another attack the next day.

The last major operation by 23rd Division in the battle of the Somme was highly successful. However, away from the battlefield the division's reputation was under threat. Ironically, Second-Lieutenant Poole, who had deserted the fighting two days earlier, was arrested on the day of the division's most significant achievement. After his initial treatment for shell-shock arising from the fighting around Contalmaison in early July, Poole was taken to a convalescent home where he was examined by Lieutenant-Colonel Foster, of the Royal Army Medical Corps. Foster recorded:

> [Poole's] Condition improved in C. C. Home but [he] did not look well and some objective nervous symptoms [were] complained of. I brought him up to Sir James Fowler (Medical Consultant) on 19/8/16 who found some degree of irregular action of heart and tachycardia, but no signs of any lesion either cardiac or nervous. He [Fowler] agreed with me he [Poole] was at present still unfit for duty at the front and considered he should be sent to Temporary Base Duty for a time. [Poole was] Discharged [from the convalescent home] on 22.8.16.[62]

Poole was indeed sent to an Infantry Base Depot on 23 August 1916. A few days later he was again examined, this time at Etaples where Lieutenant-Colonel Martin (RAMC), certified that Poole was classified as 'A', or 'fit for duty'.[63] Poole was returned to his unit just as it was going back into action.

The division was positioned in the front-line trenches on 5 October in readiness for its attack on Le Sars. The company commander, Captain Armstrong, inspected the troops at midnight on 5 October and discovered that Poole had absconded from the trenches leaving behind the troops in his charge. Poole managed to avoid capture until after the attack, whereupon he was charged with desertion. His claim that he had left to seek treatment for rheumatism was rejected by the court, which sat on 24 November 1916. Poole, who was described by his battalion commander, Lieutenant-Colonel Barker, as 'rather stupid' – a view supported by other witnesses, including those for the defence – was executed on 10 December 1916.[64]

There was a steady flow of condemnations in the spring and summer of 1917, a total of 13 between February and July, involving men from each brigade, but none was carried out. Most had probably resulted from the division's deployment in the Battle of Messines in mid-June; there were five condemnations in June and another four in July. The next execution was carried out on the eve of another attack by the division, once again indicating that the death penalty was often employed as a deliberate means of stiffening unit discipline at specific moments.

Again, the unfortunate man, a private in 8th Battalion, York and Lancaster Regiment (70th Brigade), was an ideal candidate: the commander-in-chief had suspended a previous sentence of death against him. Deployment to the Ypres area and the opening of the offensive at the end of July had proved too much and he had deserted, only to be recaptured and tried on 5 September. This time the sentence of death was confirmed by the commander-in-chief and the execution went ahead on 19 September.[65] The following morning the division went into action in what became known as the Battle of Menin Road Ridge.

The division's attack that morning appears to have been a great success. All the objectives were taken despite stiff resistance from German machine-gunners in concrete bunkers around Veldhoek. These were captured and a number of counter-attacks repulsed in the afternoon. The division was relieved from the frontline on 25 September, but a few days later it was deployed once more. On 30 September a determined attack by Germans armed with flame-throwers was beaten off.[66] Another German attack on the line held by 23rd Division, this time supported by aircraft, resulted in some ground being lost on 1 October. The Division was again relieved on 9 October and a few days later handed over its section of the line in readiness for the transfer to the Italian Front, which began on 31 October.

It appears that the division utilised the time out of the line to resolve any outstanding disciplinary matters and the courts martial were busy during this period of relative peace. A number of condemnations followed and although in the absence of the case papers it cannot be ascertained whether they were connected, five involved men of 70th Brigade, the formation involved in repelling the flame-thrower attack. Another two men in 70th Brigade who had both deserted in separate incidents near the end of August were executed in November. One, Private Charles Nicholson, 8th Battalion, York and Lancaster Regiment, had deserted his unit for the second time. He appeared before a court martial on 8 October and was sentenced to death.[67] Two others who had appeared alongside him had their sentences commuted to periods of penal servitude, but Nicholson's record, which included a conviction for absence, singled him out. The other, Private Davis of 11th Battalion, Sherwood Foresters, again a persistent offender with a previous death sentence to his name, was condemned near the end of October.[68]

Both men had remained behind on the Western Front while the division moved elsewhere. Davis was executed at Wizernes near St Omer on 15 November and Nicholson was shot two days later. The rest of the division had left for Italy on 6 November.[69] It is unlikely that these executions were intended to address any particular disciplinary concerns in the brigade because with the division being absent the specific deterrent effect was minimal. Accordingly, we should view these two executions as the removal of undesirable soldiers rather than as examples to their comrades. As with all capital cases the army ensured wide dissemination of their fate – intended as a more general deterrent.

The Italian Expeditionary Force

Due to the collapse of the Italian army in the face of the Austro-German offensive during October 1917, a joint Franco-British force was hastily dispatched to Italy as reinforcements. The force initially comprised five divisions (23rd, 41st, 7th, 48th and 5th in order of arrival) under the command of General Sir H. C. O. Plumer, except for a brief period shortly after its arrival in Italy when Lieutenant-General the Earl of Cavan was appointed temporary commander. By the time it was involved in action during the following summer the force was reduced to three divisions (23rd, 7th and 48th) and was again under the command of the Earl of Cavan, who was promoted to General in June 1918. This arrangement did not change for the remainder of the war. The command structure of the force was further complicated when it was temporarily placed directly under the Italian commander at the end of 1917. However, the essential features are that by the spring of 1918 the British force in Italy, constituting 23rd, 7th and 48th Divisions under the command of the Earl of Cavan, was deployed in the mountainous Asiago sector of the Piave front. The stark differences between their new surroundings and those they had left behind on the Western Front were obvious. The magazine of 1/5th Glosters (48th Division) featured a cartoon depicting a fully-laden British soldier climbing a sheer rock face in its July 1918 edition.[70] Towards the end of 1918 7th and 23rd Divisions were transferred to another sector, still under the command of Lord Cavan, leaving 48th Division behind under the Italian XII Corps. For the majority of their time in Italy, therefore, the divisions' experiences were broadly similar.

The idea of transferring British troops from the Western Front to Italy was not supported by a High Command that continued to be irritated by the retention of valuable troops in Salonika. The subject had been raised by the French Minister of War, Paul Painlevé, as early as April 1917 – at the time that British troops launched their successful offensive at Arras in support of Nivelle's offensive on the Chemin des Dames. General Sir William Robertson, Chief of the Imperial General Staff, reassured Haig in a message sent on 10 April 1917: 'You may depend on me doing the right thing so far as it is in my power to do it with respect to the despatch of troops to Italy,' adding that 'It would be folly to send them'.[71] To a large extent the Italian force was a political gesture rather than a military necessity aimed at maintaining the alliance. Significantly, the Prime Minister, Lloyd George, appears to have been more enthusiastic for it than his military commanders. Lloyd George's promise of delivering a 'big-blow' in Italy, in July 1917 on the eve of the Passchendaele offensive, was described by Robertson as 'damned madness'.[72] Although, following the Italian collapse in October, even Robertson conceded that 'We must not get rattled over this business [the rout of the Italian army], but of course we must stop the rot if we can'.[73] As described above, the divisions despatched were in no way second-rate: they had all shown good fighting spirit in the recent Flanders operation.

Of the first months in Italy Captain Hardie, the mail censor, reported 'there is widespread indication of good Morale in the Italian Expeditionary Force'.[74] It appears that most troops were glad to get away from the slaughter of the Western Front. According to Hardie, 'most men look on the Italian campaign as a "picnic" compared with that in Belgium and France'.[75] This was despite earlier fears to the contrary: on 27 October 1917 Robertson had remarked, 'it is really very hard on our men after what they have recently gone through [Passchendaele!] to send them to Italy'.[76] The men, it seems, preferred to take their chances in the unknown Italian theatre than to continue the war in Flanders. In short, their morale was influenced as much by notions of safety as by any other factors. Statistics produced by the War Office after the war suggest that the men were right: there were 653 total casualties (from all causes, including sickness) per 1000 troops in Italy compared with 1139 on the Western Front.[77] Furthermore, in Italy the figure for casualties resulting from battle only was far lower still: 64 (2.13 per cent of whom were killed) per 1000 troops as opposed to 493 (6.13 per cent killed) on the Western Front.[78] Italy was a safer posting and the men knew it better than the Chief of the Imperial General Staff did.

The first British court martial in Italy took place before the arrival of the main force. A member of the Royal Engineers – presumably sent ahead to prepare for the arrival of the British force – was convicted on 25 October 1917 (the day after the opening of the main Austro-German offensive) of absence and sentenced to six months' hard labour.[79] In the early days of November, 11 other courts martial heard cases ranging from drunkenness to manslaughter.[80] This was still prior to the arrival of the first infantry division (23rd) which did not reach Italy until 16 November.[81] As the British force steadily grew so too did the number of courts martial. These were mostly for minor offences such as drunkenness, but also included trials for various capital offences: within two weeks of arrival one man had been convicted of desertion, one of sleeping at his post, four of striking a senior officer and several for insubordination and disobedience. The usual sentence for these offences during this early period was between two to three months' field punishment and none was sentenced to death.[82]

The first death sentence was passed by a court martial on 8 December 1917. Private W. Simpson, serving with 9th Battalion, Yorkshire Regiment, escaped execution when the commander-in-chief commuted his sentence for desertion to ten years' penal servitude. This case was swiftly followed by a similar one on 12 December. Private P. Montgomery, 10th Battalion, West Riding Regiment, was also condemned for desertion. His sentence was commuted to fifteen years' penal servitude.[83] There were two factors surrounding both cases that are especially significant. First, these were just the second and third convictions for desertion in Italy. The seemingly harsh response should be viewed as a deliberate demonstration of authority designed to reinforce discipline at an early stage. Second, both men's units were in Babington's 23rd Division where, as we have already discussed, discipline frequently involved the death penalty. Consequently, this case was merely a continuation of a disciplinary practice that had been firmly established on the Western Front.

Other Western Front practices were also retained in Italy. Desertion had been taken particularly seriously by courts martial in France and Flanders and these early cases are suggestive of an identical approach in Italy. The next case to be heard (18 December) involving a charge of desertion (it is not necessary to refer to convictions because acquittals were extremely rare in the ranks) resulted in two years' hard labour for a soldier serving in 22nd Manchesters (7th Division).[84] Then on 20 December another soldier serving with 10th West Riding, again 23rd Division, was sentenced to death for desertion.[85] Although his sentence was commuted to five years' penal servitude it was once more an indication of the seriousness that was attached to desertion at such an early point of the Italian campaign: three out of five convicted deserters had been sentenced to death – all were in 23rd Division. Death sentences in Italy became less frequent after this initial demonstration of authority, but desertion remained the offence most likely to attract the ultimate response from the courts – all but five of the fifteen capital condemnations in Italy were for offences of desertion.

Desertion attracted a relatively consistent response from the courts, which usually passed sentences clearly aimed at deterring potential offenders. During the period November 1917 to March 1918 there were 55 trials involving cases of alleged desertion.[86] This period is particularly important from a comparative point of view because 5th Division left Italy on 1 March 1918 and was followed one month later by 41st Division.[87] It is only during this period that all five British divisions were in Italy and, therefore, can be regarded as distinct from the period following 1 April 1918 when the British contingent was reduced to three divisions – which we will deal with later. There were six death sentences passed on deserters during this initial phase of the Italian campaign – two on men in 7th Division, but all the others on men serving with 23rd Division. Does this suggest that desertion was a greater problem in the latter division, or can this be attributed to differences in the approach adopted by the respective commanders of the five divisions as I have previously argued?

Conditions in Italy were by no means easy for the British troops. Poor communications in the Piave River region – where all the British divisions were initially posted – made transportation and supply difficult. Captain Hardie identified the effect this had on troop morale in his report of February 1918; a 'downturn' in morale was, according to Hardie, the result of food shortages.[88] Equally difficult was the evacuation of the wounded and sick. These problems increased when the British took over the mountainous Asiago region, but this was not until 29 March – the later phase – and we need not be concerned with this at this stage. The British divisions shared the same front and conditions for most of the Italian campaign. There was little serious fighting until June 1918 and the courts martial were concerned with general disciplinary issues during the first winter in Italy.

There appear to have been great variations between discipline in the five divisions. Almost half the trials for alleged desertion involved men serving with 23rd Division. There were 20 such trials in 23rd Division, eight in 41st, seven in 7th and none in either 5th or 48th. Perhaps it is no surprise that there were no trials brought in the Territorial Force formation (48th), but that the two New Army divisions (23rd and 41st) tried so many more than their Regular counterparts (5th and 7th) requires an explanation.

Overall this appears to have been little more than a continuation of practices already established on the Western Front. In the two Regular divisions there were 81 and 60 condemnations respectively with eight and nine executions on the Western Front before their removal to Italy. This compares with 40 condemnations and six executions in 23rd Division and another 14 condemnations with three executions in 41st. At first glance this might appear to suggest a more rigid and harsher discipline in the Regular divisions than in these particular New Army formations. But this is misleading and takes no account of the actual time each division was posted to the front. The Regular divisions had been at the front for over a year by the time 23rd Division arrived in France and it was a further nine months before 41st Division joined them (May 1916). The consequent direct comparison suggests that the death penalty was at least as frequent in 23rd Division in particular. There is also a noticeable trend towards less frequent recourse to the threat of execution in the Regular divisions while in the New Army divisions the reverse is true.[89] This is probably a reflection of the shifting burden of the fighting, which after the end of 1915 was less reliant on the Regular formations. Furthermore, the ratio of executions to condemnations is far higher in the New Army divisions. All this suggests that discipline was becoming harsher in these two particular New Army formations – a trend that appears to have continued after their transfer to the Italian Front.

Illness and disease were a particular problem in Italy, but there is no reason to suppose that this affected one division any more than others, at least during the initial phase of the campaign. The situation was monitored by the Director of Medical Services (DMS) who, on 14 January 1918, noted a 'slow but steady increase of Enteric and Para-typhoid' fever amongst the troops.[90] By 31 January, though, the situation appeared to be improving:

> The health of the troops during the month has been very good, an improvement on the previous month as witnessed by the Admissions to Casualty Clearing Stations from Field Ambulances. The number of

infectious cases reported during the latter part of the month was less than in the earlier part. The number of Enteric Fever reported has considerably decreased. Evacuated to Base: Officers 28, Other Ranks 393.[91]

This is especially interesting because courts martial appear to have been particularly busy during the month of January. In fact there were 310 trials during January – the highest of the winter period. This was approximately half as many again as during December 1917, with a noticeable downturn in February and March 1918. The overwhelming majority of these trials were for minor infractions of discipline such as drunkenness. It seems, therefore, that courts martial were busiest at times when the men were subjected to the greatest discomfort: food shortages and illness. Courts martial statistics, as far as can be ascertained for this period are as given in Table 5.1.

A further 23 trials convened during this period involved officers; the overwhelming majority of which (17) were for drunkenness.[93] Of the remaining six, two were for absence and three officers were accused of conduct prejudicial to military discipline – the precise circumstances of which are unknown and could involve almost anything. Interestingly, the two officers accused of absence – arguably the most serious of these particular offences – were acquitted by the respective courts.[94] But the apparently high level of drunkenness among officers and men was probably little more than a symptom of the miserable conditions in Italy. Similar patterns can be detected in courts martial of officers and men alike. The highest number of officers court-martialled occurred in January 1918 (eight cases including one of absence). The next highest was in February (six cases) and thereafter the number of officers being tried gradually declined. It was rare for more than one or two officers to be tried in any one month, although the figure did rise to eight once more in July 1918 following the Austrian offensive.[95] Most trials were for drunkenness or an unspecified act prejudicial to military discipline (Section 40, Army Act), but in April 1918 Lieutenant W. H. Aitken, Royal Engineers, was convicted of inflicting a wound on himself, and

Table 5.1   Courts martial statistics for British Army in Italy (other ranks only)[92]

Month	Number of courts martial	Month	Number of courts martial
October 1917	1	June 1918	173
November 1917	17	July 1918	243
December 1917	194	August 1918	150
January 1918	310	September 1918	140
February 1918	258	October 1918	123
March 1918	268	November 1918	149
April 1918	236	December 1918	184
May 1918	134		

reprimanded.[96] This particular offence was indicative of low morale, but it is impossible to identify this officer with any division. Of those officers whose units can be identified with specific divisions six were serving with 48th, five with 23rd, and one with 7th Division. These cases also appear to be concentrated in certain brigades: four in 68th Brigade (23rd Division) and three in 143rd Brigade (48th Division). It might, therefore, be significant that the Deputy-Director Medical Services (DDMS) noted in May 1918 that the fever was proving to be difficult to eradicate in certain units of 70th Brigade.[97]

There is further evidence to suggest a relationship between illness and minor indiscipline. By mid-February the Director Medical Services reported that sick wastage 'is the lowest since the arrival of the force in Italy' although there was little change in the numbers evacuated to Base: 23 officers and 439 Other Ranks.[98] If the corner had indeed been turned then the effects of the epidemic on army discipline was still felt – hence the number of courts martial for February, while declining, remained relatively high. The gradual reduction in cases brought to trial after March should be viewed in the context of the improving health of the troops throughout February. Indeed, on the last day of February the Director Medical Services was able to report that the 'health of the troops during the month has been very good, no epidemic disease'. Furthermore, he recorded in his diary that no evacuations to Base had been carried out during the final week of February.[99] The reduction in the number of courts martial continued with the exception of June and July. This was probably the result of the Austrian offensive during June, but even this did not result in as many cases being tried as in the months of February and March.

The Austrian offensive during June had an impact on the nature of courts martial. Exposure to battle resulted in four trials for cowardice: there was only one other trial for cowardice during the entire Italian campaign.[100] Two men of the Royal Warwickshire Regiment (48th Division) were sentenced to 15 years' penal servitude by a court on 7 June 1918. Another man, serving with the York and Lancaster Regiment (23rd Division), and another with the Pay Corps (HQ) received lesser sentences for the same offence on 27 June and 1 July respectively.[101] The inclusion of a man in the Pay Corps might be suggestive of a manpower problem in the front line during the offensive.

Surprisingly, the number of trials for desertion following the June offensive did not increase markedly from the preceding months – as shown in Table 5.2.

Table 5.2 clearly shows that trials for desertion were highest during the period December 1917 to February 1918 when the influenza epidemic was at its worst. The Austrian offensive during June, which resulted in an increase in cases of cowardice, did not lead to an increase in desertion. The cases of desertion during November 1918, all in 23rd Division, occurred after the armistice (see Appendix) and were probably part of a more general act of indiscipline whereby troops were less willing to cooperate with the military authorities

Table 5.2 Number of trials for desertion in Italian Expeditionary Force[102]

Month	Total	No. in 7th Div.	No. in 23rd Div.	No. in 48th Div.
Nov. 1917	1			
Dec. 1917	14	3	9	
Jan. 1918	15	1	8	
Feb. 1918	12	3	3	
Mar. 1918	5		2	
Apr. 1918	8	3	1	
May 1918	5	1	1	2
Jun. 1918	3	1	2	
Jul. 1918	6	2	2	1
Aug. 1918	5	1	2	
Sep. 1918	7	2	2	2
Oct. 1918	4	1	1	
Nov. 1918	12		12	
Dec. 1918	1		1	
Total	98	18	46	5

after the cessation of hostilities. This can be detected in all theatres.[103] Few cases were brought in 48th (Territorial Force) Division, but the number of trials in 23rd (New Army) Division was greater than in 7th (Regular) Division, all of which conforms to the patterns we have already identified. Discipline, it appears, was being more rigidly enforced in 23rd Division.

Despite the constant tightening-up of discipline in 23rd Division the general approach to discipline in Italy was probably more lenient than in other theatres. The acquittal rate for trials in Italy was roughly 10 per cent – comparable to the overall average of 10.1 per cent for trials overseas during the war.[104] Other features point to a disciplinary code less rigidly enforced in Italy. First, no British or Dominion troops were executed. One black soldier of the British West Indies Regiment was shot for mutiny just after the armistice. This reflected more general trends in the British army, which tended to treat black troops more harshly.[105]

There is another striking feature about desertion in Italy, but it is only apparent if we scrutinise each individual case. Cases of desertion in Italy were often downgraded to absence. As desertion was the most important capital offence, this is an important distinction because it effectively turned the crime into a non-capital one. Of the 98 cases involving men charged with desertion during the Italian campaign, 61 (approximately two-thirds) were found guilty of absence only. It is possible that this resulted from inadequate evidence to support the higher charge. This certainly occurred in the German army where it was increasingly difficult to secure convictions for desertion and charges of absence were generally preferred because they were more likely to succeed. This, though, was probably not the case in the

British army where the law was more flexible and desertion was far easier to prove than in the German code.[106] It is more likely that the lesser charge was preferred for other reasons, but it is unclear from the records if this was the actual finding of the court or whether the commander-in-chief had adjusted the conviction upon review. It might have been a mixture of both, but there is no obvious difference between the divisions – the percentage varied from 60 in 48th Division to 63 in 23rd Division. Nor is there a discernible difference between the periods of the two respective commanders-in-chief.

While this practice can be detected in all theatres, the ratio for these cases in Italy seems to be remarkably high. Analysis of more than 2500 cases tried on the Western Front during the same period shows that fewer than 45 per cent of men charged with desertion had their convictions reduced in this manner. The ratio would be even lower but for an apparent increased use of the practice during the period of the German offensive in the Spring of 1918.[107] It is also salutary to compare the rate of 'downgrading' of offences for the men in Italy with the cases of British officers. Sixty-three officers were tried for desertion during the war, 16 of whom had their convictions downgraded to absence – a rate of only 25 per cent. The ratio is further reduced if we confine ourselves to trials abroad where the figures are 33 cases, seven of which were reduced to absence.[108] Such wide use of this practice in Italy, reminiscent of a long-established judicial practice, known as 'pious perjury', is significant.

This feature of British military discipline, which has largely gone unnoticed, was also a well-established practice in criminal law across Western Europe. Juries in French criminal courts often found 'extenuating circumstances' in murder cases to avoid a death sentence.[109] Its application in English criminal law can be detected as early as the eighteenth century. Juries then, often with the connivance of the judges, would convict for theft of a quantity of 'metal' (coins) or 'paper' (bills of exchange) rather than theft of a specific sum in excess of ten pounds, which was the sum necessary to make an offence capital. It was Judge Blackstone who referred to the practice as 'pious perjury'.[110] Nor was this confined to the eighteenth century. In 1819 the Sheriffs of London and Middlesex presented a petition to the House of Commons opposing the death penalty. In it they suggested:

> That some Jurymen are deterred from a strict discharge of their duty, and acquit guilt or mitigate the offence so as not to subject the offender to the punishment of death, and thus assume a discretion never intended to be invested in juries, and relax the sanctity of a judicial oath . . .[111]

Charles Dickens took up the same theme in a letter to the *Daily News* in 1847 in which he drew attention to juries 'evading their oaths' by acquitting 'on a fiction of his being insane' to avoid condemning alleged murderers.[112]

The military precedents are unclear, but it is likely that courts martial also practised a form of 'pious perjury', especially, it seems, in Italy. There is evidence that the practice of 'pious perjury' by courts martial had previously caused concern among commanders on the Western Front. In a General Routine Order dated 27 January 1915 Douglas Haig, then commander of 1st Army, attempted to discourage courts from finding a man charged with desertion guilty of the lesser charge of absence:

> Proof that the absence did in fact lead to the avoidance of any such duty raises a presumption that the accused absented himself with that object in view; and the Court is entitled to act on that presumption unless the accused can prove that it is not well founded . . . if a soldier is charged with desertion, it will depend upon the evidence adduced by the accused whether the Court find him guilty of that graver [capital] charge, or the less serious [non-capital] one of absence only.[113]

Although originating from an earlier part of the war this might go some way to explaining why the practice of 'pious perjury' was less in evidence on the Western Front whereas in Italy, it appears, the commanders-in-chief were more tolerant of it.

By the spring of 1918 a distinctly separate phase of the Italian campaign can be discerned. 5th and 41st Divisions had returned to France, where the BEF was fighting for its very existence. In Italy the remaining British divisions had survived the winter and the Earl of Cavan took over command of the force on 10 March 1918. On 29 March the British force was moved to the mountainous Asiago sector and a new GHQ was established in mid-April.[114] With the arrival of spring came also preparations for action against the enemy. All these factors affected the morale and discipline of the troops; they could also have an adverse effect on the morale of officers. Only three days after a court martial had reprimanded Lieutenant W. H. Aitken for inflicting a wound on himself a further two Royal Engineer officers were convicted of minor acts of indiscipline.[115]

The threat of disease remained a constant concern for the army in Italy. The 7th Division appears to have had a particularly difficult time during the spring months. In April two men of the division were convicted of desertion and sentenced to death.[116] Both sentences were commuted and although the circumstances of their crimes remain obscure there is evidence that the division was not in a healthy state. An inspection on 13 May 1918 by 7th Division's commander, Major-General Shoubridge, resulted in a complaint being lodged with the Deputy-Director Medical Services that the men were in a 'dirty and shabby' condition. The following day staff from the medical services discovered an army bakery at Novoledo to be in an unsatisfactory state; no protection against flies or mosquitoes had been introduced as had apparently been ordered following a previous inspection.[117]

The miserable conditions caused discontent to spread throughout the three divisions and HQ troops. A medical officer in 23rd Division reported many of his men affected by headaches and dizziness. An outbreak of pyrexia in 48th Division was noted on 17 May and similar illnesses occurred in the French division based in the same area. By 20 May the medical services had reached the conclusion that the illness was 'an infectious condition with a short incubation period' and arranged for the billets of the men to be vacated and disinfected.[118] The Director of Medical Services had reported on 17 May that 'the onset symptoms etc. appear to point to the cases being phlebotomus fever, which is prevalent in the North of Italy in the Spring'. He further noted that the worst affected units were those resting in the area of the Piave plain rather than in the mountains.[119] On 21 May the consulting physician, Lieutenant-Colonel Gates, arranged for a search for sandfly, and stated that he was 'rather of the opinion that it is an influenzal condition'.[120] Despite a report dated 23 May that the number of cases was diminishing, the situation continued to worsen and by 10 June the DDMS recorded in his war diary that there were more than 2000 cases in two casualty clearing stations alone. The worst affected unit was undoubtedly 8th Battalion, York and Lancaster Regiment (23rd Division), which alone had suffered 114 cases by 21 May.[121] During this period two men were sentenced to death for mutiny. It is unclear whether the miserable conditions were a cause, but the timing is significant. Pioneer Jelly of the Royal Engineers was condemned on 27 April and Gunner Edwards of the Royal Field Artillery on 30 May 1918.[122] The circumstances of the offences, which are unknown, were probably not serious because the sentences were commuted to five and three years' penal servitude respectively: an extremely lenient response even by standards in Italy. This suggests that the commander-in-chief had taken into consideration extenuating circumstances such as the unbearable conditions and illness.

The other main factor affecting morale during this period was concern for the plight of the BEF on the Western Front, causing Captain Hardie to remark that 'the shadow of events in France has lain dark across the Italian Expeditionary Force'.[123] This remark probably reflected the frustration of both officers and men alike. Inactive troops were of great concern to their commanders at the best of times, but when events in France had taken an apparent turn for the worse these concerns were heightened. However, their relative inactivity did not last long and the war in Italy entered a new phase with the opening of an offensive by the Austrian army on 15 June 1918. Fifty-one Austrian divisions attacked the Piave sector of the front while a further 55 launched an assault across the Asiago plateau. This part of the sector was held by the Italian Sixth Army, which included the British 23rd and 48th Divisions with 7th in reserve. The preliminary bombardment started at midnight and by 3 am it was reported to be particularly intense. At 8 am the attack proper began and 7th Division – the reserve – were put on two hours' notice to move to positions as required. 23rd Division, holding the right-hand side of the British lines, was driven back off the ridge, but the ground was swiftly retaken by a counter-attack. On the left 48th Division was forced to give up roughly 2500 metres of its line to a depth of 1000 metres. This caused some reorganisation of the British medical services and those suffering from influenza were evacuated to base to free-up room for the wounded in the field ambulances and hospitals. By 6 pm 575 wounded had passed through the dressing stations. The following day the line was restored and the Austrian firstline trenches were captured. But British casualties had been considerable: 23rd Division had lost 351 all ranks, 48th Division suffered 420 casualties of all ranks, while the reserve (7th Division) had lost 34 men and GHQ a further 50.[124] Among the dead was Captain Edward Brittain MC, brother of the writer Vera Brittain. By 18 June casualty figures had increased: more than 1100 British casualties were reported, worst affected was the 48th Division which lost 33 officers and 537 other ranks, followed by 23rd Division with 19 and 417 respectively.[125]

Immediately the worst of the fighting was over, a soldier of 23rd Division was tried for desertion. The circumstances of Private Jackson's case are unknown, but the timing of his trial was probably influential and the court sentenced him to death.[126] Jackson's sentence was commuted, but his was the only capital sentence during the period of the Austrian offensive. Significantly, the soldier concerned was serving with 23rd Division, with its apparent tradition of a harsher disciplinary code than the other divisions in Italy, and not in 48th Division, which suffered most casualties during the Austrian offensive. Perhaps equally important was the fact that Jackson was serving with 8th Battalion York and Lancaster Regiment – the unit most affected by the influenza outbreak. Morale in this unit was probably lower than in others because of the effects of illness and its role in countering the enemy offensive. However, Captain Hardie did not identify this as a concern in his report. Instead Hardie's evaluation reflected more general concerns of commanders worried about the effects of inactivity on the morale and discipline of their men, noting that a renewed 'sense of purpose following the Austrian attack has been good for the men'.[127]

Although each British division took part in a number of operations, most especially during the autumn of 1918, Jackson's was the last death sentence to be passed on a British soldier in Italy.[128] On 28 June the DMS reported that 'the epidemic of fever has now practically ceased' and turned his attention to other matters. Concerns about venereal disease had resulted in the cancellation of soldiers' leave (but not that of officers). A number of brothels and the town of Vicenza were placed out of bounds. Furthermore, the men were warned that courts martial would take a serious view of cases of concealment of venereal disease.[129]

The apparent abandonment of the death penalty for desertion in Italy during the second half of 1918 reflected the general trend throughout the

British army. On the Western Front the transformation from a volunteer to a conscript army was one of the main causes of this shift in disciplinary practice,[130] but it is unlikely that this was as important a factor in Italy. Death sentences had been rare in the Italian Expeditionary Force and none were carried out for purely military offences. Cases of alleged desertion had usually been downgraded to the non-capital offence of absence. Of the 15 condemnations throughout the Italian campaign, 11 had been passed during the first five months – a time when the command was establishing its authority. Paradoxically, there were fewer condemnations during the period of the main fighting in Italy. The outbreak of influenza towards the end of 1918, which affected the Italian and French armies more than the British force, remained a significant preoccupation of the British command. Illness rather than desertion was regarded as the greatest threat to military efficiency. Accordingly, the outbreak was monitored closely. Dysentery and diarrhoea were major problems for the medical services: 255 cases of dysentery and 498 of diarrhoea were recorded in August 1918.[131] Influenza – the greatest concern – caused 3375 admissions to hospital and 142 deaths in October alone.[132] Given the pervasive attitude of the commanders in Italy towards the death penalty, coupled with the effects of the outbreak of influenza, it is no surprise that the death penalty ceased to be employed as a disciplinary instrument during the last months of the campaign.

All three divisions had comparable war experience. Each had taken part in the major battles of 1916 and 1917 before being transferred to Italy. Yet the approach to discipline in each division appears to have varied considerably. This depended on a number of factors. First, the type of formation undoubtedly did much to shape the nature of discipline. Initially, discipline in the Regular 7th Division was more harshly enforced than in the other two. Yet, in common with many other New Army formations, 23rd Division was undergoing something.of a change in its approach. Gradually 23rd Division abandoned its Territorial Force-style discipline and increasingly adopted Regular division practices. As Gary Sheffield has shown, there was a tendency for this to occur in the New Armies, which 'lacked a longstanding tradition of informal discipline, and were perhaps more vulnerable to Regular discipline creeping in'.[133] By the time the divisions reached Italy the 23rd had become harsher in its approach than Regular 7th Division. This was probably a continuation of the process of the commander asserting his control over the division. Certainly discipline in 23rd Division appears to have leant towards the harsher of the New Army formations. By contrast, 7th Division, which in common with other Regular divisions had maintained a harsh approach to discipline from the earliest clashes with the enemy, appears to have adopted a more lenient approach as the war progressed. Many of the decisions in capital cases in 7th Division were based on individual rather than unit considerations. This was especially so during the battles of the Somme and Third Ypres. In keeping with Territorial Force traditions, the death penalty had never been a significant feature of discipline in 48th Division, but appears to have been deliberately applied at significant moments such as at the beginning of battles. In terms of the death penalty men serving with the 48th Division on the Western Front appear to have been at greatest risk when the division was entering or leaving the line. In Italy the threat of the death penalty was non-existent in 48th Division. The timing of trials was often an important factor in every division. Moreover, the differing approaches to capital punishment was little affected by the apparent state of troop morale in each division, or even by its experience in battle. 48th had been singled out for the poor condition of its troops, yet maintained its fighting efficiency without recourse to capital punishment in any great numbers. There is no evidence to suggest that death sentences were more likely after reversals in action. In fact during the Austrian assault and the subsequent counter-attacks by British forces in June 1918, 7th Division, which had suffered most casualties, did not find a need to condemn any of its men, unlike 23rd Division.

Factors other than purely military and tactical considerations were of equal importance to troop morale. First among these was undoubtedly concern for family at home, as we have discussed in the previous chapter. But next probably came the conditions under which the men were living: their billets, food and so on. These factors were consistent regardless of the location. In Italy conditions were miserable and compounded by the spread of illness among the troops. Evidence suggests that there was a close relationship between these conditions and military crime, with men in units worst affected being most likely to desert. The death penalty, as a disciplinary weapon, was variously applied not only according to tradition, but also depending on the commander-in-chief's assessment of conditions at the time. In Italy at least this assessment appears to have reached beyond the purely military.

Conclusion

What kept men in the line – why did most of them 'stick it' through to the end? It seems unlikely that the threat of the death penalty was by itself sufficient to ensure obedience. Yet it undoubtedly formed a vital part of pre-1914 thought, much of which survived to the end of the war. These ideas, though, were continually revised as the army learned to cope with the pressures and changes that modern warfare forced on it. The army never abandoned its faith in deterrence and continued to execute men until the final days of the war, but by 1918 use of the death sentence, and of execution itself, was in decline. The relationship between commanders and their men had been redefined. The balance had shifted.

Despite changes in the army's approach to discipline it remains an inescapable fact that the British Army executed far more of its own troops than the other major armies engaged on the Western Front. In 1918 alone – when the death penalty was most sparingly used by the British – the number of men executed still exceeded that of the German army for the whole war. If we are fully to comprehend the reasons for this we must look beyond the war and beyond the military. The pre-existing legal, social and cultural structures combined to create the circumstances necessary – the preconditions – that made possible this disparity.

British military law was constructed in a manner that encouraged harsh discipline: the principle of deterrence dominated ideas about control of the army. This was partly the result of lingering notions of British troops as ignorant and immoral, recruited from the lowest strata of society, but also owed much to more general ideas about deviance, crime and the nature of punishments. The criminal code was also dominated by ideas of deterrence, especially when it came to serious crime. Speaking of the criminal code between the wars, Professor Victor Bailey suggests that 'the "classical" jurisprudential axioms of personal responsibility, deterrence, and a due proportion between crime and punishment retained much of their authority'.[1] Of all the western countries, Britain clung most steadfastly to corporal and capital punishments, reflecting the importance attached to deterrence, which remained an essential element of penal policy throughout the nineteenth and early twentieth centuries. This reliance on deterrence was particularly evident in the military code. But unlike the criminal code, which had to wait until 1965 for the abolition of capital punishment for murder,[2] there was sufficient concern at the standards applied by courts martial to ensure that the death penalty was effectively abolished for military crimes by 1930.[3] The events of the First World War, and in particular the execution of so many British soldiers, were crucial in focusing those concerns and mobilising the political opinion that eventually led to abolition.

In common with the criminal law, the military code was reformed during the mid-to-late-nineteenth century: first public whippings for criminals and then branding and flogging of soldiers were abolished. Concerns about the impact of public brutality on society provided the impetus for the former, but the death of Private Slim in 1867 focused attention on the nature of military punishments. Branding was abolished in 1871 despite the resistance of some military commanders and an increased use of flogging in the 1870s ensured that it too was abolished in 1881. However, this does not mean that the army had been brought under the control of parliament. Moves to wrest authority away from the commander-in-chief were fiercely resisted, nowhere more so than in matters of discipline. In the decades before the First World War the army resisted challenges to its autonomy from the Judge Advocate General and from politicians, for example, when the dismissal of Colonal Kinlock in 1903 brought the whole issue of military authority under the close scrutiny of both chambers of parliament. Invariably, defenders of the *status quo* cited the army's political independence as sacrosanct and any attempt to alter this potent status was doomed to failure. With flogging no longer available to them, some British commanders increasingly looked towards capital punishment as the only effective deterrent to desertion during the war. Unlike other armies the British did not have penal battalions, and the options available to commanders were severely limited. Field Punishments were frequent, but unpopular. Certainly no soft option, Field Punishments were most often inflicted for minor offences such as drunkenness and this suggests that they were not generally believed to be an effective deterrent for a determined deserter. The failure of the British legislators and military alike to envisage alternative punishments before the war or to develop other strategies to manage indiscipline during it merely heightened the problem.

In many ways military traditions had triumphed over the modernising reforms. The commander-in-chief retained his absolute power in matters of military discipline and the Judge Advocate General remained on the margins of the disciplinary process. Furthermore, there were few safeguards in place to prevent any abuse of authority and no structure to allow for any direct political involvement. In this respect Britain was alone among the major Western democracies – the codes of both France and the United States allowed for some form of political restraint of military authority – and had more in common with the old empires of Eastern Europe. During wartime the power of the commander-in-chief was consolidated rather than limited and many forms of military-style discipline even crept into civilian life. Nevertheless, there was sustained criticism of the use of the death penalty in spite of the restrictions of censorship, and the criticism commonly highlighted the unfettered nature of military authority. Later, this became a potent element in the movement to abolish the death penalty for military offences after the war. Despite the apparent restraint of Haig and the others, the untrammelled authority of the commander-in-chief eventually proved to be the Achilles heel of traditional forms of military discipline.

Comparisons with the French and American codes reveal deficiencies in the construction of British military law. Most marked of all, though, were the differences between the British and German codes. The fierce Prussian code was abandoned shortly after the unification of Germany. The new code of 1872 was arguably the most liberal of all the belligerents of the First World War. Without doubt the construction of the state governed by law, or *Rechtsstaat,* played a large part in this. The law was more tightly constructed than the British code. Desertion, for example, was not as loosely defined as it was in the British code. Sentencing and the rights of soldiers were also written into the law rather than being left to the whim of the commander-in-chief. This caused some consternation to General Ludendorff and his staff, who clearly felt constrained by the nature of German military law, but the significance of the differences between the two codes cannot be overstated. It appears likely, from what he had to say after the war, that Ludendorff would have preferred to preside over a disciplinary code every bit as harsh as did Haig. That he did not suggests that popular notions of pre-war Germany being dominated by a severe Prussian militarism do not apply, or at least need qualification even with regard to discipline in the army. The further liberalisation of the military code suggests that even during the war politicians were able to impose their will on the military. The same cannot be said of Britain.

Unlike their French and German equivalents, British soldiers were regarded as subjects rather than citizens at least in the early years of the war. This was largely because of contrasting traditional forms of recruitment. The British Army was intolerant of desertion by its volunteer soldiers, which contrasts with the French and German armies where certain types of desertion by those the state compelled to serve were excused. Only during the final year of the war did the British Army change its harsh approach to discipline. During this period, when conscripted soldiers formed the bulk of the army, the number of death sentences meted out by courts martial fell dramatically. There had been no liberalisation of the British military code as there had been in Germany. Nor had there been any direct political intervention such as the French army had experienced. Instead changes occurred within the army itself.

At the end of 1917 the British Army, mindful of the situation in Russia, increasingly concerned about the quality of its own troops and aware of deteriorating morale following the failure of the Flanders campaign, implemented subtle changes, which would have dramatic implications for discipline. First, the strategic emphasis shifted from moral to *matériel* superiority: no longer was it believed to be sufficient to undermine the morale of the enemy. This represented an abandonment of much pre-war military thought, but also placed less emphasis on the individual character of British troops. Second, a programme of citizenship education was introduced, which indicates a tacit acceptance of consent as the basis for future discipline rather than mere coercion.

These changes had been forced on the army by a number of developments – social, political and military. Undoubtedly, the altered recruitment of the army had placed enormous strain on the existing structures including disciplinary ones. Men who had volunteered under Kitchener's scheme resented old-army forms of discipline based on deterrence. Later, the army was seemingly uncomfortable with the thought of shooting men who had been compelled to serve. Such an act would no doubt have brought down on the army some form of direct political control – a situation the commander-in-chief could not tolerate. Failure on the battlefield had forced the army to question its own practices by the end of 1917. Practices rooted in old-fashioned ideas about individual character – this time of the enemy – were found to be wanting. Wholesale changes in personnel followed. Less obvious were the changes in attitude. Lessons learned from the collapse of the Tsarist armies accelerated the need for change. Maxse, commander of XVIII Corps, urged other commanders to place greater trust in their men in an effort to retain their consent and thereby avoid 'what has happened in Russia through indiscipline'.[4]

It is incorrect, however, to view military discipline as conforming to two phases: coercion prior to 1918 and consent thereafter. The need for the consent of the troops was recognised long before 1918 – it was the emphasis that shifted. Even in the preceding three years the death sentence had been carried out in only approximately one tenth of the cases referred to the commander-in-chief. Given the importance attached to the principle of deterrence, one in ten is a surprisingly low proportion and without the checks and tolerance enshrined in other codes it is no small wonder that there was not a greater abuse of authority. But one in ten was probably thought to be sufficient to deter potential offenders while keeping politicians at bay and maintaining the consent of the troops. It also conformed to a long-established military precedent, itself no doubt rooted in the desire to balance authority and consent. There is evidence that commanders were mindful of this need from the first moments of the war even when inflicting punishments designed to deter, such as Field Punishments. The exigencies of the war presented a challenge to conventional military thought on matters of discipline and morale. This was partly because of the sheer scale of the war and of the armies deployed, but also because so much pre-war thought had its roots in much older models that placed the emphasis on individual qualities. Like so many other features of total war, both discipline and morale defied attempts to comprehend them in individualist terms. Military punishments, constructed around the concept of individual deterrent, were found to be ineffective; prosecutions for desertion increased and the number of condemnations rose each year until 1918. The importance attached to individual character gradually diminished also until 1918 when it too was effectively abandoned. In their place emerged a programme of collective education. The relationship between coercion and consent had varied, with the emphasis shifting decidedly in favour of the latter by 1918.

The decision whether or not to execute was undoubtedly an administrative one, probably taken by the Director of Personal Services rather than by the commander-in-chief himself. The criteria applied are not always obvious. Unit discipline and individual character were of undoubted importance here, but so too was timing. Most executions were carried out at critical moments of the war. Often, an ideal candidate would present himself to the confirming authority, but not always, and those cases which seem to defy rationale should be viewed in this context. The most obvious examples are the two officers, Dyett and Poole, who were executed at the very moment that there was increasing disquiet at the inequality of punishment between officers and men. The army had its examples, but it restricted itself to an acceptable number by a confirmation process that amounted to 'bureaucratic decimation'.

Discipline was *the* central tenet of military efficiency in pre-war British military thinking. The pervasive belief was that victory would be achieved by the most disciplined army; a view that also prevailed after the war. Indeed, the length of the war was often understood in the context of a struggle between two highly disciplined armies – of Britain and Germany – and military collapses were placed in the context of poor discipline, in society as well as in the army. This was believed to be the reason for the mutinies and collapse in Russia, Italy and even France. Military law was constructed to ensure that the authority of the commander-in-chief was upheld. It is a mistake to regard the military code as a legal framework designed to ensure that justice was dispensed. The unique judicial role granted to the British commander-in-chief was an essential element in this. The apparent contradiction of the dual responsibilities of his office – the maintenance of discipline and final arbitration in capital cases – was no mistake. The stated intention of military law was 'to maintain discipline'.[5] The legal process not only provided a framework for the authority of the commander-in-chief, but legitimised its implementation.

Pre-war thought placed the emphasis on good leadership. However, during the war disciplinary problems were often blamed on the troops, utilising explanations centring on degeneracy or poor moral fibre. Commanders were concerned about the enormous expansion of the army, and as the army was enlarged to encompass most elements of society, so the fear of military crime rose. The enlistment of so many men from urban centres caused great concern, but not nearly as much as the arrival at the front of colonial troops and native labourers – 'racially inferior' men. The approach to discipline and punishments often reflected these anxieties, with black and oriental troops and labourers having to endure severe restrictions on their movements and harsh punishments for those who deviated.

Shell-shock was often regarded as a disciplinary issue rather than a medical problem. Although the Army did respond to the psychological issues in a muted form, it still sought a disciplinary solution. Even those concerned with the (medical) treatment of shell-shock, such as Charles Myers, saw a connection between the condition and discipline. The frequency of shell-shock cases was regarded as an indicator of the state of discipline in a particular unit – a view which persisted after the war. Some of those executed were undoubtedly suffering from the condition, but we should view these cases in the context of contemporary concerns about discipline and degeneracy.

Morale posed several problems for the Army. First, no single definition existed. This was at once problematic in addressing concerns, yet helpful to those who wished to interpret assessments of morale in a positive light. The ambiguity of the term enabled the British mail censor to write positively of morale even at times of profound war-weariness in the British army. Secondly, assessing troop morale proved to be beyond quantitative methods, forcing the army to adopt qualitative means, as the French had before them. However, these were subject to such dubious interpretation that we must question the extent to which the High Command and, therefore, the Government, had any notion of the state of troop morale in the British army. Although there is no evidence to suggest that the army deliberately misled the Government, it was nevertheless in the army's interests to present an optimistic evaluation to the Cabinet if it was to avoid direct political interference in military matters. Lastly, the relationship between morale and discipline remained an ambiguous one. Most commanders believed that the two were linked and that good morale was the outcome of strong (though not necessarily harsh) discipline. Even the more progressive military pundits such as Maxse adopted this approach.

Pre-war military traditions were highly influential in disciplinary matters and were reflected in the frequency of the use of the death penalty. Greater severity was reserved for those serving in Regular Army formations than in Territorial Force divisions. Furthermore, the disparate approaches proved to be remarkably resilient despite the dilution of the original character of divisions. However, variations did exist and none was more marked than in the New Armies where, more than in other formations, the divisional commander could shape discipline to his own model. Usually this leant more towards the harshness of the Regular Army than to the more democratic Territorial Force, but there were significant exceptions. The strong tradition of the Territorial Force acted as a counter against the frequent use of the death penalty, but this often gave way at times of battle when disciplinary concerns became heightened.

A number of factors caused men to desert. Some simply gave in to fear during battle, perhaps exhibiting symptoms of shell-shock. For others it was a culmination of long-term factors such as absence from their family and community. A threat, whether real or imagined, to these familial and communal ties often caused an individual soldier to perform irrational acts. The prospect of returning home, whether by ending the war or even the remote possibility of leave, was paramount in most soldiers' minds. The erosion of *esprit de corps* could be rapid in those units with distinct local identities that suffered large casualties in battle. Furthermore, large losses in these units often magnified men's concerns about their communities. The preservation of community ties preoccupied men's minds on the war front; 'alienation' was what they feared the most. A significant number of capital cases arose out of fear that ties with home were in some way threatened. We cannot afford to ignore the impact on soldiers' state of mind at these moments.

Was discipline rigidly applied in the British army as Crown Prince Rupprecht suggested? At times it certainly was, but there were great variations. Different commanders approached discipline in their own ways and practices also varied over time. There is evidence to suggest that the law was even circumvented on occasions; courts could find prisoners guilty of lesser offences to avoid harsh punishments. This certainly occurred in Italy and probably elsewhere too. But why would courts behave in this manner? The retention of consent cannot be ruled out and we must view the simplistic view that soldiers were coerced into some form of blind obedience with great suspicion.

Nevertheless the death penalty was used with some regularity. Most often its purpose was to reassert the authority of the divisional commander. The evidence suggests that rarely was there any disciplinary advantage to be gained from an execution. The deterrent value of executions was of a more general nature rather than as a response to specific disciplinary problems in divisions. Condemnations usually followed criticisms or concerns from the High Command rather than arising from problems on the battlefield. Accordingly, we must view condemnations as a demonstration of the divisional commander's authority – an overt demonstration of disciplinary resolve – mainly for the benefit of the High Command.

British army discipline was hampered by the lack of alternatives. Some commanders were able to develop strategies to manage their troops, but others simply fell back on traditional methods of control characterised by harsh punishments. In these divisions the death penalty was often regarded as the only means to prevent the increasing problem of desertion. It could also be used to prop up flagging morale. Once more, though, this became less apparent as the character and structure of the army was altered over time.

That the Army was able to accommodate these changes should not be forgotten, but there were signs that it was modernising its attitudes towards discipline, morale and the relationship between officers and men. The pervasive notion of a harsh disciplinary code enforced by callous commanders, of whom Haig was a paradigm, should be treated with caution. Unit commanders were able to express their opposition to the death penalty and some divisional commanders were able to avoid executions in their units. This is not suggestive of an oppressive hierarchy where leniency was never tolerated. Commanders at all levels from battalion to army were able to object to executions, though not always successfully. Perhaps this is why a practice of 'pious perjury' developed.

Appendix

Trials for Desertion and Cowardice in Italy 1917–18[1]

Name	Rank	Regiment	Brigade	Division	Date	Offence	Sentence	Disposal	Information
Slater E	Pte	10 Queens	124	41	03/11/17	Desertion	2 yrs HL		Guilty of Absence only
Simpson W	Pte	9 Yorkshire	69	23	08/12/17	Desertion	**DEATH**	10 yrs PS	
Montgomery P	Pte	10 W Riding	69	23	12/12/17	Desertion	**DEATH**	15 yrs PS	
Craven A	Pte	22 Manchester	91	7	18/12/17	Desertion	2 yrs HL		Guilty of Absence only
Orriss A	Pte	19 Middx (pnr)	Pnr	41	21/12/17	Desertion	28 days FP2		Guilty of Absence only
Lomas H	Pte	21 Manchester	91	7	24/12/17	Desertion	2 yrs HL		Guilty of Absence only
Manders T	Pte	1 S Staffs	91	7	24/12/17	Desertion	2 yrs HL		Guilty of Absence only
Sewell R	Pte	10 W Riding	69	23	26/12/17	Desertion	2 yrs HL	Susp	Guilty of Absence only
Leach G	Pte	10 W Riding	69	23	26/12/17	Desertion	2 yrs HL	Susp	Guilty of Absence only
Abbott J	Pte	9 Yorks & Lancs	70	23	27/12/17	Desertion	1 yr HL	90 days FP1	Guilty of Absence only
Mallinson J	Pte	10 W Riding	69	23	27/12/17	Desertion	2 yrs HL	Susp	Guilty of Absence only
Monk E	Pte	10 W Riding	69	23	27/12/17	Desertion	2 yrs HL	Susp	Guilty of Absence only
Willcock H	Pte	10 W Riding	69	23	27/12/17	Desertion	2 yrs HL	Susp	Guilty of Absence only
Mellish A	Pte	26 R Fusiliers	124	41	29/12/17	Desertion	5 yrs PS	FP com for pay	Guilty of Absence only
Jackson W	CQMS	9 Yorks	69	23	31/12/17	Desertion	56 days FP1/ reduced to ranks		
Watson J	Pte	9 Yorks	69	23	02/01/18	Desertion	2 yrs HL	Susp	Guilty of Absence only

Name	Rank	Regiment	Brigade	Division	Date	Offence	Sentence	Disposal	Information
Collins G	Pte	9 Yorks & Lancs	70	23	03/01/18	Desertion	2 yrs HL		Guilty of Absence only
Eaton E	Pte	8 Yorks & Lancs	70	23	03/01/18	Desertion	28 days FP1	28 days FP2	
Butcher W	Pte	11 Northumb Fusiliers	68	23	03/01/18	Desertion	2 yrs HL	90 days FP1	Guilty of Absence only
Welsby J	Pte	2 King's Own Scot Borderers	13	5	04/01/18	Cowardice/ Desertion /S 40	2 yrs HL		Guilty of Absence only
Parker E	Pte	19 Middx	Pnr	41	12/01/18	Desertion	2 yrs HL	Susp	Guilty of Absence only
McHugh P	Dvr	Army Service Corps			12/01/18	Desertion	56 days FP2		Guilty of Absence only
Pareezer S	Pte	21 Manchester	91	7	14/01/18	Desertion	**DEATH**	15 yrs PS	
McMillan R	Pte	11 Northumb Fusiliers	68	23	17/01/18	Desertion	**DEATH**	15 yrs PS	
Walton I	Pte	12 Durham Lt Infantry	68	23	17/01/18	Desertion /Absence /Esc	2 yrs HL	90 days FP1	Guilty of Absence only
Rabjohn F	Pte	10 W Riding	69	23	17/01/18	Desertion	**DEATH**	15 yrs PS	
Newman P	Pte	11 Sherwood Foresters	70	23	17/01/18	Desertion	2 yrs HL	90 days FP1	Guilty of Absence only
Lester A	Pte	32 R Fusiliers	124	41	25/01/18	Desertion	5 yrs PS	Susp	
Beck HC	Gnr	Royal Field Artillery			30/01/18	Desertion × 2	3 yrs PS	6 months HL susp	
Gibbons M	Pte	8 Yorks	69	23	31/01/18	Desertion	2 yrs HL		Guilty of Absence only
Cook J	Pte	10 Queens	124	41	08/02/18	Desertion	5 yrs PS		
Campbell H	Pte	10 Queens	124	41	08/02/18	Desertion × 2	10 yrs PS		Guilty of Absence only

Wooley T	Pte	10 Queens	124	41	08/02/18	Desertion ×2	10 yrs PS		Guilty of Absence only
Caunt H	Pte	1 S Staffs	91	7	11/02/18	Desertion	90 days FP1		Guilty of Absence only
Porter A	Pte	2 Border	20	7	11/02/18	Desertion	1 yr HL	90 days FP1	Guilty of Absence only
Cresswell C	Pte	1 S Staffs	91	7	11/02/18	Desertion	2 yrs HL	90 days FP1	Guilty of Absence only
Thompson W	Pte	11 Sherwood Foresters	70	23	13/02/18	Desertion	2 yrs HL		Guilty of Absence only
Bloom W	Pte	11 Sherwood Foresters	70	23	13/02/18	Desertion	2 yrs HL		Guilty of Absence only
Shuttleworth J	Pte	10 [?] Durham Lt Infantry	68	23	17/02/18	Desertion /Esc	2 yrs	Susp HL	Guilty of Absence only
Spriggs J	Dvr	Army Service Corps			26/02/18	Desertion	5 yrs PS	Susp	
Wood A	Dvr	Army Service Corps			26/02/18	Desertion	5 yrs PS		
Hewlett H	Fitter	Royal Field Artillery			28/02/18	Desertion /Esc	2 yrs	Susp HL	Guilty of Absence only
Larson A	Pte	Army Ordnance Corps			07/03/18	Desertion /Esc	DEATH	10 yrs PS	
Golding H	Cpl	11 W Yorks	69	23	20/03/18	Desertion	1 yr HL	Susp	Guilty of Absence only
Vale S	Pte	Royal Field Artillery			22/03/18	Desertion	2 yrs HL	Susp	Guilty of Absence only
Smith E	Gnr	Royal Field Artillery			22/03/18	Desertion	2 yrs HL	Susp	Guilty of Absence only
Ripsher S	Sgt	11 Northumb Fusiliers	68	23	23/03/18	Desertion	5 yrs PS	reduced /susp 2 yrs HL	
Massey H	Pte	Machine Gun Coy			02/04/18	Desertion	**DEATH**	2 yrs HL	

Name	Rank	Regiment	Brigade	Division	Date	Offence	Sentence	Disposal	Information
Horton HS	Pte	1 S Staffs	91	7	14/04/18	Desertion	**DEATH**	7 yrs PS	
McLeod J	Pte	2 King's Own Scot Borders	13	5	15/04/18	Desertion	90 days FP1		Guilty of Absence only
Stone R	Pte	11 Sherwood Foresters	70	23	17/04/18	Desertion	2 yrs HL	Susp	Guilty of Absence only
Cahill J	Pte	1 Devonshire	95	5	20/04/18	Desertion	NG		Guilty of Absence only
Reilly P	Sgt	18 Lancs Fusiliers			26/04/18	Desertion	reduced to ranks		Guilty of Absence only
Deakin R	Pte	2 R Warwicks	22	7	30/04/18	Desertion	2 yrs HL	Susp	
Steven W	Pte	20 Manchester	22	7	30/04/18	Desertion	3 yrs PS	90 days FP1	
Olsen C	Pte	1/6 Gloster	144	48	25/05/18	Desertion	2 yrs HL		Guilty of Absence only
Wilson VR	Pte	1/6 Gloster	144	48	25/05/18	Desertion	2 yrs HL		Guilty of Absence only
Rutter J	Cpl	Royal Field Artillery			27/05/18	Desertion	1 yr HL	Susp	Guilty of Absence only
McLean A	Pte	2 Gordon Highlanders	20	7	28/05/18	Desertion	1 yr imprisonment	90 days FP1	Guilty of Absence only
Johnson JA	Pte	8 Yorks & Lancs	70	23	30/05/18	Desertion	2 yrs HL		Guilty of Absence only
Williams J	Pte	1/5 Royal Warwicks	143	48	07/06/18	Cowardice /Quitting	15 yrs PS		
Wenburn CE	Pte	1/5 Royal Warwicks	143	48	07/06/18	Cowardice /Quitting	15 yrs PS	Susp	
Farrell B	Pte	8 Devonshire	20	7	18/06/18	Desertion	60 days FP1		Guilty of Absence only
Richardson JA	Pte	8 Yorks & Lancs	70	23	21/06/18	Desertion	5 yrs PS		

Name	Rank	Unit			Date	Offence	Sentence	Commuted	Notes
Fulton A	Pte	8 Yorks & Lancs	70	23	21/06/18	Desertion	NG		
Clee R	Pte	9 S Staffs	Pnr	23	26/06/18	Desertion	NG		
Farrar SH	Pte	9 Yorks & Lancs	70	23	27/06/18	Cowardice /Quitting	5 yrs PS		
Filles WS	Cpl	Army Police Corps			01/07/18	Cowardice /Absence	2 yrs HL	Susp	Guilty of Absence only
Snell H	Pte	1/5 Gloster	145	48	01/07/18	Desertion	90 days FP1		
Martin EW	Pte	22 Manchester	91	7	08/07/18	Desertion	NG		
James N	Pte	12 Durham Lt Infantry	68	23	10/07/18	Desertion	10 yrs PS	Susp	
Firth J	Gnr	Royal Field Artillery			12/07/18	Desertion	18 months HL		Guilty of Absence only
Jones JT	Pte	1 R Welh Fusiliers	22	7	15/07/18	Desertion	NG		
Beck H	Gnr	23 DAC	HQ	23	17/07/18	Desertion	2 yrs HL	15 months HL	Guilty of Absence only
Davies J	Pte	22 Manchester	91	7	06/08/18	Desertion	15 yrs PS	Susp	Guilty of Absence only
Dolphin J	Pte	11 Sherwood Foresters	70	23	13/08/18	Desertion	6 months HL	90 days FP1	
Cook J	Pte	12 Durham Lt Infantry	68	23	19/08/18	Desertion	2 yrs HL	Not confirmed	
Hunt R	Gnr	Royal Field Artillery			27/08/18	Desertion	10 yrs PS	Susp	
Turner R	Pte	13 R Scots			30/08/18	Desertion	2 yrs HL		
Allen JH	Pte	22 Manchester	91	7	06/09/18	Desertion	6 months HL	30 days HL	Guilty of Absence only
Collins J	Pte	1/4 Gloster	144	48	07/09/18	Desertion	20 yrs PS	Susp	Guilty of Absence only
Griffith JF	Pte	Ox & Bucks Lt Infantry	145	48	07/09/18	Desertion	7 yrs PS	Susp	
Fulton A	Pte	8 Yorks & Lancs	70	23	12/09/18	Desertion	6 months HL		Guilty of Absence only

Name	Rank	Regiment	Brigade	Division	Date	Offence	Sentence	Disposal	Information
Slater J	Pte	8 Yorks & Lancs	70	23	12/09/18	Desertion	6 months HL		Guilty of Absence only
Avis J	Pte	2 Queen's	91	7	24/09/18	Desertion	10 yrs PS	5 yrs	
Powell G	Gnr	Royal Field Artillery			27/09/18	Desertion	90 days FP1	/Susp	Guilty of Absence only
Harrison CV	Pte	1 S Staffs	91	7	08/10/18	Desertion	90 days FP1	76 days FP2	Guilty of Absence only
Garland CB	Pte	Army Service Corps			23/10/18	Desertion /Drunk	90 days FP1	£1 fine	Guilty of Absence only
Hurst J	Pte	11 W Yorks	69	23	31/10/18	Desertion	90 days FP1	76 days FP2	Guilty of Absence only
Knight JS	Pte	Army Service Corps			31/10/18	Desertion	90 days FP1		Guilty of Absence only
Evenden G	Pte	13 Durham Lt Infantry	68	23	11/11/18	Desertion	90 days FP1		Guilty of Absence only
Hislop R	Pte	10 Northumb Fusiliers	68	23	17/11/18	Desertion	18 months imprisonment	90 days FP1	
Armour J	Pte	12 Durham Lt Infantry	68	23	17/11/18	Desertion	2 yrs imprisonment	90 days FP1	Guilty of Absence only
Dartford J	Pte	10 Northumb Fusiliers	68	23	17/11/18	Desertion	90 days FP1		Guilty of Absence only
Norton J	Pte	10 Northumb Fusiliers	68	23	17/11/18	Desertion	10 yrs PS		
Pierce G	Pte	10 Northumb Fusiliers	68	23	17/11/18	Desertion	90 days FP1		Guilty of Absence only
Brown T	Pte	10 Northumb Fusiliers	68	23	17/11/18	Desertion	90 days FP1		Guilty of Absence only
McNulty J	Pte	10 Northumb Fusiliers	68	23	17/11/18	Desertion	90 days FP1		Guilty of Absence only

Name	Rank	Unit	Number	Age	Date	Offence	Sentence	Commuted	Notes
Stainton T	Pte	1/6 Royal Warwicks	143	48	18/11/18	Desertion	10 yrs PS		Guilty of Absence only
Orton W	Pte	9 S Staffs	Pnr	23	20/11/18	Desertion	10 yrs PS		
McKenna J	Pte	11 W Yorks	69	23	27/11/18	Desertion	3 yrs PS		
Graham FS	Pte	8 Yorks	69	23	27/11/18	Desertion	2 yrs HL	Susp 18 months HL	
Norman E	Pte	9 S Staffs	Pnr	23	11/12/18	Desertion	2 yrs HL		

Notes:

Com	Commuted
CQMS	Company Quartermaster Sergeant
Dvr	Driver
Esc	Esaping arrest or confinement
FP	Field Punishment
Gnr	Gunner
HL	Hard labour
NG	Found Not Guilty
Pnr	Pioneer
PS	Penal servitude
Susp	Suspended
S40	Section 40: Conduct prejudicial to military discipline

Notes

Introduction

1 Major-General Sir Wyndham Childs, *Episodes and Reflections* (Cassell, London, 1930) pp. 143, 145.
2 Ian F. W. Beckett, 'The Military Historian and the Popular Image of the Western Front, 1914–1918' *The Historian*, no. 53 (1997) p. 12.
3 Anthony Babington, *For the Sake of Example: Capital Courts-Martial 1914–18, the Truth*, revised edition (Leo Cooper, Barnsley, 1993) and Julian Putkowski and Julian Sykes, *Shot at Dawn*, revised edition (Leo Cooper, Barnsley, 1992). These have been followed by a steady flow of newspaper articles about the campaign to pardon the executed soldiers. See, for example, *The Independent*, 16 August 1993.
4 The work of Babington, and Putkowski and Sykes are frequently cited in other works on the First World War. For instance, Martin Gilbert, *The First World War* (Weidenfeld & Nicolson, London, 1994), cites both works in his bibliography. Another of Babington's works, *Shell-shock: A History of the Changing Attitudes to War Neuroses* (Leo Cooper, Barnsley, 1997), was even cited as an influential study by Sir Edward Sommers in his *Review of Deaths by Execution in the Great War of 1914–1918*, which was placed before the New Zealand Government in October 1999. Although far from the definitive work on the subject, this indicates just how Babington's name has become synonymous with the study of military executions.
5 Ernest Thurtle, *Shootings at Dawn* (Victoria House, London, 1924).
6 A. P. Herbert, *The Secret Battle* (Methuen, London, 1919). The story was loosely based on the case of Sub-Lieutenant Edwin Dyett of the Royal Naval Division. Dyett was executed in early 1917 – only the second officer to be shot during the war – and his case was the cause of considerable media and political reaction in Britain. Dyett's case, of all those executed, continues to arouse most interest and is the sole subject of Leonard Sellers' book, *For God's Sake Shoot Straight* (Leo Cooper, London, 1991). Once again, though, it is void of historical analysis, focusing instead on revelations of apparent injustice.
7 John Peatty, 'Capital Courts-Martial during the Great War' in Brian Bond et al., *'Look to Your Front': Studies in the First World War by the British Commission for Military History* (Spellmount, Staplehurst, 1999), p. 102.
8 Cathryn Corns and John Hughes-Wilson, *Blindfold and Alone: British Military Executions in the Great War* (Cassell, London, 2001). The misquoting of General Sir Hubert Gough's comments in the case of Edwin Dyett (p. 268) might be mere carelessness. But the manner in which other evidence is used gives rise to more serious concerns. For example, a passage from a novel is cited in support of a key argument without any attempt to identify it as a work of fiction (p. 461) and the source of other evidence is not cited and, therefore, cannot be verified – all of which raises doubts about its reliability. In particular, the statistical analysis of desertion during the war (p. 504) needs to be more transparent.
9 David French, 'Discipline and the Death Penalty in the British Army in the War against Germany during the Second World War', *Journal of Contemporary History*,

vol. 33 (4), 1998, pp. 531–45; David Englander, 'Mutinies and Military Morale', in Hew Strachan (ed.), *The Oxford Illustrated History of the First World War* (Oxford University Press, Oxford, 1998), pp. 191–203.

10   *Statistics of the Military Effort of the British Empire during the Great War 1914–1920* (War Office, HMSO, London, 1922), p. 649 suggests that there were 3080 condemnations during the war, with 346 executions carried out. This, though, is a highly conservative figure which does not include Indian troops or civilians. It is unlikely that the actual figure will ever be known, but there is evidence to suggest that it is far greater than officially recorded. See G. Oram, *Death Sentences passed by military courts of the British Army 1914–1924* (Francis Boutle, London, 1998).

11   See, for example, T. H. E. Travers, 'Technology, Tactics and Morale: Jean de Bloch, the Boer War, and British Military Theory, 1900–1914' *Journal of Modern History,* vol. 51 (June 1979), pp. 264–86.

12   Gary Sheffield, 'Officer–Man Relations: Morale and Discipline in the British army 1902–1922', PhD thesis, King's College, London, 1994.

13   PRO WO213/1-34 and WO90/6-8 and WO92/3&4, Courts-Martial registers. Also PRO WO71/387-690, Judge Advocate General's Records.

14   There is no record of Indian executions. If a record was maintained then it has not survived.

15   Two executions of British soldiers have been omitted from the official records. These are Corporal William Price and Private Richard Morgan of 2 Bn Welsh Regiment who were executed in early 1915 for the murder of their own CSM. Neither Price's nor Morgan's details are recorded in the Judge Advocate General's Records or in the Courts-Martial registers at the PRO.

16   Ian F. W. Beckett, 'The Military Historian', p. 12. See also John Peatty, 'Capital Courts-Martial'.

17   *Report of the Committee Constituted by the Army Council to Enquire into the Law and Rules of Procedure Regulating Military Courts-Martial* (HMSO, 1919) [hereafter referred to as *The Darling Report*].

18   See David Englander and James Osbourne, 'Jack, Tommy and Henry Dubb: the Armed Forces and the Working Class', *Historical Journal,* no. xxi (1978) pp. 593–621.

19   By 1930 the only offences punishable by death were treason and mutiny.

20   *The Darling Report*. In particular see paragraph 105.

21   Thurtle, *Shootings at Dawn.*

22   Thurtle, *Shootings at Dawn*, p. 7.

23   Thurtle, *Shootings at Dawn*, p. 3.

24   William Moore, *The Thin Yellow Line* (Leo Cooper, Barnsley, 1974).

25   Guy Pedroncini, *Les Mutineries de 1917* (PUF, Paris, 1967).

26   Babington, *For the Sake of Example*, p. ix.

27   Anthony Babington, *Shell-Shock: A History of the Changing Attitudes to War Neuroses* (Leo Cooper, Barnsley, 1997).

28   Eric Leed, *No Man's Land: Combat and Identity in World War One* (Cambridge University Press, Cambridge, 1979) contains an excellent section on discipline and war neuroses. Martin Stone, 'Shellshock and the Psychologists', in W. F. Bynum, R. Porter and M. Shepherd (eds) *Anatomy of Madness*, vol. II (Tavistock Press, London, 1985) explores the perception of psychological treatment of neuroses before the war and the impact of the war on both psychology and psychiatry.

29   Peter John Lynch, 'The Exploitation of Courage: Psychiatric Care in the British Army 1914–1918, MPhil thesis, University College London, 1977. Peter Jeremy

Leese, 'A Social and Cultural History of Shellshock, with particular reference to the experience of British soldiers during and after the Great War' PhD thesis, Open University, 1989.

30   Douglas Gill and Gloden Dallas, *The Unknown Army* (Verso, New York, 1985).

31   David Englander and James Osbourne, 'Jack, Tommy and Henry Dubb'.

32   Putkowski and Sykes, *Shot at Dawn*.

33   Putkowski and Sykes, *Shot at Dawn*, p. 5.

34   Works such as John Terraine, *The Great War* (Wordsworth Editions, Ware, 1997) and A. J. P. Taylor, *The First World War: An Illustrated History* (Penguin Books, Harmondsworth, 1966) refer to executions of French soldiers following the 1917 mutinies, but make no mention of the more numerous British executions, or any others for that matter.

35   Martin Gilbert, *First World War* (Weidenfeld & Nicolson, London, 1994); John M. Bourne, *Britain and the Great War 1914–1918* (Edward Arnold, London, 1989).

36   Martin Gilbert, *First World War*, p. 288.

37   Martin Gilbert, *The Routledge Atlas of the First World War: The Complete History*, second edition, (Routledge, London, 1994).

38   J. M. Bourne, *Britain and the Great War*, p. 216.

39   A complete annotated list of over three thousand death sentences passed by British courts martial, the 'raw material' of this research, has been published. See Gerard Oram, *Death Sentences Passed by Military Courts of the British Army 1914–1924* (Francis Boutle, London, 1998).

40   Gerard Oram, 'Worthless Men: Death Sentences in the British Army during the First World War', unpublished MPhil thesis, University of Hertfordshire, 1997.

41   G. Oram, *Worthless Men: Race, Eugenics and the Death Penalty in the British Army during the First World War* (Francis Boutle, London, 1998). Hereafter referred to as *Worthless Men*.

42   Oram, *Worthless Men*, pp. 84–101.

43   Joanna Bourke, 'Effeminacy, Ethnicity and the End of Trauma: the Sufferings of "Shell-Shocked" Men in Great Britain and Ireland, 1914–39' *Journal of Contemporary History*, vol. 35 (1) (2000), pp. 57–69. See also George Mosse, 'Shell-shock as a Social Disease' also *Journal of Contemporary History*, vol. 35 (1) (2000), pp. 101–8.

44   Timothy Bowman, 'The Discipline and Morale of the British Expeditionary Force in France and Flanders 1914–18, with Particular Reference to Irish Units', PhD thesis, Unversity of Luton, 1999.

45   Christopher Pugsley, *On the Fringe of Hell* (Hodder & Stoughton, Auckland, 1991); Desmond Morton, *When Your Number's Up: The Canadian Soldier in the First World War* (Random House of Canada, Toronto, 1993) and 'The Supreme Penalty: Canadian Deaths by Firing Squad in the First World War', *Queen's Quarterly*, no. 79 (1972) pp. 345–52.

46   Pugsley, *On the Fringe of Hell*, p. 119.

47   Pugsley, *On the Fringe of Hell*.

48   Morton, *When Your Number's Up*, p. 251.

49   Morton, 'Deaths by Firing Squad', p. 350.

50   Morton, 'Deaths by Firing Squad', p. 346.

51   Pedroncini. *Les Mutineries*.

52   Pedroncini, *Les Mutineries*.

53   Pedroncini, *Les Mutineries*.

54   Leonard V. Smith, *Between Mutiny and Obedience* (Princeton University Press, Princeton, New Jersey, 1994).

55 The ratio of executions to death sentences passed is strikingly similar to that in the British Army. In both the French and British cases it is approximately 11%.

56 Leonard V. Smith, 'War and "Politics": The French Army Mutinies of 1917' in *War in History* 2 (2) (1995) p. 198.

57 Smith, 'War and 'Politics', p. 181.

58 Smith, 'War and 'Politics', p. 200.

59 Pedroncini, *Les Mutineries*, p. 204. Smith, *Between Mutiny and Obedience*, p. 210, concurs with Pedroncini's findings.

60 Smith, *Between Mutiny and Obedience*, p. 211.

61 David Englander, 'The French Soldier 1914–18' *French History*, vol. 1, no. 1 (1987) pp. 49–67.

62 Nicholas Offenstadt, *Les Fusillés de la Grande Guerre et la mémoire collective (1914–1999)* (Editions Odile Jacob, Paris, 1999), p. 36.

63 Christoph Jahr, *Gewöhnliche Soldaten. Desertion und Deserteure im deutschen und britischen Heer 1914–1918* (Vandenhoeck und Rupprecht, Göttingen, 1998).

64 Jahr made a detailed comparison of two German and two British Divisions on the Western Front.

65 Leonard V. Smith, 'The Disciplinary Dilemma of French Military Justice, September 1914 – April 1917: The Case of the 5e Division d'infanterie' *Journal of Military History*, no. 55 (January 1991) pp. 47–68.

66 Out of 3118 death sentences passed on soldiers in the British Army, 2004 were for desertion; 272 of these resulted in execution.

67 *The Darling Report*, p. 11.

68 Professor Sophie de Schaepdrijver, in her introduction at the Unquiet Graves International Conference at Ieper, Belgium, 19 May 2000. See also Sophie de Schaepdrijver, 'Theirs was Precisely to Reason Why: On Slaughter, Sacrifice, and Shootings at Dawn', *In Flanders Fields Magazine*, vol. 2 (July 2000), p. 18.

69 Robert Williams, unpublished MPhil thesis, University of Birmingham. In particular, see chapter 3 'Orders is Orders'.

70 I am most grateful to my Open University colleague, Chris Williams, for his help in formulating my own ideas about military crime along lines already developed in criminology. For a discussion of crime and its relationship to criminal statistics see, for example, Chris Williams, 'Counting crimes or counting people: some implications of mid-nineteenth century British police returns' *Crime, Histoire et Sociétés/Crime, History and Societies*, 2000, vol. 4, no. 2, pp. 77–93.

71 For an excellent discussion of the Australian 'problem' see Peter A. Pedersen, '"Thou Shalt Not Kill": the Death Penalty in the Australian Imperial Force 1914–18' in Gerard Oram (ed.), *Unquiet Graves: Comparative Perspectives on Military Executions during the Great War and Modern Memory* (Francis Boutle, London – forthcoming 2003).

72 Major A. F. Becke, *History of the Great War Based on Official Documents: Order of Battle of Divisions – Part 3B New Army Divisions* (HMSO, London, 1945), p. 58.

Chapter 1 'The administration of discipline by the English is very rigid'

1 David Englander, 'Mutinies and Military Morale' in Hew Strachan (ed.) *The Oxford Illustrated History of the First World War* (Oxford University Press, Oxford, 1998), p. 191. I would like to acknowledge the enormous debt I owe to Dr Englander, who supervised my research until his tragic death.

2   William Moore, *The Thin Yellow Line* (Leo Cooper, London, 1974); Julian Putkowski and Julian Sykes, *Shot at Dawn*, revised edition (Leo Cooper, London, 1992). Anthony Babington, *For the Sake of Example*, revised edition (Leo Cooper, London, 1993).

3   Gerard Oram, *Worthless Men: race, eugenics and the death penalty during the First World War* (Francis Boutle, London, 1998), pp. 51–6. In theatres far from home the British could afford to be less severe with deserters who in reality had nowhere to flee to and would inevitably return to their units after a short period of time. Disciplinary concerns in these far off places tended to focus on other matters such as men sleeping at their posts – an offence for which capital punishment was rarely carried out.

4   Figures quoted for the French army vary greatly – they are usually cited at anything between 300 and 700. However, for his recent study, Nicholas Offenstadt, who was granted unprecedented access to the military records, puts the figure at 600. See Nicholas Offenstadt, 'Enquête sur les fusillés de 1914–1918' *L'histoire*, no. 237 (November 1999), p. 65.

5   British figures are based on the War Office publication *Statistics of the Military Effort of the British Empire in the Great War 1914–1920* (HMSO, London, 1922), p. 648. However, this figure does not include native labourers, nor does it include Indian troops for whom no official records survive. A recent survey of the registers of courts martial kept by the army has cast doubt on the accuracy of the official number of condemnations which, it appears, have been slightly underestimated. See G. Oram, *Death Sentences Passed by Military Courts of the British Army 1914–1924* (Francis Boutle, London, 1998). The number of executions in the British army, including Indian troops, certainly exceeded 400 although by how many it is difficult to say.

6   Robert Blake (ed.), *The Private Papers of Douglas Haig 1914–1919* (Eyre & Spottiswoode, London, 1952), p. 234.

7   Edward M. Spiers, *The Late Victorian Army 1868–1902* (Manchester University Press, Manchester, 1992), p. 246.

8   Quoted in Babington, *For the Sake of Example*, p. 191.

9   Moore, *The Thin Yellow Line*, p. 167.

10 Erich Ludendorff, *Kriegführung und Politik*, (E. S. Mittler u. Sohn, Berlin, 1922), p. 149. See also Christoph Jahr, *Gewönliche Soldaten. Desertion und Deserteure im deutschen und britischen Heer 1914–1918* (Vandenhoek & Rupprecht, Göttingen, 1998), p. 330.

11 Christoph Jahr excepted, even in recent studies historians have concerned themselves with the consequences of the executions rather than the underlying causes. Gary Sheffield, 'Officer–Man Relations, Morale and Discipline in the British Army 1902–22', PhD thesis (King's College, London, 1994), analyses many of the army's traditions, but has largely avoided military law. The most recent publication on the subject of executions, Nicholas Offenstadt, *Les Fusillés de la Grande Guerre et la mémoire collective 1914–1999* (Editions Odile Jacob, Paris, 1999), as the title suggests, is concerned with processes that occurred after the executions rather than before them.

12 Peter Burroughs, 'Crime and Punishment in the British Army, 1815–1870' in *English Historical Review*, no. 386, vol. C (July 1985), pp. 545–71, argues that improved recruiting procedures after 1870 led to a reduction in the incidence of offences (p. 571).

13 *Manual of Military Law*, 1914 edition (HMSO, 1914), p. 7.

14 The British aversion to a standing army developed during the period of Charles I and Cromwell when princes such as Louis XIV were creating them. The aversion was again apparent during the Restoration, after the Glorious Revolution and again during the eighteenth century.

15 For an analysis of the debate surrounding military crime at this time see Burroughs, 'Crime and Punishment in the British Army'.

16 Spiers, *The Late Victorian Army*, p. 73.

17 Spiers, *The Late Victorian Army*, p. 74.

18 Howard Taylor, 'The Politics of the Rising Crime Statistics of England and Wales, 1914–1960' in *Crime, histoire et sociétés/Crime, History and Societies* 1998, no. 1, vol. 2, p. 6.

19 Martin J. Wiener, *Reconstructing the Criminal: Culture, Law and policy in England, 1830–1914* (Cambridge University Press, Cambridge, 1990), pp. 92–101.

20 Clive Emsley, *Crime and Society in England 1750–1900*, 2nd edition (Longman, London, 1996), pp. 276–7.

21 Seán McConville, *Next Only to Death: English Local Prisons 1860–1900* (Routledge, London, 1995), p. 246.

22 *The Report of the Courts-Martial Commission 1869*, hereafter referred to as either *The First Report* or *The Second Report*.

23 G. R. Rubin, 'Parliament, Prerogative and Military Law: who had legal authority over the army in the later nineteenth century?' *Legal History*, vol. 18, no. 1 (April 1997), pp. 45–84.

24 *The Second Report*, p. 216.

25 István Deák, *Beyond Nationalism: A Social and Political History of the Habsburg Officer Corps 1848–1918* (Oxford University Press, Oxford, 1992), p. 146.

26 *The Second Report*, pp. 211–23.

27 Rubin, 'Parliament, Prerogative and Military Law', p. 75.

28 *Parliamentary Debates* (Hansard), vol. CXXI, column 618.

29 *Parliamentary Debates* (Hansard), vol. CXXI, column 1177.

30 Report of Colonel W. Claremont in *The Second Report*, p. 222.

31 *The Second Report*, pp. 211–23.

32 *The Army Act 1881*, s. 51 allowed British soldiers to 'object, for any reasonable cause, to any member of the court, including the president . . .'.

33 Geoffrey Wawro, 'Morale in the Austro-Hungarian Army: The Evidence of Habsburg Army Campaign Reports and Allied Intelligence Officers', in Hugh Cecil and Peter Liddle (eds), *Facing Armageddon: The First World War Experienced* (Leo Cooper, London, 1997), p. 400. Also Benjamin Ziemann, 'Fahnenflucht im deutschen Heer 1914–1918', in *Militärgeschichtliche Mitteilungen* 55 (1996), pp. 93–130.

34 Report of Colonel Hope-Crealock in *The Second Report*, p. 212.

35 Report of Colonel Blane in *The Second Report*, p. 217.

36 Irina Davidian, 'The Russian Soldier's Morale from the Evidence of Tsarist Military Censorship', in Hugh Cecil and Peter Liddle (eds), *Facing Armageddon: The First World War Experienced* (Leo Cooper, London, 1997), p. 429.

37 John Gooch, 'Morale and Discipline in the Italian Army, 1915–1918' in Hugh Cecil and Peter Liddle (eds), *Facing Armageddon: The First World War Experienced* (Leo Cooper, London, 1997), p. 439.

38 *The Second Report*, p. 221.

39 Cited in Gooch, 'Morale and Discipline in the Italian Army', p. 436.

40 Englander, 'Mutinies and Military Morale', p. 192.

41   John Whittam, *The Politics of the Italian Army 1861–1918* (Croom Helm, London, 1977), pp. 194–95.
42   *The Second Report*, p. 223.
43   Robert Tombs, 'Crime and the Security of the State: The "Dangerous Classes" and Insurrection in Nineteenth-Century Paris', in V. A. C. Gattrell, Bruce Lenman and Geoffrey Parker (eds), *Crime and the Law: the Social History of Crime in Western Europe since 1500* (Europa Publications, London, 1980), p. 234.
44   Paddy Griffith, *Military Thought in the French Army 1815–51* (Manchester University Press, Manchester, 1989), p. 172.
45   Fewer than 8 per cent of British courts martial resulted in acquittal during the First World War. *Statistics of the Military Effort*, p. 645.
46   Burroughs, 'Crime and Punishment in the British Army', p. 560.
47   *The Second Report*, pp. 219–20.
48   Griffith, *Military Thought in the French Army*, pp. 86–7.
49   In 1830 it was estimated that the Irish made up approximately 42 per cent of the British army. This proportion steadily decreased up to 1914, but the number of Irishmen serving in the pre-Great War British army remained disproportionately high. See Terence Denman, 'The Catholic Irish Soldier in the First World War', *Irish Historical Studies*, vol. 27 (November 1991), pp. 352–65.
50   Cited in Burroughs, 'Crime and Punishment in the British Army', p. 548.
51   Parliamentary debate on the Army (Annual) Bill reported in *The Times*, 11 April 1912.
52   Soldiers could be sentenced to imprisonment with or without hard labour. The court could also sentence them to solitary confinement, again with or without hard labour. The figures presented here are an aggregate of all these categories. Only a minority (just over 600 in each year) underwent solitary confinement.
53   Compiled from statistics contained in the appendix to *The Second Report*, pp. 255–78.
54   *The Second Report*, p. x. See also Burroughs, 'Crime and Punishment in the British Army', p. 570.
55   Appendix to *The Second Report*, pp. 255–78.
56   Edward M. Spiers, *The Army and Society 1815–1914* (Longman, London, 1980) p. 37.
57   *The Second Report*, p. 212.
58   Deák, *Beyond Nationalism: A Social and Political History of the Habsburg Officer Corps*, p. 147.
59   Report on the Various Methods of Punishment adopted by Foreign Armies in the Field (1879), PRO WO32/6045, pp. 2–3. Hereafter referred to as the Ellice Report.
60   The Ellice Report, p. 5.
61   *The First Report*, p. viii.
62   *The First Report*, pp. ix–x.
63   *Mutiny Act*, Section 15.
64   *Mutiny Act*, Section 23.
65   *Mutiny Act*, Section 22.
66   *Mutiny Act*, Section 24.
67   *Mutiny Act*, Section 8.
68   *The Handbook of the German Army in War, January 1917* (EP Publishing, Wakefield, 1973) pp. 30–7. Also, *Militärstrafgesetzbuch für das Deutsche Reich vom 20. Juni 1872* (Berlin, 1912).
69   The Ellice Report, p. 5. The 12 capital offences listed by Ellice are: treason, unjustifiable surrender, repeated desertion, instigating a conspiracy to desert, deserting

a post in the presence of the enemy, cowardice, disobedience, assaulting a superior, instigating a mutiny, participating in a mutiny, plundering (only if accom-
panied by killing) and breach of parole by POWs.

70 David Englander, 'Manpower in the British Army, 1914–1918', in Gerard Canini
(ed.), *Les Fronts Invisibles* (Presse Universitaires de Nancy, 1984), pp. 93–102.
71 Ellice Report, p. 2.
72 Ellice Report, p. 2.
73 The 'Ansell–Crowder dispute' lingered long after the war, taking on an increasingly personal and public face. See Jonathon Lurie, *Arming Military Justice, Volume
1, The Origins of the United States Court of Military Appeals, 1775–1950* (Princeton
University Press, Princeton, New Jersey, 1992). Also Gerard Oram, ' "The greatest
efficiency": British and American military law 1866–1918' in B. Godfrey, C.
Emsley and G. Dunstall (eds) *Comparative Histories of Crime* (Willan Publishing,
Cullompton, Devon – forthcoming).
74 David A. Schleuter, 'The Court-Martial: An Historical Survey', *Military Law Review*,
vol. 87 (1980), p.154.
75 Gerald B. Hurst, 'The Administration of Military Law', *Contemporary Review*, vol.
CXV (1919), p. 323.
76 There were 895 condemnations in the British army during 1916 and a further 904
in 1917 – equivalent to a monthly average of 75.
77 *Army Discipline and Regulation (Annual) Act 1881.*
78 Draft Rules as to Summary Punishments Proposed to be made by the Secretary of
State under Section 4 of the Army Discipline and Regulation (Annual) Bill
1881–2.
79 McConville, *Next Only to Death*, p. 148.
80 Oram, *Death Sentences*, p. 15.
81 Captain Francis F. Grierson, *The A.B.C. of Military Law: a concise guide for the use
of officers, NCOs and men* (T. Fisher Unwin, London, 1916), p. 52.
82 Army Act 1881, Section 12.1 as published in *The Public General Acts passed in the
forty-fourth and forty-fifth years of the reign of Her Majesty Queen Victoria* (Eyre &
Spottiswoode, London, 1881), p. 209.
83 Militärstrafgesetzbuch für das Deutsche Reich von 20. Juni 1872 (Berlin, 1912).
84 *Parliamentary Debates* (Hansard), vol. XXXVI, column 1286. Also reported in *The
Times* (11 April 1912).
85 *Parliamentary Debates* (Hansard), vol. XXXVI, column 1286. Also reported in *The
Times* (11 April 1912).
86 Figures based on comparative tables in Richard Evans, *Rituals of Retribution,
Capital Punishment in Germany 1600–1987* (Oxford University Press, Oxford,
1996), statistical appendix. See also L. Radzinowicz and R. Hood, *A History of
English Criminal Law, Volume 5, The emergence of penal policy* (Clarendon Press,
London, 1986), pp. 671–7.
87 Cited in Radzinowicz and Hood, *A History of English Criminal Law*, p. 672.
88 J. F. Galliher, G. Ray and B. Cook, 'Abolition and Reinstatement of Capital
Punishment during the Progressive Era and Early 20th Century', *Journal of
Criminal Law and Criminology*, vol. 83, no. 3 (USA, 1992), pp. 538–78.
89 Roger Chadwick, *Bureaucratic Mercy: The Home Office and the Treatment of Capital
Cases in Victorian Britain* (Garland, New York, 1992), pp. 231–85.
90 During the First World War the President was slow to exercise this power and the
army commanders were unrestrained for the first year or so. However, the existence of this safeguard was an important feature of French military law. The same

type of power was conferred on the President of the USA where tighter control was taken of military justice following the execution of 13 black soldiers for a mutiny in Texas in 1917.

91   It should be noted that appeals remained problematic in both the Russian and Austrian armies, but were certainly not unprecedented.

92   *Manual of Military Law*, p. 6.

93   This feature of capital cases during the First World War is a recurrent theme in Babington, *For the Sake of Example*, and Putkowski and Sykes, *Shot at Dawn*.

94   Benjamin Ziemann, *Front und Heimat: Ländliche Kriegserfahrungen im südlichen Bayern 1914–1923* (Klartext, Leipzig, 1997), pp.106–20.

95   *Gesetz betreffend die Aenderung der Paragraphen 66, 70 Militärstrafgesetzbuch* (14 July 1914).

96   *Gesetz betreffend die Herabsetzung von Mindeststrafen* (25 April 1917).

97   Hew Strachan, 'Ludendorff and Germany's Defeat', in Cecil and Liddle (eds), *Facing Armageddon*, (Leo Cooper, London, 1998), pp. 55–6.

98   *Gesetz betr. Milderung im Militärstrafgesetzbuch* (25 July 1918).

99   Erich Ludendorff, *Kriegführung und Politik*, (E. S. Mittler u. Sohn, Berlin, 1922), p. 149. See also Christoph Jahr, *Gewönliche Soldaten. Desertion und Deserteure im deutschen und britischen Heer 1914–1918* (Vandenhoek & Rupprecht, Göttingen, 1998), p. 330.

100 I am most grateful to Dr Christoph Jahr for his assistance with this translation, but the responsibility for any error rests solely with me.

101 Gerald B. Hurst, 'The Administration of Military Law', cited cases where corps commanders required divisional commanders to account for acquittals as well as other instances of interference with the judicial process. See also Chapter 2.

102 Hew Strachan, *The Politics of the British Army* (Oxford University Press, Oxford, 1997). Chapter 5, pp. 92–117 is most relevant here, not only for its assessment of the Curragh incident, but for the analysis of the army's political activities during our period.

103 See G. Oram, *Death Sentences*, p. 14, and *Worthless Men*, p. 42.

104 Private Scotton, executed February 1915. PRO WO71/396.

Chapter 2   Military Discipline and the Nation at War

1   Commitment to the war effort was the fundamental feature of troop morale – the subject of the next chapter.

2   The two principal published works, Anthony Babington, *For the Sake of Example*, revised edition (Leo Cooper, London, 1993), and Julian Putkowski and Julian Sykes, *Shot at Dawn* (Leo Cooper, Barnsley, 1989) both focus on the issue of possible miscarriages of justice. Babington's premise that the troops were shot 'for the sake of example' is not disputed by Putkowski and Sykes. In my own previous work I have argued that the 'examples' were carefully selected: that Irish soldiers and those thought to be 'degenerate' made irresistible targets for demonstrations of military authority. Furthermore, I argued that a defence of 'shell-shock' was likely to have the exact opposite of the desired effect because it amounted to an admission that the soldier was of no further military value. See Gerard Oram, *Worthless Men: race, eugenics and the death penalty in the British army during the First World War* (Francis Boutle, London, 1998).

3   John Baynes, Morale: *A Study of Men and Courage* (Cassell, London, 1967), p. 181.

4   Tim Travers, *The Killing Ground: The British Army, The Western Front and the Emergence of Modern Warfare* 1900–1918 (Routledge, London, 1993).

5   Gary Sheffield, 'Officer–Man Relations, Morale and Discipline in the British Army 1902–1922', PhD thesis, King's College, London, 1994.

6   David Englander, 'Manpower in the British Army', in Gerard Canini (ed.), *Les Fronts Invisibles* (Presse Universitaire de Nancy, 1984), p. 102.

7   See Bernard Waites, 'Black Men in White Men's Wars: 1914–18, 1939–45', in Peter Liddle, John Bourne and Ian Whitehead (eds), *Lightning Strikes Twice*, forthcoming. I am grateful to Dr Waites for allowing me to see this paper prior to publication.

8   Cited in Baynes, *Morale*, p. 265.

9   Brigadier General F. P. Crozier, *A Brass Hat in No Man's Land* (Cedric Chivers, Bath, 1930), p. 38.

10 Thirty-seven executions had been carried out by the British army between 1865 and 1898 with a further four during the war in South Africa. See Edward Spiers, *The Late Victorian Army 1868–1902* (Manchester University Press, Manchester, 1992), p. 73. Also Gerard Oram, ' "A serious example is necessary": The British Army and the Death Penalty 1900–1918', forthcoming article.

11 John M. Bourne, *Britain and the Great War 1914–1918* (Edward Arnold, London, 1989), p. 217.

12 Baynes, *Morale*, p. 190.

13 Figures compiled from courts-martial registers. See also G. Oram, *Death Sentences*.

14 Peter J. Lynch, 'The Exploitation of Courage: Psychiatric Care in the British Army, 1914–1918', MPhil thesis, University College, London, 1977.

15 Craig Gibson, 'Relations between the British Army and the Civilian Populations on the Western Front, 1914–18', unpublished PhD thesis, University of Leeds, 1998.

16 See also Craig Gibson, ' "My Chief Source of Worry": An Assistant Provost Marshal's View of Relations between 2nd Canadian Division and Local Inhabitants on the Western Front, 1915–1917' *War in History*, 2000, vol. 7, no. 4, pp. 413–41.

17 *Statistics of the Military Effort*, p. 667.

18 Courts-Martial Registers 1914–1920, PRO WO213/1–34, WO86/62–90, WO90/6–8 & WO92/3–4.

19 Oram, *Death Sentences*, p. 15.

20 Oram, *Death Sentences*, p. 15.

21 Oram, *Death Sentences*.

22 It is, however, debatable whether Afrikaner settlers in the province of Transvaal could be considered loyal. Britain had annexed the territory in 1877 in the face of opposition led by Paul Kruger. Given the circumstances it is more likely that the occupying British forces regarded the Boer people as hostile. Only one year after this report was written the British were at war with the Boers in Transvaal: the First South African War, 1880–81.

23 William Russell, 'The Zulu War' in Roger Hudson (ed.), *William Russell Special Correspondent of The Times* (Folio Society, London, 1995), pp. 378–9.

24 The Act refers to them as civil offences when the acts to which they refer were actually covered by criminal law rather than civil law (contract, torts, etc). While it is appreciated that a differentiation between military and civilian law was sought by the legislators it is more satisfactory for the purpose of this study to remove the ambiguity and refer to offences against military or criminal law.

25 Case of Private Kirk, PRO WO71/403.

26 *Manual of Military Law* (HMSO, London, 1914).

27 Baynes, *Morale*, pp. 189–90.

28 Baynes, *Morale*, p. 189.

29 Graves, *Goodbye To All That* (Penguin, London, 1960), p. 147.

30 There appears to be a Celtic bias here. Those concerned were as follows: Private Stevenson, Scottish Rifles on 26 December 1914 (PRO WO213/3); Private Taggart, North Staffs. On 26 February 1915 (PRO WO213/3), Private Lynch, Inniskillings; on 1 July 1917 (PRO WO213/16), Private Bell, Highland Light Infantry on 17 September 1917 (PRO WO213/18). The first three cases occurred on the Western Front, the last one in Egypt.

31 *Statistics of the Military Effort*, p. 667.

32 See Putkowski and Sykes, *Shot at Dawn*, in particular the cases of Dale, Skone, Morgan, Price, Knight, Moore and Reid, all of whom it was alleged were intoxicated at the time of their offences. To this list we can add the names of Private Murray (PRO WO71/504) and Sapper Oyns (PRO WO71/613) who both killed other soldiers while drunk.

33 Unfortunately the surviving records are incomplete. What does survive, however, shows that at least sixteen cases involved the murder of fellow soldiers or labourers and at least nine cases involved the murder of civilians.

34 See papers of Captain Hardie, Imperial War Museum, 84/64/1, report dated May 1916.

35 Hardie papers, report dated October 1918.

36 See the comparative tables in the Statistical Appendix of Richard Evans, *Rituals of Retribution: Capital Punishment in Germany 1600–1987* (Oxford University Press, Oxford, 1996), p. 934.

37 PRO WO71/636.

38 All British and Dominion recruits totalled together. *Statistics of the Military Effort*, p. 363.

39 PRO WO71/676.

40 Privates Harris and Davids, PRO WO71/684 & 685.

41 PRO WO71/629.

42 See for example the comments of Tim Travers concerning the preparations for the Battle of the Somme. Travers, *The Killing Ground*, chapter 6, especially pp. 144–6.

43 Lord Moran, *The Anatomy of Courage*, 2nd edition (Constable, London, 1966), p. 163.

44 Peter Simkins, 'The Four Armies' in David Chandler and Ian Beckett (eds), *The Oxford History of the British Army* (Oxford University Press, Oxford, 1996), pp. 235–5.

45 Baynes, *Morale*, p. 193.

46 'Notes and Hints on Training' in Maxse Papers. IWM 69/53/13.

47 'Notes and Hints on Training' in Maxse Papers. IWM 69/53/13.

48 'Notes and Hints on Training' in Maxse Papers. IWM 69/53/13.

49 Fourth Army 'Tactical Notes', Rawlinson Papers, National Army Museum. See also Travers, *The Killing Ground*, pp. 144–6.

50 Gary Sheffield, 'Officer–Man Relations, Morale and Discipline in the British Army 1902–22', PhD thesis, King's College, London, 1994, p. 2.

51 G. Oram, *Worthless Men*, especially chapter 4.

52 Sheffield, 'Officer–Man Relations', pp. 51–3.

53 Colonel G. F. R. Henderson, *The Science of War: the Author's Essays from 1891–1903*, edited by Colonel Niell Malcolm (Longman, London, 1919), p. 173.

54 Report on Training of NCOs, PRO WO32/8386, pp. 15–16.

55 See, for example, T. H. E. Travers, 'Technology, Tactics and Morale: Jean de Bloch, the Boer War, and British Military Theory, 1900–1914', *Journal of Military History*, vol. 51 (June 1979), pp. 264–86.

56 Report of the Committee on Military Training of the Royal Army Medical Corps 1909, PRO WO32/6940, p. 5.

57 See Oram, *Death Sentences*, p. 14, and also Oram, *Worthless Men*.

58 Case of Rifleman James Crozier, who was executed for desertion on 22nd February 1916. PRO WO71/450.

59 G. Sheffield, 'Officer–Man Relations', p. 38.

60 Rawlinson papers. 'Notes on Operations between 14th September and 3rd October 1916', p. 13. NAM 5201–33–69.

61 Lord Moran, *The Anatomy of Courage*, 2nd edition (Constable, London, 1966), p. 171.

62 For a more detailed discussion of this see G. Oram, *Worthless Men*, pp. 37–41.

63 Cecil Lewis, *Saggitarius Rising* (Folio Society, London, 1998), p. 86.

64 Siegfried Sassoon, *The Complete Memoirs of George Sherston* (Faber, London, 1937), p. 257.

65 Babington, *For the Sake of Example*, and Putkowski and Sykes, *Shot at Dawn*, both follow this line of argument. So too does Sheffield, 'Officer-Man Relations', p. 70.

66 See Oram, *Worthless Men*, pp. 84–101.

67 PRO WO71/531.

68 There are some notable exceptions to these trends, but each can be explained. Analysis of this aspect of military executions is beyond the scope of this thesis – the author's own assessment can be found elsewhere – but it is important to note the existence of a remarkable consistency in confirmation of death sentences. See Oram, *Worthless Men*.

69 Major-General Sir Wyndham Childs, *Episodes and Reflections* (Cassell, London, 1930), p. 135.

70 *Statistics of the Military Effort of the British Empire During the Great War* 1914–1920 (War Office, London, 1922), p. 643.

71 Wroughton had entered the army in 1893 and was commissioned in the Royal Sussex Regiment and served in the South African War. A Staff Captain at the outbreak of war, he was appointed Deputy-Adjutant-General and Assistant-Quartermaster-General in 1914 and headed the Personal Services Branch from February 1916 with the nominal rank of Brigadier General; a rank made substantive on 10 November 1917.

72 Maxse Papers, IWM 69/53/6.

73 Oram, *Death Sentences*, p. 15.

74 Maxse Papers, IWM 69/53/6.

75 PRO WO213/7.

76 Gerald B. Hurst, 'The Administration of Military Law', *Contemporary Review*, vol. CXV (1919), p. 324.

77 Hurst, 'The Administration of Military Law', p. 325.

78 *The Darling Report*, p. 8.

79 *The Darling Report*, p. 8.

80 PRO WO71/401.

81 PRO WO71/401.

82 PRO WO71/402.

83 PRO WO71/402.

84   PRO WO71/403.
85   PRO WO71/403.
86   PRO WO71/403.
87   Oram, *Worthless Men*, pp. 84–101.
88   Lord Moran, *The Anatomy of Courage*, p. 174.
89   Peter J. Lynch, 'The Exploitation of Courage: Psychiatric Care in the British Army, 1914–1918', MPhil thesis, University College, London (July 1977), pp. 7–8.
90   John Bourne, 'The British Working Man in Arms', in Peter Liddle and Hugh Cecil (eds), *Facing Armageddon: The First World War Experienced* (Leo Cooper, London, 1997), pp. 336–52.
91   John Bourne, 'The British Working Man in Arms', p. 345.
92   See, for example, Doris Kaufmann 'Science as Cultural Practice: Psychiatry in the First World War and Weimar Germany', *Journal of Contemporary History*, vol. 34 (1), pp. 125–44.
93   Martin Stone, 'Shellshock and the psychologists' in W. F. Bynum, R. Porter and M. Shepherd (eds), *The Anatomy of Madness*, vol. II (Tavistock Press, London, 1985), pp. 242–71.
94   Lynch, 'The Exploitation of Courage', p. 234.
95   George Mosse, 'Shell-shock as a Social Disease', *Journal of Contemporary History*, vol. 35 (1) (2000), pp. 101–8.
96   Joanna Bourke, 'Effeminacy, Ethnicity and the End of Trauma: the Suffering of "Shell-shocked" Men in Great Britain and Ireland, 1914–39', *Journal of Contemporary History*, vol. 35 (1) (2000), p. 59.
97   Bourke, 'Effeminacy, Ethnicity and the End of Trauma', p. 62.
98   Mosse, 'Shell-shock as a Social Disease', pp. 102–3.
99   Oram, *Worthless Men*.
100 Peter J. Leese, 'A Social and Cultural History of Shellshock, with particular reference to the experience of British soldiers during and after the Great War', PhD thesis, Open University (1989).
101 *Southborough Report*, p. 13.
102 *Southborough Report*, p. 39.
103 PRO WO93/49.
104 PRO WO93/49.
105 Case of Private Arthur Earp, 1/5 Royal Warwickshire Regiment. PRO WO71/485.
106 Moran, *The Anatomy of Courage*, p. 177.
107 W. H. R. Rivers, *Instinct and the Unconscious* (Cambridge University Press, Cambridge, 1922), especially chapter IV 'Suppression and Inhibition'.
108 Colonel G. F. R. Henderson, *The Science of War: the author's essays from 1891 to 1903*, edited by Colonel Niell Malcolm (Longman's, Green and Co., London, 1919), p. 189.
109 *Southborough Report*. In particular see footnote inserted in support of Lord Gort's assertion that there was practically no shell-shock in first-class divisions (p. 50), a view clearly shared by Lord Moran.
110 PRO WO71/1027.
111 Poole's case is discussed in more detail in Chapter 5.
112 PRO WO71/530.
113 PRO WO71/530.
114 See evidence of Squadron Leader W. Tyrell, Royal Air Force Medical Service. *Southborough Report*, p. 35.
115 *The Times*, 1 October 1917 (p. 8) and 20 February 1918 (p. 8).

116 'Lord Knutsford's Appeal' in *The Times*, 4 November 1914, p. 5.
117 Martin Stone, 'Shellshock and the Psychologists', p. 256.
118 Siegmund Freud, 'Memorandum on the Electrical Treatment of War Neurotics', in *The Standard Edition*, vol. XVII (1920), p. 214
119 Sir Martin Conway, *The Crowd in Peace and War* (Longmans, Green and Co., London, 1915), p. 303.
120 Arthur Marwick, *The Deluge: British Society and the First World War*, 2nd edition (Macmillan – now Palgrave Macmillan, Basingstoke, 1991), p. 102.
121 David Englander, 'Military Intelligence and the defence of the realm: the surveillance of soldiers and civilians during the First World War', *Bulletin of the Society for the Study of Labour History*, vol. 52, no. 1 (1987), p. 25.
122 Conway, *The Crowd in Peace and War*, p. 299.
123 Englander, 'Military Intelligence and defence of the realm', p. 24.
124 Marwick, *The Deluge*, pp. 243–50.
125 Marwick, *The Deluge*, p. 246.
126 Findings of Appeal Tribunal No. 12, convened at Fernie, B. C., Canada on 26 January 1918. British Columbia Records Office, Victoria, B. C., Canada, ref. 274686–2 (hereafter referred to as Fernie Miners' Judgement), pp. 2–3.
127 Appeal by 49 miners at Fernie, pp. 3–4.
128 Marwick, *The Deluge*, p. 122.
129 Oram, *Death Sentences*, pp. 35–6.
130 PRO WO71/387–441.
131 Childs, *Episodes and Reflections*, p. 137.
132 *Statistics of the Military Effort*, p. 670.
133 Private Brown, executed December 1914. PRO WO71/390.
134 Private Scotton, executed February 1915. PRO WO71/396.
135 Private Burden, executed July 1915. PRO WO71/424.
136 John Bourne, 'The British Working Man in Arms', p. 345.
137 Childs, p.145.

Chapter 3 Military Theory and Redefining Troop Morale

1 G. Sheffield, 'Officer–Man Relations: Morale and Discipline in the British Army 1902–1922', PhD thesis, King's College, London, 1994', p. 63.
2 J. G. Fuller, *Troop Morale and Popular Culture in the British and Dominion Armies 1914–1918* (Clarendon Press, Oxford, 1990), p. 21.
3 Carl von Clausewitz, *On War*, edited by Anotol Rapaport (Penguin, London, 1982), p. 252.
4 Colonel G. F. R. Henderson, *The Science of War: Author's Essays from 1891 to 1903*, edited by Colonel N. Malcolm (Longmans, Green and Co., London, 1919), p. 101.
5 *The Southborough Report*, p. 29.
6 Henderson, *The Science of War*, p. 189.
7 Niall Ferguson, *The Pity of War* (Allen Lane, London, 1998), pp. 342–56.
8 Clausewitz, *On War*, p. 253.
9 Clausewitz, *On War*, p. 262.
10 Letter to Marshal Berthier, 10 April 1806, in J. M. Thompson (ed.), *Napoleon's Letters* (Prion, London, 1998), p. 122.
11 Clausewitz, *On War*, p. 253.

12   *Infantry Training* (HMSO, 1914), p. 12.
13   Thomas R. Metcalf, *Ideologies of the Raj* (Cambridge University Press, Cambridge, 1997).
14   Cited in Metcalf, *Ideologies of the Raj*, pp. 228–9.
15   *The Times* (10 April 1912).
16   Henderson, *The Science of War*, p. 412.
17   Henderson, *The Science of War*, p. 379.
18   Niccolò Machiavelli, *The Prince* (Penguin Books, London, 1981), pp. 79–87.
19   *The Southborough Report*, p. 27.
20   George Mosse, 'Shell-shock as a Social Disease', *Journal of Contemporary History*, vol. 35 (1), (2000), p. 105.
21   Henderson, *The Science of War*, p. 243.
22   *Napoleon's Letters*, p. 219.
23   *Napoleon's Letters*, p. 280.
24   Sheffield, 'Officer–Man Relations', p. 68.
25   Cited in T. H. E. Travers, *The Killing Ground The British Army, the Western Front and the Emergence of Modern Warfare, 1900–1918* (Routledge, London, 1990), p. 20.
26   Travers, *The Killing Ground*, p. 17 and pp. 127–46.
27   The case of 35th Division; see extended discussion in Chapter 4. See also, G. Oram, ' "A serious example is necessary": the Death Penalty and the British Army 1900–1918', forthcoming article.
28   A most extreme case of this occurred in December 1916 when the commander of 8th Division and his staff officer were sacked in response to concerns of poor discipline.
29   More than 6500 Belgian and French civilians were executed by German firing squads in the first months of the war. In most cases this appears to have been a case of an over-reaction by the army units concerned: a 'great fear' of a *franc-tireur*-type resistance had taken hold in the invading forces. John Horne, 'German War-Crimes in Belgium and France, August–October 1914', conference paper given at the Unquiet Graves Conference at Ieper, Belgium on 20 May 2000.
30   Denis Winter, *Haig's Command: A Reassessment* (Penguin, London, 1992), pp. 164–5.
31   Jay M. Winter, 'Propaganda and the Mobilization of Consent', in Hew Strachan (ed.), *The Oxford Illustrated History of the First World War* (Oxford University Press, Oxford, 1998), p. 216.
32   Brigadier General F. P. Crozier, *A Brass Hat in No Man's Land* (Cedric Chivers, Bath, 1930), p. 42.
33   Winter, 'Propaganda and Mobilization of Consent', pp. 219–20.
34   Henderson, *The Science of War*, pp. 173–4.
35   Henderson, *The Science of War*, p. 174.
36   Colonel F. N. Maude, 'Introduction' to Clausewitz, *On War* (Penguin, London, 1982), p. 89.
37   Lord Moran, *The Anatomy of Courage*, 2nd edition (Constable, London, 1966), p. 166.
38   John Baynes, *Morale: A Study of Men and Courage* (Cassell, London, 1967), p. 253.
39   Moran, *The Anatomy of Courage*, p. 175.
40   Moran, *The Anatomy of Courage*, p. 178.
41   Moran, *The Anatomy of Courage*, p. 166.
42   Sheffield, 'Officer–Man Relations', p. 65.

43 Brigadier General Edmonds in a letter to G. C. Wynne, 17 February 1944. Cited by Travers, *The Killing Ground*, p, 20. This account should, however, be treated with caution. Not only was there some antipathy between Edmonds and Gough, but he also suggests that two executions of officers were carried out in 1918. This is patently untrue; the only officers executed for military offences were both shot in early 1917.

44 Crozier, *A Brass Hat in No Man's Land*, p. 47.

45 Henderson, *The Science of War*, p. 412.

46 Lieutenant-Colonel S. V. Riddell, Memorandum on Field Punishments, 9 November 1915 (p. 2) in Maxse Papers, IWM, 69/53/6, File 14/1.

47 *Instructions for the training of Platoons for Offensive Action* Part III, ss (d), 2000 reprint (The Military Press, Milton Keynes, 2000), p. 99.

48 Fuller, *Troop Morale and Popular Culture*, p. 175.

49 Brigadier General John Charteris, *At G. H. Q.* (Cassell, London, 1931), p. 214. Charteris was another British general who was fond of quoting Napoleon; see pp. 237 and 274.

50 It appears that Charteris and Lieutenant-General Sir George MacDonogh, Director of Military Intelligence, did not agree about the state of German morale during 1916–17. See Travers, *The Killing Ground*, pp. 115–18.

51 Charteris, *At G.H.Q.*, p. 260.

52 See, for instance, Travers, *The Killing Ground*, p. 96.

53 David R. Woodward (ed.), *The Military Correspondence of Field-Marshal Sir William Robertson, Chief Imperial General Staff December 1915–February 1918* (Army Records Society, The Bodley Head, Chatham, 1989), p. 265.

54 Letter from Robertson to General Sir Henry Wilson, 16 December 1917 in Woodward (ed.), *The Military Correspondence of Field Marshal Sir William Robertson*, p. 268.

55 Hew Strachan, 'The Morale of the German Army, 1917–18' in Peter Liddle and Hugh Cecil (eds), *Facing Armageddon: The First World War Experienced* (Leo Cooper, London, 1997), pp. 386–7.

56 John Gooch, 'Morale and Discipline in the Italian Army, 1915–1918' in Hugh Cecil and Peter Liddle (eds), *Facing Armageddon: The First World War Experienced* (Leo Cooper, London, 1997), p. 435.

57 Major-General Sir Wyndham Childs, *Episodes and Reflections* (Cassell, London, 1930), p. 139.

58 John Bourne, 'The British Working Man in Arms' in Hugh Cecil and Peter Liddle (eds), *Facing Armageddon: The First World War Experienced* (Leo Cooper, London, 1997), p. 340.

59 G. Oram, *Death Sentences*, p. 14, and *Worthless Men*, pp. 37–51.

60 Fuller, *Troop Morale and Popular Culture*.

61 Rudyard Kipling, *The New Army in Training* (Macmillan, London, 1915), p. 62.

62 Clausewitz, *On War*, p. 258.

63 Sheffield, 'Officer–Man Relations', p. 65.

64 Sheffield, 'Officer–Man Relations', p. 66.

65 Sheffield, 'Officer–Man Relations', p. 68.

66 Clausewitz, *On War*, p. 257.

67 Travers, *The Killing Ground*, p. 55.

68 Winston S. Churchill, *The Boer War: London to Ladysmith via Pretoria and Ian Hamilton's March* (Leo Cooper, London, 1989), p. 110.

69 Gary Sheffield, ' "A very good type of Londoner and a very good type of colonial"': Officer–Man Relations and Discipline in the 22nd Royal Fusiliers,

1914–18', in Brian Bond et al, *'Look to Your Front': Studies in the First World War* (Spellmount, Staplehurst, 1999), p. 145.

70   *Southborough Report*, p. 21.

71   Nick Bosanquet, 'Health Systems in Khaki: The British and American Medical Experience' in Hugh Cecil and Peter Liddle (eds), *Facing Armageddon: The First World War Experienced* (Leo Cooper, London, 1997), p. 457.

72   See for example the execution of three men of the Durham Light Infantry whose unit 'has not done well in the fighting line', PRO WO71/534.

73   War Diary – Director-General Medical Services, 3rd Army, PRO WO95/381.

74   Crozier, *A Brass Hat in No Man's Land*, p. 77.

75   R. Graves, *Goodbye to All That* (Penguin, London, 1960), pp. 144–5.

76   Maxse papers. IWM 69/53/13.

77   Fuller, *Troop-Morale and Popular Culture*, p. 175 and pp. 7–20. Both entertainments and sport often reflected humbler preferences, see below.

78   *The Fifth Glo'ster Gazette 1915–1919: A Trench Magazine of the First World War* (Sutton, Stroud, 1993), pp. 131, 153–5 and 169–73.

79   S. Hynes, *The Soldiers' Tale: Bearing Witness to Modern War* (Pimlico, London, 1998), p. 37.

80   *The Fifth Glo'ster Gazette*, p. 234.

81   *The Fifth Glo'ster Gazette*, p. 176.

82   Maxse papers. IWM 69/53/13.

83   Maxse papers. IWM 69/53/6.

84   *The Fifth Glo'ster Gazette*. Almost every edition featured a list of awards and promotions.

85   Jeffrey, K. (ed.), *The Military Correspondence of Field Marshal Sir Henry Wilson 1918–1922* (Bodley Head, London, 1985), p. 42.

86   J. G. Fuller, *Troop Morale and Popular Culture*, p. 175.

87   Maxse papers. IWM 69/53/13.

88   Fuller, *Troop Morale and Popular Culture*, pp. 175–80.

89   Guy Pedroncini, *Les Mutineries de 1917* (PUF, Paris, 1968). Leonard Smith, *Between Mutiny and Obedience: The Case of the French Fifth Infantry Division in World War I* (Princeton, 1994); David Englander, 'The French Soldier, 1914–18', *French History*, Vol. 1, No. 1, pp. 49–67.

90   Papers of Captain Hardie. IWM 84/64/1. Report on morale, November 1916, p. 4.

91   Papers of Captain Hardie. IWM 84/64/1.

92   Papers of Captain Hardie. IWM 84/64/1. Report on morale, November 1916, p. 3.

93   Papers of Captain Hardie. IWM 84/64/1. Report on morale, January 1917, p. 5.

94   Letter of Private E. C. Perham, 22nd London Regiment, dated 8 October 1915. Private collection.

95   Letter of Private E. C. Perham, 22nd London Regiment, dated 6 July 1916. Private collection. Private Perham was killed in action eleven days after writing this letter.

96   Papers of Captain Hardie. IWM 84/64/1. Report on morale for period February to July 1918, p. 1.

97   According to Hew Strachan, 'Morale and Discipline in the German Army, 1917–18', 'One of the principal grouses of the German soldier was food' (p. 390). It appears that the realisation of impending defeat was also a major factor in the collapse in German morale in the autumn of 1918. See Benjamin Ziemann, 'Fahnenflucht im deutschen Heer 1914–1918' in *Militärgeschichtliche Mitteilungen* 55 (1996), pp. 93–130.

98 Papers of Captain Hardie. IWM 84/64/1. Report on morale for period December 1917 to February 1918, p. 3. See also Chapter 5, below.

99 Ferguson, *The Pity of War*, p. 350.

100 PRO WO71/488. The case of Private Nelson is particularly tragic. His father was a prisoner of war in Germany and Private Nelson was about to embark for the Western Front when he was given news of his mother's death, leaving the young soldier the sole provider for his young siblings. His neighbour had arranged to care for his sister, but had clearly found the task too difficult and wrote to Nelson informing him of the termination of the arrangements.

101 Case of Private Phillips, PRO WO71/430.

102 PRO WO71/526.

103 PRO WO71/526.

104 Simkins, 'The Four Armies', in Chandler, D. (ed.), *The Oxford History of the British Army* (Oxford University Press, Oxford, 1994), pp. 235–55.

105 Baynes, *Morale,* p. 190.

106 Moran, *The Anatomy of Courage,* p. 177.

107 Moran, *The Anatomy of Courage,* p. 178.

108 Moran, *The Anatomy of Courage,* p. 177.

109 Diary of A. H. Roberts. IWM.

110 Diary of unidentified soldier. IWM, Misc. 550.

111 This is one of the central themes identified by Nicolas Offenstadt in *Les Fusillés de la Grande Guerre et la mémoire collective (1914–1999)* (Editions Odile Jacob, Paris, 1999).

112 Thurtle, *Shootings at Dawn,* p. 4.

113 Leading Seaman T. MacMillan, unpublished diary, pp. 169–70. IWM.

114 Thurtle, *Shootings at Dawn.*

115 John McCauley, 'A Manxman's Diary', p. 29. IWM 97/10/1.

116 McCauley, 'A Manxman's Diary', p. 32.

117 Putkowski and Sykes, *Shot at Dawn,* p. 59.

118 Babington, *For the Sake of Example,* pp. 88–9. Putkowski and Sykes, *Shot at Dawn,* pp. 126–7.

119 Private John Braithwaite, an Australian serving with the New Zealand Rifle Brigade, was executed on 29 October 1916. PRO WO790/6.

120 Note on the Morale of British troops in France as disclosed by the censorship. PRO CAB24/26.

121 Papers of Captain Hardie. IWM 84/64/1. Report on morale, dated 25 August 1917, p. 1.

122 Note on morale of the British Armies in France as gathered from censorship (18th December 1917). PRO CAB24/36.

123 Papers of Captain Hardie. IWM 84/64/1. Report for period December 1917 to February 1918, p. 3.

124 Papers of Captain Hardie. IWM 84/64/1. Report dated November 1916, p. 6.

125 Siegfried Sassoon, *The War Poems* (Faber & Faber, London, 1983), p. 148.

126 Papers of Captain Hardie. IWM 84/64/1. Report for period February to July 1918, p. 1.

127 Papers of Captain Hardie. IWM 84/64/1. Report for period February to July 1918, p. 4.

128 Papers of Captain Hardie. IWM 84/64/1. Report dated January 1917, pp. 6–7.

129 Papers of Captain Hardie. IWM 84/64/1. Report dated May 1917, p. 1.

130 Papers of Captain Hardie. IWM 84/64/1. Report dated 25 August 1917, p. 1.

131 Note on morale of the British Armies in France as gathered from censorship (18 December 1917). PRO CAB24/36.
132 Note on morale of the British Armies in France as gathered from censorship (18 December 1917). PRO CAB24/36.
133 Papers of Captain Hardie. IWM 84/64/1. Report dated 25 August 1917, p. 1.
134 See Oram, *Death Sentences*.
135 Benjamin Ziemann, 'Fahnenflucht im deutschen Heer 1914–1918', *Militär-geschichtliche Mitteilungen* 55 (1996), pp. 93–130.
136 Papers of Captain Hardie. IWM 84/64/1. Report dated January 1917, pp. 6–7.
137 Papers of Captain Hardie. IWM 84/64/1. Report dated 20 July 1918.

Chapter 4 *Pour encourager les autres*

1 For example, Brigadier-General F. P. Crozier, *A Brass Hat in No Man's Land* (Cedric Chivers, Bath, 1930), p. 204, recalls ordering the machine-gunning of fleeing Portuguese troops during 1918. See also G. Oram, *Worthless Men: race, eugenics and the death penalty in the British army during the First World War* (Francis Boutle, London, 1998), p. 33.
2 On 15 February 1915 Private Morgan and Lance Corporal Price, 2 Welsh Regiment, were executed for murder, but their names were not recorded in the courts-martial registers.
3 G. Sheffield, 'Officer–Man Relations, Morale and Discipline in the British Army 1902–22', PhD thesis (King's College, London, 1994).
4 Private Whittle, 5 Dragoon Guards was sentenced to death by court martial on 23 August 1914 for sleeping at his post. His sentence was commuted to two years' hard labour. PRO WO213/2.
5 Robert Blake, *The Private Papers of Douglas Haig 1914–1919* (Eyre & Spottiswoode, London, 1952), p. 77.
6 Major A. F. Becke, *Order of Battle, Part 1: The Regular British Divisions* (HMSO, London, 1945).
7 See graph in Oram, *Death Sentences*, p. 14, or *Worthless Men*, p. 38.
8 If 43rd and 44th Divisions are removed from the calculation, the average number of condemnations in Territorial Force Divisions rises slightly to 24 – still significantly fewer than in Regular units.
9 Alan Moorhead, *Gallipoli* (Wordsworth Editions, Ware, 1997), p. 138.
10 For ease of reference and for the sake of completeness I have included Royal Naval Division as a New Army formation.
11 Maxse papers, IWM 11/1.
12 Quoted in T. Travers, *The Killing Ground: The British Army and the Emergence of Modern Warfare 1900–1918* (Routledge, London, 1990), p. 51.
13 Curiously, the divisional history, Lieutenant-Colonel H. M. Davson, *History of the 35th Division* (Cassell, London, 1926) virtually ignores this unprecedented phenomenon.
14 Crozier, *A Brass Hat in No Man's Land*, p. 204.
15 See remarks made in the case of Rifleman James Crozier, PRO WO71/450, also discussed below.
16 Crozier's unit, 9th Royal Irish Rifles had more than its share of condemnations – almost half the division's total until the end of 1916.
17 This is one of the themes of Travers, *The Killing Ground*.

18 It is worth noting here that by the summer of 1917 second line Territorial Force units were posted to the Western Front to join the first line units, most of which had been there since 1915, and unlike the Somme offensive many second line Territorials were deployed at Third Ypres.

19 Case of Rifleman James Crozier, PRO WO71/450. See also Chapter 2 above.

20 Travers, *The Killing Ground*, p. 146.

21 Maxse papers, IWM 69/53/11 (Box 11/1).

22 Maxse papers, IWM 69/53/11 (Box 11/1).

23 Case of Private Scotton, PRO WO71/396.

24 Case of Private Kershaw, PRO WO71/410.

25 Case of Private Reid, PRO WO71/406.

26 See Chapter 1.

27 James Brent Wilson, 'Morale and Discipline in the British Expeditionary Force 1914–1918', MA thesis (University of New Brunswick, 1978).

28 Oram, *Death Sentences*, p. 14, and *Worthless Men*, p. 38.

29 WO95/2683 and 2686.

30 WO71/490.

31 Wilson, 'Discipline and Morale', p. 341.

32 PRO WO213/12.

33 PRO WO71/516.

34 PRO WO71/516.

35 PRO WO71/516.

36 PRO WO71/516.

37 Putkowski and Sykes, *Shot at Dawn*, p. 138.

38 PRO WO95/2176.

39 PRO WO71/525.

40 Hardie papers. Report re troop morale for November 1916, p. 4.

41 PRO WO71/525.

42 PRO WO71/526.

43 Hardie papers. Report re troop morale for November 1916, p. 3.

44 PRO WO71/525.

45 PRO WO71/526.

46 Maxse papers, file 14/1.

47 The war diary shows that the battalion was being moved steadily forward from 1 until 13 July in readiness for the assault on Trônes Wood on 14 July.

48 Hurst, 'The Administration of Military Law', *Contemporary Review*, vol. CXV (1919), p. 325.

49 Hurst, 'The Administration of Military Law', p. 325.

50 PRO WO95/2468.

51 A more complete discussion of this case can be found in Oram, *Worthless Men*, pp. 89–95.

52 PRO WO95/2468.

53 Remarks of commander of 106th Infantry Brigade. PRO WO71/534.

54 PRO WO95/2468.

55 Blake, *The Private Papers of Douglas Haig*, p. 77.

56 PRO WO95/2468.

57 Davson, *The History of the 35th Division*, p. 48.

58 Wilson, 'Morale and Discipline', p. 219.

59 Hardie papers. Report re troop morale for November 1916, p. 6.

60 Niall Ferguson, *The Pity of War* (Allen Lane, London, 1998), pp. 350–7.

61 Ferguson, *The Pity of War*. Paul Fussell, *The Great War and Modern Memory* (Oxford University Press, Oxford, 1975).
62 Sheffield, 'Officer–Man Relations', p. 62.

Chapter 5 Discipline and Morale in the Three Armies

1 Peter Simkins, 'The Four Armies' in Chandler, D. (ed.), *The Oxford History of the British Army* (Oxford University Press, Oxford, 1996), pp. 235–55, identifies four armies: the Regular army; the Territorial Force; the 'Kitchener' volunteers and the conscript army. To this we might add the Dominion and Colonial forces. For our purposes, however, there were three armies – Regular, Territorial and New Army – each characterised by different approaches to discipline.
2 Major A. F. Becke, *History of the Great War based on Official Documents: Order of Battle of Divisions, Part I – The Regular British Divisions* (HMSO, London, 1935), Appendix 1, pp. 126–7.
3 See the comparative tables in G. Oram, *Death Sentences passed by Military Courts of the British Army 1914–1924* (Francis Boutle, London, 1998), p. 15, and *Worthless Men: race, eugenics and the death penalty in the British Army during the First World War* (Francis Boutle, London, 1998), p. 120, a synopsis of which is as follows:

Condemnations for desertion: 2004 (272 executions)
                    cowardice: 213 (14 executions)
                    sleeping on post: 449 (2 executions)
                    quitting post: 82 (6 executions)
4 Although there were 449 condemnations for sleeping on post only two were carried out. I have argued elsewhere that courts martial did not expect the commander-in-chief to confirm these sentences and so passed them all too frequently in order to enforce their authority on the ranks. However, after the execution of two men in Mesopotamia for this particular offence, courts martial could not afford to regard a condemnation with such impunity. Consequently the number of condemnations for sleeping on post fell dramatically.
5 See, for example, Routine Orders for 4th Division issued on 16 December 1914. PRO WO95/1449.
6 Some trends in 23rd Division that are not typical of other New Army formations will be discussed later.
7 Gary Sheffield, 'Officer–Man Relations: Morale and Discipline in the British Army 1902–22', PhD thesis, King's College, London (1994).
8 PRO WO95/ 1664 – battalion war diary, 2nd Royal Warwickshire Regiment.
9 Cases of Privates Hargreaves, Jones, Parnell (all 2nd Warwickshires), Carter and Clark (both 2nd Bedfordshires). PRO WO213/3.
10 PRO WO95/1664.
11 PRO WO95/ 1658 – war diary, 2nd Bedfordshire Regiment.
12 PRO WO71/398.
13 PRO 213/3.
14 PRO WO71/404.
15 IWM – Misc. 550. Diary of unknown British soldier discovered in a captured German trench at Hulloch by Captain N. J. Sievers on 17 November 1915 – quoted in full in Chapter 3.
16 PRO 95/1655 – battalion war diary, 2nd Border Regiment.

17   PRO 95/1655 – battalion war diary, 2nd Border Regiment.
18   Privates Abraham Acton and James Smith were each awarded the Victoria Cross for rescuing wounded comrades under heavy fire from the enemy.
19   PRO WO71/406.
20   Becke, *Order of Battle, Part I*, p. 82.
21   PRO WO71/406.
22   PRO WO71/413 & 414.
23   Only nine death sentences were passed between Watts's appointment in charge of 7th Division on 26 September 1915 and 7 January 1917, the date his successor took over.
24   PRO WO213/10.
25   J. H. Boraston (ed.), *Sir Douglas Haig's Despatches* (J. M. Dent, London, 1919), p. 30.
26   PRO WO213/11.
27   Private J. Coley, 1st South Staffords, was condemned for desertion on 1 November 1916, and Private T. Roberts, 1st Royal Welsh Fusiliers, was condemned for sleeping on post on 6 November 1916. Both PRO WO213/12.
28   Becke, *Order of Battle, Part I*, p. 82.
29   Becke, *Order of Battle, Part I*, p. 82.
30   PRO WO71/558.
31   *Sir Douglas Haig's Despatches,* pp. 75 and 102.
32   Privates James and Wooding, 2nd Battalion Royal Warwickshires and Private Kinsey, 21st Battalion Manchesters. PRO WO213/18.
33   Private Goff. PRO WO213/19.
34   Private T. Hawkins. PRO WO71/622.
35   Putkowski and Sykes, *Shot at Dawn*, pp. 218–19.
36   PRO WO213/13 & 15.
37   PRO WO71/657.
38   Major A. F. Becke, *Order of Battle of Divisions, Part 2A – The Territorial Force Mounted Divisions and The 1st-Line Territorial Force Divisions (42–56)* (HMSO, London, 1936), p. 77.
39   War Diary – DGMS – 3rd Army. PRO WO95/381.
40   *Sir Douglas Haig's Despatches,* p. 30.
41   PRO WO71/485.
42   PRO WO213/11.
43   PRO WO71/501.
44   War diary – 1/4th battalion, Royal Berkshire Regiment. PRO WO95/2762.
45   *Sir Douglas Haig's Despatches,* p. 72.
46   *Sir Douglas Haig's Despatches,* pp. 118–19.
47   *Sir Douglas Haig's Despatches,* p. 119.
48   PRO WO95/2746 – War diary, 48th Division.
49   PRO WO71/586.
50   PRO WO95/954, War diary of A. G., XVIII Corps.
51   PRO WO213/17.
52   Becke, *Order of Battle – Part 2A*, p. 83.
53   Major A. F. Becke, *Order of Battle of Divisions, Part 3A – New Army Divisions (9–26)* (HMSO, London, 1938), pp. 119–25.
54   According to Becke, *Order of Battle of Divisions, Part 3A*, p. 124, concentration of the Division around Tilques in France was completed on 29 August 1915. Private J. Bird, 11 Sherwood Forresters, and Private T. Roach, 11 West Yorks, were sentenced to death on 1 and 16 October respectively. PRO WO213/6.

55 *Sir Douglas Haig's Despatches,* p. 27.
56 PRO WO71/1027.
57 PRO WO95/2184 – War Diary, 8th Battalion, Yorkshire Regiment.
58 PRO WO213/11.
59 Private R. Clee, 9th Battalion South Staffordshire Regiment. PRO WO213/11.
60 PRO WO71/543.
61 PRO WO71/508.
62 PRO WO71/1027.
63 PRO WO71/1027.
64 PRO WO71/1027.
65 Private Leonard Mitchell. PRO WO71/590.
66 PRO WO95/ 2170 – War diary, 23rd Division.
67 PRO WO71/619.
68 PRO WO71/617.
69 According to Becke, *Order of Battle of Divisions, Part 3A,* p. 125, 23rd Division en-trained for Italy on 6 November, arriving near Mantua on the 16th.
70 *The Fifth Glo'ster Gazette 1915–1919: A Trench Magazine of the First World War* (Sutton, Stroud, 1993), p. 257.
71 David R. Woodward (ed.), *The Military Correspondence of Field-Marshal Sir William Robertson, Chief of the Imperial General Staff, December 1915–February 1918* (Army Records Society, London, 1989), p. 168.
72 *The Military Correspondence of William Robertson,* p. 235.
73 *The Military Correspondence of William Robertson,* p. 240.
74 Papers of Captain Hardie, IWM 84/64/1. Report for period December 1917–February 1918.
75 Papers of Captain Hardie, IWM 84/64/1. Report for period December 1917–February 1918.
76 *The Military Correspondence of William Robertson,* p. 240.
77 Because this refers to casualties from all causes it includes the wounded and sick, many of whom were wounded or fell sick on more than one occasion and so were counted more than once.
78 Major T. J. Mitchell and Miss G. M. Smith, *History of the Great War, based on official documents – Medical Services: Casualties and Medical Statistics of the Great War* (HMSO, London, 1931), pp. 107 and 177.
79 Private A. Greene, 23 Middlesex Regiment (attached to Royal Engineers). PRO WO213/19.
80 PRO WO213/19.
81 Becke, *Order of Battle – Part 4,* p. 66.
82 PRO WO213/19.
83 PRO WO213/19.
84 Private A. Craven. PRO WO213/19.
85 Private E. Rickett. PRO WO213/19.
86 Figures collated from courts martial registers – PRO WO213/19 & 20.
87 Becke, *Order of Battle – Part IV,* p. 66.
88 Hardie Papers, Report on Troop Morale based on Mail Censorship for period December 1918 – February 1918, p. 3.
89 Compiled from courts-martial registers PRO WO213/1–34 inclusive. Also pub-lished in G. Oram, *Death Sentences.*
90 War Diary – DMS (Italy), PRO WO95/4198.
91 War Diary – DMS (Italy), PRO WO95/4198.

92 Figures compiled from courts martial registers. PRO WO213/19–27.
93 Compiled from Register of General-Courts Martial – PRO WO90/8.
94 2/Lt G. Brown of 14 London Regiment was cleared of absence on 22 January 1918 by a court martial sitting at Taranto, and 2/Lt A. Harmer of 13 Durham Light Infantry was cleared of the same offence by a court convened in the field on 25 February 1918. PRO WO90/8/16.
95 Figures compiled from Register of General-Courts-Martial, PRO WO90/8.
96 PRO WO90/8/21.
97 War Diary – DDMS (Italy), PRO WO95/4198.
98 War Diary – DMS (Italy), PRO WO95/4198.
99 War Diary – DMS (Italy), PRO WO95/4198.
100 Private J. Welsby, 2 King's Own Scottish Borderers (5th Division) had been tried for cowardice and desertion in January 1918, but had been found guilty only of absence. PRO WO213/19, p. 82.
101 PRO WO213/23, pp. 168, 182 and 183. See also Appendix.
102 Compiled from courts martial registers. PRO WO 213/19–27.
103 See Chapter 3.
104 *Statistics of the Military Effort of the British Empire during the Great War 1914–1920* (HMSO, 1922), pp. 644–5.
105 Oram, *Worthless Men*, pp 102–19.
106 For a comparison of desertion in the British and German armies on the Western Front, including the military and judicial responses to it, see Christoph Jahr, *Gewönliche Soldaten. Desertion und Deserteure im deutschen und britischen Heer 1914–1918* (Göttingen, 1998). See also G. Oram, ' "The administration of discipline by the English is very rigid": British Military Law and the Death Penalty 1868–1918', in *Crime, histoire et sociétés/Crime, History and Societies* 2001, V, no. 1, pp. 93–110.
107 There are 2634 trials for desertion on the Western Front recorded in the courts-martial registers for the period November 1917 to August 1918. In 1178 of these cases (44.72%) a final conviction of absence has been recorded. Only 33 cases were found not guilty (approximately 1.25%). What these statistics hide, though, is the increased incidence of downgrading during the Spring of 1918 when 177 cases out of 309 (or 57.3%) were found guilty of absence rather than desertion. Figures collated from PRO WO213/19–23 inclusive.
108 Figures compiled from courts-martial registers. PRO WO 90/6 – 8 & 92/3–4. Official statistics put the number at 43, which omits those tried for other offences as well as desertion. Even if analysis is confined to the official figure the rate of 'downgrading' (37%) remains comparatively low.
109 Radzinowicz and Hood. See also Oram, 'The administration of discipline'.
110 J. M. Beattie, *Crime and Courts in England, 1660–1800* (Oxford, 1986), pp 424–30. Clive Emsley, *Crime and Society in England 1750–1900*, 2nd edition (London, 1996), pp. 185 and 197.
111 The Petition of the Corporation of London (January 25, 1819), cited in Louis Blom-Cooper QC and Gavin Drewry (eds), *Law and Morality* (London, 1976), p. 44.
112 Cited in Blom-Cooper and Drewry, *Law and Morality*, p. 47.
113 *Extracts from General Routine Orders issued to the British Armies in France by Field Marshal Sir Douglas Haig*, Part I (London, 1918), p. 59.
114 Becke, *Order of Battle – Part IV*, p. 66.
115 PRO WO90/8/21

116   Private H. Horton, condemned on 14 April 1918, and Private A. Maunders, condemned on 20 April 1918. Both were serving with 1st Battalion South Staffordshire Regiment. PRO WO213/21.
117   War Diary – DDMS – Italy. PRO WO95/4198.
118   War Diary – DDMS – Italy. PRO WO95/4198.
119   War Diary – DMS – Italy. PRO WO95/4198.
120   War Diary – DMS – Italy. PRO WO95/4198.
121   War Diary – DDMS – Italy. PRO WO95/4198.
122   PRO WO213/22.
123   Hardie Papers – Report on Troop-Morale based on Mail Censorship for period February–July 1918, p. 1. IWM 84/64/1.
124   War Diary – DDMS – Italy (16/6/18). PRO WO95/4198.
125   War Diary – DDMS – Italy (18/6/18). PRO WO95/4198.
126   PRO WO213/24.
127   Hardie Papers – IWM. Report for period February – July 1918, p. 1.
128   Two men of the British West Indies Regiment were condemned after the war: one for murder and another for mutiny – the former sentence was carried out.
129   War Diary – DMS – Italy (14 and 31 July 1918). PRO WO95/4198.
130   Oram, *Worthless Men*, p. 42.
131   War Diary – DMS – Italy (31/8/18). PRO WO95/4198.
132   War Diary – DMS – Italy (31/10/18). PRO WO95/4198.
133   Gary Sheffield, 'Officer–Man Relations', p. 307.

Conclusion

1   Victor Bailey, 'The Shadow of the Gallows: The Death Penalty and the British Labour Government, 1945–51' in *Law and History Review*, vol. 18, no. 2 (summer 2000), p. 349.
2   Capital punishment for murder was suspended for five years in 1965. Its eventual abolition came at the end of that term.
3   The capital offences of Treason and Mutiny remained. The death sentence for these, together with the last few remaining capital offences in the criminal code, was abolished in 1998. See John McHugh, 'The Labour Party and the Parliamentary Campaign to Abolish the Military Death Penalty 1919–1930', *Historical Journal*, vol. 42, no. 1 (1999), pp. 233–49.
4   General Sir Ivor Maxse, *Notes and Hints on Training* (February 1918). Maxse Papers, IWM, 69/53/1–18.
5   *Manual of Military Law*, 1914 edition (HMSO, London, 1914), p. 6.

Appendix

1   Compiled from Courts-Martial Registers. PRO WO21319-27.

Bibliography

National archives

Public Record Office

CAB24/26 & 36 – Notes on Morale of British Troops as gathered from Mail Censorship.
WO32/4747 – Minutes of the Southborough Committee.
WO32/6045 – Memorandum on the Various Methods of Punishment Adopted in Foreign Armies for Soldiers in the Field.
WO32/6930 – Notes on Training of RAMC.
WO32/8386 – Notes on Training of NCOs.
WO71/387-1027 – Papers of Judge Advocate General's Office (capital trials).
WO90/3-4 – Courts-Martial Registers – General Court Martial (Foreign).
WO92/3-8 – Courts-Martial Registers – General Court Martial (Home).
WO93/42 – Nominal Role of Court-Martial proceedings, Australian Imperial Force.
WO93/43 – Nominal Role of Canadian Officers tried by Courts-Martial.
WO93/44 – Nominal Role of Canadian Other Ranks tried by District Court-Martial.
WO93/45 – Nominal Role of Canadian Other Ranks tried by Field-General Court-Martial.
WO93/49 – Summary of Capital Trials (Judge Advocate General's Office).
WO95/381 – War Diary, Director-General Medical Services, 3rd Army.
WO95/596 – War Diary, I Corps.
WO95/1265 – War Diary, 10th Battalion, Gloucestershire Regiment.
WO95/1361-71 – War Diaries, 1st Battalion, Royal Berkshire Regiment.
WO95/1449 – War Diary, 4th Division.
WO95/1658 – War Diary, 2nd Battalion, Bedfordshire Regiment.
WO95/1664 – War Diary, 2nd Battalion, Royal Warwickshire Regiment.
WO95/1665 – War Diary, 2nd Battalion, Border Regiment.
WO95/2167-70 – War Diaries, 23rd Division.
WO95/2184 – War Diary, 8th Battalion, Yorkshire Regiment.
WO95/2468 – War Diary, 35th Division.
WO95/2745-6 – War Diaries, 48th Division.
WO95/4198 – War Diary, Director Medical Services, Italy.
WO95/4198 – War Diary, Deputy Director Medical Services, Italy.
WO213/1-34 – Courts-Martial Registers – Field General Court Martial.
WO329 – Great War Medal Role.

Imperial War Museum

Papers of:
Beer, E., 91/3/1
Cox, C. H., 88/11/1
Cullen, G. H.
Dibble, Captain A. H., Con Shelf
Dickinson, A. H.
Gell, Lieutenant

Hardie, Captain Martin, 84/64/1
Harrison, W., Con Shelf
Hirst, F.
Lennard, H., 86/86/1
Lye, E.
Mackay, Lieutenant R. L., MC
MacMillan, Leading Seaman T.
Maxse, General Sir Ivor, 69/53/1-18
J. McAuley, 'A Manxman's Diary', 97/10/1
McElwaine, Sir Percy, 92/35/1
Munro, A. M., Con Shelf
Murfin, F. J., 88/11/1
Murray, J.
Packham, F. M.
Pears, R.
Preston, J.
Roberts, A. H.
Rogers, Canon T. G.
Schweder, Major R. P., MC, 86/65/1
Spencer, Brigadier-General F. E.
Unknown Soldier's Diary, Misc. 550
West, W. F., 92/10/1

Other Papers:
Battalion Orders of 2nd Battalion, Royal Munster Fusiliers, 22 June 1916 – 8 August
    1916
Papers re: Singapore Mutiny, Misc. 1722

National Army Museum
Papers of General Sir Henry Rawlinson

Other Archives

Archive and Record Service of British Columbia, Victoria, Canada
Military Service Act 1917 – Disposition of Schedules for Appeal Tribunal No. 12
    Showing Copies of Findings Filed with District Registrar at Fernie: Fernie Miners
    Judgment, January 1918.
Papers relating to conscientious objectors – GR 2369 & GR 2498.
Papers of Department of Justice, Military Service Branch, Chilliwack, British
    Columbia.

Printed Sources

Official publications
Army (Courts-Martial) Return for 1879 (HMSO, London, 1880).
Army Act 1881.
Army Act 1914.

Army Discipline and Regulation Act 1881.

Army Discipline and Regulation Bill (Rules for Punishments) 1879.

Handbook of the German Army in War, January 1917, reprint (E. P. Publishing, Wakefield, 1973).

Infantry Training (HMSO, London, 1914).

Instructions for the Training of Platoons for Offensive Action issued by The General Staff, February 1917 (The Military Press, Milton Keynes, 2000).

Manual of Military Law, 1914 edition (HMSO, London, 1914).

Memorandum by the Director-General, Army Medical Service, on the Physical Unfitness of Men Offering Themselves for Enlistment in the Army (HMSO, London, 1903).

Memorandum on Army Training (HMSO, London, 1910).

Memorandum on the Censorship (HMSO, London, 1915).

Militärstrafgesetzbuch für das Deutsche Reich vom 20. Juni 1872 (J. Güttentag Verlags, Berlin, 1912).

Mutiny Act 1876.

Parliamentary Papers (Hansard).

Report of the Commissioners Appointed to Enquire into the Constitution and Practice of Courts-Martial in the Army, and the Present System of Punishment for Military Offences – Two Parts (HMSO, London, 1869).

Report of the Committee Constituted by the Army Council to Enquire into the Law and Rules of Procedure Regulating Military Courts-Martial (Darling Committee) (HMSO, London, 1919).

Report on Recruiting in Ireland (HMSO, London, 1916).

Report of the War Office Committee of Enquiry into 'Shell-Shock' (Southborough Committee) (HMSO, London, 1922).

Soldiers Died in the Great War, vols 1–80 (HMSO, London, 1921).

Statistics of the Military Effort of the British Empire during the Great War 1914–1920 (HMSO, London, 1922).

Official histories and unit histories

Becke, Major A. F., *History of the Great War Based on Official Documents by Direction of the Historical Section of the Committee of Imperial Defence – Order of Battle, Part 1: The Regular British Divisions* (HMSO, London, 1935).

Becke, Major A. F., *History of the Great War Based on Official Documents by Direction of the Historical Section of the Committee of Imperial Defence – Order of Battle, Part 2A: The Territorial Force Mounted Divisions and The 1st Line Territorial Force Divisions (42–56)* (HMSO, London, 1936).

Becke, Major A. F., *History of the Great War Based on Official Documents by Direction of the Historical Section of the Committee of Imperial Defence – Order of Battle, Part 3A: New Army Divisions (9–26)* (HMSO, London, 1938).

Becke, Major A. F., *History of the Great War Based on Official Documents by Direction of the Historical Section of the Committee of Imperial Defence – Order of Battle, Part 3B: New Army Divisions (30–41); & 63rd (R. N.) Division* (HMSO, London, 1945).

Becke, Major A. F., *History of the Great War Based on Official Documents by Direction of the Historical Section of the Committee of Imperial Defence – Order of Battle, Part 4: The Army Council, G. H. Q.s, Armies, and Corps 1914–1918* (HMSO, London, 1945).

Davson, Lieutenant-Colonel H. M., *The History of the 35th Division* (Cassell, London, 1926).

History of the Great War Based on Official Documents: Italy, reprint (Imperial War Museum, 1996).

Mitchell, Major T. J. and Smith, Miss G. M., *History of the Great War Based on Official Documents: Medical Services, Casualties and Medical Statistics of the Great War*, reprint (Imperial War Museum, London, 1997).

Memoirs, diaries, poetry, and other published correspondence

Blake, R. (ed.), *The Private Papers of Douglas Haig 1914–1919* (Eyre & Spottiswoode, London, 1952).

Boraston, J. H. (ed.), *Sir Douglas Haig's Despatches (December 1915–April 1919)* (J. M. Dent, London, 1919).

Chair, S. de (ed.), *Napoleon on Napoleon: an Autobiography of the Emperor* (Brockhampton Press, London, 1992).

Charteris, Brigadier General J., *At G. H. Q.* (Cassell, London, 1931).

Childs, Brigadier General Sir W., *Episodes and Reflections* (Cassell, London, 1930).

Churchill, W. S., *The Boer War: London to Ladysmith via Pretoria and Ian Hamilton's March* (Leo Cooper, London, 1989).

Crozier, Brigadier General F. P., *A Brass Hat in No Man's Land* (Jonathan Cape, London, 1930).

Glover, J. and Silkin, J. (eds), *The Penguin Book of First World War Prose* (Penguin, London, 1990).

Graves, R., *Goodbye to All That* (Penguin, London, 1957).

Gurney, I., *Severn and Somme and War's Embers*, Thornton edition (Mid Northumberland Arts Group, Ashington, 1997).

Hastings, M. (ed.), *William Russell Special Correspondent of The Times* (Folio Society, London, 1995).

Jeffrey, K. (ed.), *The Military Correspondence of Field-Marshal Sir Henry Wilson 1918–1922* (Bodley Head, London, 1985).

Jünger, E., *The Storm of Steel* (Constable, London, 1994).

Lawrence, T. E., *Seven Pillars of Wisdom* (Wordsworth, Ware, 1997).

Lewis, C., *Sagittarius Rising* (Folio Society, London, 1998).

Ludendorff, E., *Kriegführung und Politik*, (E. S. Mittler u. Sohn, Berlin, 1922).

Owen, W., *The Poems of Wilfred Owen*, Stallworthy edition (Chatto & Windus, London, 1990).

Reiter, M. M., *Balkan Assault: The Diary of an Officer 1914–1918* (Historical Press, London, 1994).

Sassoon, S., *The Complete Memoirs of George Sherston* (Faber & Faber, London, 1972).

Sassoon, S., *The War Poems* (Faber & Faber, London, 1983).

Silkin, J. (ed.), *The Penguin Book of First World War Poetry*, 2nd edition (Penguin, London, 1981).

Thompson, J. M. (ed.), *Napoleon's Letters* (Prion, London, 1998).

Vaughan, E. C., *Some Desperate Glory: The Diary of a Young Officer 1917* (Macmillan – now Palgrave Macmillan, Basingstroke, 1984).

Woodward, D. R. (ed.), *The Military Correspondence of Sir William Robertson, Chief Imperial General Staff, December 1915–February 1918* (Bodley Head, London, 1989).

Newspapers, journals and periodicals

The Derry Standard

The Fifth Glo'ster Gazette 1915–1919: A Trench Magazine of the First World War (Sutton, Stroud, 1993).

The Lancet
The Times

Polemical works, articles and other published studies

Baynes, J., *Morale: A Study of Men and Courage* (Cassell, London, 1967).

Clausewitz, C. von, *On War*, 1908 edition (Penguin, London, 1982).

Conway, Sir M., *The Crowd in Peace and War* (Longmans, Green, London, 1915).

Forsyth, Dr D., 'Functional Nerve Disease and Shock in Battle: A Study of the So-called Traumatic Neuroses Arising in Connection with the War', *The Lancet* (25 December 1915), pp. 1399–1400.

Grierson, Captain F. D., *The ABC of Military Law* (T. Fisher Unwin, London, 1916).

Henderson, Colonel G. F. R., *The Science of War: Author's Essays from 1891 to 1903, edited by Colonel Niell Malcolm* (Longmans, Green, London, 1919).

Hurst, G. B., 'The Administration of Military Law', *Contemporary Review*, vol. CXV (1919), pp. 321–7.

Kentish, Brigadier General R. J., *The Maxims of the Late Field-Marshal Viscount Wolseley, KP, GCB, GCMG, and the Addresses on Leadership, Esprit de Corps and Morale* (Gale & Polden, London, 1918).

Kipling, R., *The New Army in Training* (Macmillan, London, 1915).

Lavery, F., *Great Irishmen in War and Politics* (Andrew Melrose, London, 1920).

Machiavelli, N., *The Prince* (Penguin, London, 1981).

Maude, Colonel F. N., 'Introduction' to Clausewitz, C. von, *On War*, 1908 edition (Penguin, London, 1982).

Maudsley, H., 'War Psychology: English and German', *Journal of Mental Science*, vol. LXV, no. 269 (April 1919), pp. 5–87.

Melville, Colonel C. H., 'Eugenics and Military Service', *Eugenics Review*, vol. 2 (1910–11), pp. 53–60.

Moran, Lord, *The Anatomy of Courage*, 2nd edition (Constable, London, 1966).

Myers, C., *Shell-Shock in France* (Cambridge University Press, Cambridge, 1940).

Thurtle, E., *Shootings at Dawn* (Victoria House, London, 1924).

Secondary sources

Books

Adams, R. J. Q. and Poirier, P. P., *The Conscription Controversy in Great Britain 1900–18* (Macmillan – now Palgrave Macmillan, Basingstroke, 1987).

Babington, A., *For the Sake of Example: Capital Courts-Martial 1914–18*, revised edition (Leo Cooper, London, 1993).

Babington, A., *Shell-Shock: A History of the Changing attitudes to War Neuroses* (Leo Cooper, Barnsley, 1997).

Beattie, J. M., *Crime and Courts in England, 1660–1800* (Clarendon Press, Oxford, 1986).

Beckett, I. F. W. and Simpson, K. (eds), *A Nation in Arms* (Manchester University Press, Manchester, 1985).

Blanning, T. C. W. (ed.), *The Oxford Illustrated History of Modern Europe* (Oxford University Press, Oxford, 1996).

Bond, B., *War and Society in Europe 1870–1970* (Sutton, Stroud, 1998).

Bond, B., et al., *Look to Your Front: Studies in the First World War by the British Commission for Military History* (Spellmount, Staplehurst, 1999).

Bourke, J., *An Intimate History of Killing: Face-to-Face Killing in Twentieth-Century Warfare* (Granta Books, London, 1999).

Bourne, J., *Britain and the Great War 1914–1918* (Edward Arnold, London, 1989).

Brown, M., *The Imperial War Museum Book of the Western Front* (Sidgwick & Jackson, London, 1993).

Cannini, G. (ed.), *Les Fronts Invisibles* (Presses Universitaire de Nancy, Nancy, 1984).

Castle, K., *Britannia's Children: Reading Colonialism through Children's Books and Magazines* (Manchester University Press, Manchester, 1996).

Cecil, H. and Liddle, P. (eds), *Facing Armageddon: The First World War Experienced* (Leo Cooper, London, 1997).

Chadwick, R., *Bureaucratic Mercy: The Home Office and the Treatment of Capital Cases in Victorian Britain* (Garland, New York, 1992).

Chandler, D. (ed.), *The Oxford History of the British Army* (Oxford University Press, Oxford, 1994).

Coombs, R., *Before Endeavours Fade*, 6th edition (After the Battle, London, 1990).

Corns, C. and Hughes-Wilson, J., *Blindfold and Alone: British Military Executions in the Great War* (Cassell, London, 2001).

Corvisier, A., *Armies and Societies in Europe, 1494–1789*, Siddall translation (Indiana University Press, Bloomington and London, 1976).

Deák, I., *Beyond Nationalism: A Social History of the Habsburg Officer Corps, 1848–1918* (Oxford University Press, Oxford, 1992).

Dyer, G., *The Missing of the Somme* (Penguin, London, 1994).

Eksteins, M., *Rites of Spring* (Black Swan, London, 1990).

Emsley, C., *Crime and Society in England 1750–1900*, 2nd edition (Longman, London, 1996),

Evans, R., *Rituals of Retribution: Capital Punishment in Germany 1600–1987* (Oxford University Press, Oxford, 1996).

Ferguson, N., *The Pity of War* (Allen Lane, London, 1998).

Forsyth, W. J., *The Reform of Prisoners 1830–1900* (Croom Helm, London, 1987).

Forsyth, W. J., *Penal Discipline, Reformatory Projects and the English Prison Commission 1895–1939* (University of Exeter Press, Exeter, 1990).

Foster, R., *Paddy and Mr Punch: Connections in Irish and English History* (Penguin, London, 1993).

Foucault, M., Discipline and Punish (Penguin, London, 1991).

Freedman, L., *War* (Oxford University Press, Oxford, 1994).

Fuller, J. G., *Troop Morale and Popular Culture in the British and Dominion Armies 1914–1918* (Clarendon Press, Oxford, 1990).

Fussell, P., *The Great War and Modern Memory* (Oxford University Press, Oxford, 1997).

Gilbert, M., *First World War* (Weidenfeld & Nicolson, London, 1994).

Hichberger, J. W. M., *Images of the Army: The Military in British Art 1815–1914* (Manchester University Press, Manchester, 1988).

Horne, J. (ed.), *State, Society and Mobilisation in Europe during the First World War* (Cambridge University Press, Cambridge, 1997).

Howard, M., and Louis, R. (eds), *The Oxford History of the Twentieth Century* (Oxford University Press, Oxford, 1998).

Hynes, S., *A War Imagined: The First World War and English Culture* (Pimlico, London, 1992).

Hynes, S. *The Soldiers' Tale: Bearing Witness to Modern War* (Pimlico, London, 1998).

Jahr, C., *Gewönliche Soldaten. Desertion und Deserteure im deutschen und britischen Heer 1914–1918* (Vandenhoeck & Rupprecht, Göttingen, 1998).

James, L., *Mutiny in the British and Commonwealth Forces 1797–1956* (Buchan & Enright, London, 1987).

Joll, J., *The Origins of the First World War* (Longman, London, 1984).

Joll, J., *Europe Since 1870: An International History*, 4th edition (Penguin, London, 1990).

Keegan, J., *A History of Warfare* (Hutchinson, London, 1993).

Kitchen, M., *The German Officer Corps 1890–1914* (Clarendon Press, Oxford, 1968).

Kitchen, M., *A Military History of Germany: from the Eighteenth Century to the Present Day* (Weidenfeld & Nicolson, London, 1975).

Leed, E., *No Man's Land: Combat and Identity in World War I* (Cambridge University Press, Cambridge, 1979).

Lurie, J., *Arming Military Justice* (Princeton University Press, Princeton, NJ, 1992).

Marwick, A., *The Deluge: British Society and the First World War*, 2nd edition (Macmillan – now Palgrave Macmillan, Basingstoke, 1991).

McConville, S., *Next Only to Death: English Local Prisons 1860–1900* (Routledge, London, 1995).

Metcalf, T. R., *Ideologies of the Raj* (Cambridge University Press, Cambridge, 1997).

Middlebrook, M., *The First Day of the Somme* (Penguin, London, 1984).

Middlebrook, M. and M., *The Somme Battlefields: A Comprehensive Guide from Crécy to the Two World Wars* (Penguin, London, 1994).

Millett, A. R. and Murray, W. (eds), *Military Effectiveness, Vol. 1: The First World War* (Unwin Hyman, London, 1989).

Moorhead, A., *Gallipoli* (Wordsworth, Ware, 1997).

Morton, D., *When Your Number's Up: The Canadian Soldier in the First World War* (Random House of Canada, Toronto, 1993).

Offenstadt, N., *Les Fusillés de la Grand Guerre et la mémoire collective 1914–1999* (Editions Odile Jacobs, Paris, 1999).

Oram, G., *Death Sentences Passed by Military Courts of the British Army 1914–24* (Francis Boutle, London, 1998).

Oram, G., *Worthless Men: Race, Eugenics and the Death Penalty in the British Army during the First World War* (Francis Boutle, London, 1998).

Oram, G. (ed.), *Unquiet Graves: Comparative Perspectives on Military Executions in the First World War and Modern Memory* (Francis Boutle, London) – forthcoming.

Pakenham, T., *The Boer War* (Weidenfeld & Nicolson, London, 1979).

Pedroncini, G., *Les Mutineries de 1917* (PUF, Paris, 1967).

Pick, D., *Faces of Degeneration: A European Disorder, c. 1848–c. 1918* (Cambridge University Press, Cambridge, 1993).

Pick, D., *War Machine: the Rationalization of Slaughter in the Modern Age* (Yale University Press, New Haven, 1993).

Porch, D., *The March to the Marne: The French Army 1871–1914* (Cambridge University Press, Cambridge, 1981).

Porter, R. (ed.), *Myths of the English* (Polity, London, 1993).

Porter, R., *The Greatest Benefit to Mankind: A Medical History of Humanity from Antiquity to the Present* (HarperCollins, London, 1997).

Pugsley, C., *On the Fringe of Hell* (Hodder & Stoughton, Auckland, 1991).

Putkowski, J., *British Army Mutineers 1914–22* (Francis Boutle, London, 1998).

Putkowski, J. and Sykes, J., *Shot at Dawn*, revised edition (Leo Cooper, London, 1992).

Radzinowicz, L. and Hood, R., *A History of English Criminal Law, vol. 5: The Emergence of Penal Policy* (Stevens, London, 1986).

Roberts, J. M., *Europe 1880–1945: A General History of Europe*, 2nd edition (Longman, London, 1989).

Searle, G. R., *Eugenics and Politics in Britain 1900–1914* (Noordhoff International, Leyden, 1976).

Smith, L., *Between Mutiny and Obedience* (Princeton University Press, Princeton, NJ 1994).

Spiers, E., *The Army and Society* (Longman, London, 1980).

Spiers, E., *The Late Victorian Army 1868–1902* (Manchester University Press, Manchester, 1992).

Stevenson, J., *British Society 1914–45* (Penguin, London, 1990).

Strachan, H., *The Politics of the British Army* (Oxford University Press, Oxford, 1997).

Strachan, H. (ed.), *The Oxford Illustrated History of the First World War* (Oxford University Press, Oxford, 1998).

Terraine, J., *The Great War* (Wordsworth, Ware, 1997).

Travers, T., *The Killing Ground: The British Army, the Western Front and the Emergence of Modern Warfare 1900–1918* (Routledge, London, 1990).

Varney, N., *Images of Wartime: British Art and Artists of World War I* (David & Charles, London, 1991).

Walker, N., *Crime and Punishment in Britain* (University Press, Edinburgh, 1965).

Whittam, J., *The Politics of the Italian Army* (Croom Helm, London, 1977).

Wiener, M. J., *Reconstructing the Criminal: Culture, Law, and Policy in England, 1830–1914* (Cambridge University Press, Cambridge, 1990).

Winter, D., *Death's Men: Soldiers of the Great War* (Penguin, London, 1979).

Winter, D., *Haig's Command: A Reassessment* (Penguin, London, 1992).

Winter, J. M., *The Great War and the British People* (Macmillan – now Palgrave Macmillan, Basingstoke, 1985).

Winter, J. M., *Sites of Memory Sites of Mourning* (Cambridge University Press, Cambridge, 1995).

Woodward, D., *Armies of the World 1854–1914* (Sidgwick & Jackson, London, 1978).

Ziemann, B., *Front und Heimat: Ländliche Kriegserfahrungen im südlichen Bayern 1914–1923* (Klartext, Liepzig, 1997).

Articles and essays

Bailey, V., 'The Shadow of the Gallows: The Death Penalty and the British Labour Government, 1945–51', *Law and History Review,* vol. 18, no. 2 (summer 2000), pp. 305–49.

Becker, A., 'The Avant-Garde, Madness and the Great War', *Journal of Contemporary History,* vol. 35, no. 1 (2000), pp. 71–84.

Beckett, I., 'The Military Historian and the Popular Image of the Western Front, 1914–1918', *The Historian,* no. 53 (Spring 1997), pp. 11–14.

Bessell, R. and Englander, D., 'Up From the Trenches: Some Recent Writings on Soldiers of the Great War', *European Studies Review,* vol. 11 (1981), pp. 387–95.

Best, G., 'Militarism and the Victorian Public School', in Simon, B. and Bradley, I. (eds), *The Victorian Public School* (Gill & Macmillan, Dublin, 1975), pp. 129–46.

Bogacz, T., 'War Neurosis and Cultural Change in England, 1914–22: The Work of the War Office Committee of Enquiry into "Shell-Shock"', *Journal of Contemporary History,* vol. 24 (1989), pp. 227–56.

Bourke, J., 'Effeminacy, Ethnicity and the End of Trauma: The Sufferings of "Shell-shocked" Men in Great Britain and Ireland, 1914–39', *Journal of Contemporary History,* vol. 35, no. 1 (2000), pp. 57–69.

Bourne, J., 'The British Working Man in Arms' in Cecil, H. and Liddle, P. (eds), *Facing Armageddon: The First World War Experienced* (Leo Cooper, London, 1997), pp. 336–52.

Brown, T., 'Shell Shock in the Canadian Expeditionary Force, 1914–1918: Canadian Psychiatry in the Great War', in Roland, C. G. (ed.), *Health, Disease and Medicine: Essays in Canadian History* (Hannah Institute for the History of Canada, Toronto, 1984), pp. 308–32.

Burroughs, P., 'Crime and Punishment in the British Army, 1815–1870', *English Historical Review*, vol. C, no. 386 (July 1985), pp. 545–71.

Caenegem, R. C. van, 'The "Rechtsstaat" in Historical Perspective', in Caenegem, R. C. van (ed.), *Legal History: A European Perspective* (Hambledon Press, London, 1991), pp. 185–99.

Davidian, I., 'The Russian Soldier's Morale from the Evidence of Tsarist Military Censorship', in Cecil, H. and Liddle, P. (eds), *Facing Armageddon: The First World War Experienced* (Leo Cooper, London, 1997), pp. 425–33.

Denman, T., 'The Catholic Irish Soldier in the First World War: the "Racial Environment" ', *Irish Historical Studies*, vol. XXVII, no. 108 (November 1991), pp. 352–65.

Denman, T., '"Ethnic Soldiers Pure and Simple"? The Irish in the Late Victorian British Army, *War in History*, vol. 3, no. 3, (1996), pp. 253–73.

Eksteins, M., 'Memory and the Great War', in Strachan, H. (ed.), *The Oxford Illustrated History of the First World War* (Oxford University Press, Oxford, 1998), pp. 305–18.

Emsley, C., 'A Typology of Nineteenth-Century Police', *Crime, Histoire & Sociétés/Crime, History & Societies*, vol. 3, no. 1 (1999), pp. 29–44.

Emsley, C. and Phillips, S., 'The Habsburg Gendarmerie: A Research Agenda', *German History*, vol. 17, no. 2 (1999), pp. 241–50.

Englander, D., 'Manpower in the British Army, 1914–1918', in Cannini, G. (ed.), *Les Fronts invisibles* (Presses Universitaire de Nancy, Nancy, 1984), pp. 93–102.

Englander, D., 'Mutiny and Myopia', *Bulletin of the Society for the Study of Labour History*, vol. 52, no. 1 (1987), pp. 5–7.

Englander, D., 'Military Intelligence and the Defence of the Realm: the Surveillance of Soldiers and Civilians in Britain during the First World War', *Bulletin of the Society for the Study of Labour History*, vol. 52, no. 1 (1987), pp. 24–32.

Englander, D., 'The French Soldier, 1914–18', *French History*, vol. 1, no. 1 (1987), pp. 49–67.

Englander, D., 'Soldiering and Identity: Reflections on the Great War', *War in History*, vol. 1, no. 3 (1994), pp. 300–18.

Englander, D., 'Discipline and Morale in the British Army, 1917–1918', in Horne, J. (ed.), *State, Society and Mobilisation in Europe during the First World War* (Cambridge University Press, Cambridge, 1997), pp. 125–43.

Englander, D., 'Mutinies and Military Morale', in Strachan, H. (ed.), *The Oxford Illustrated History of the First World War* (Oxford University Press, Oxford, 1998), pp. 191–203.

Englander, D. and Osbourne, J., 'Jack Tommy and Henry Dubb: The Armed Forces and the Working Class', *Historical Journal*, vol. XXXI (1978), pp. 593–621.

Gibson, C. '"My Chief Source of Worry": An Assistant Provost Marshal's View of Relations between 2nd Canadian Division and Local Inhabitants on the Western Front, 1915–1917', *War in History*, 2000, vol. 7, no. 4, pp. 413–41.

Gooch, J., 'Italy during the First World War' in Millett, A. and Murray, W. (eds), *Military Effectiveness, vol 1: The First World War* (Unwin Hyman, London, 1989), pp. 157–89.

Horne, J., 'Socialism, Peace, and Revolution, 1917–1918', in Strachan, H. (ed.), *The Oxford Illustrated History of the First World War* (Oxford University Press, Oxford, 1998), pp. 227–38.

Joll, J., *1914 – The Unspoken Assumptions*, Inaugural Lecture of the Stevenson Chair (Camelot Press, London, 1968).

Kaufmann, D., 'Science as Cultural Practice: Psychiatry in the First World War and Weimar Germany', *Journal of Contemporary History*, vol. 34, no. 1 (1999), pp. 125–44.

Killingray, D., 'Race and Rank in the British Army in the Twentieth Century', *Ethnic and Racial Studies*, vol. 10, no. 3 (July 1987), pp. 276–90.

Leed, E., 'Fateful Memories: Industrialized War and Traumatic Neuroses', *Journal of Contemporary History*, vol. 35, no. 1 (2000), pp. 85–100.

Leese, P., 'Problems Returning Home: The British Psychological Casualties of the Great War', *Historical Journal*, vol. 40, no. 4 (1997), pp. 1055–67.

Lerner, P., 'Psychiatry and Casualties of War in Germany, 1914–18', *Journal of Contemporary History*, vol. 35, no. 1 (2000), pp. 13–28.

Lyon, J. M. B., '"A Peasant Mob": The Serbian Army on the Eve of the Great War', *Journal of Military History*, vol. 61 (July 1997), pp. 481–502.

McHugh, J., 'The Labour Party and the Campaign to Abolish the Military Death Penalty, 1919–1930', *Historical Journal*, vol. 42, no. 1 (1999), pp. 233–49.

Merridale, C., 'The Collective Mind: Trauma and Shell-Shock in Twentieth-Century Russia', *Journal of Contemporary History*, vol. 35, no. 1 (2000), pp. 39–55.

Meynier, G., '"Pour l'example, Un sur Dix!" – Les Decimations en 1914', *Politique Aujourd'hui* (janvier–fevrier 1976), pp. 55–70.

Millman, B., 'British Home Defence Planning and Civil Dissent, 1917–1918', *War in History*, vol. 5, no. 2 (1998), pp. 204–32.

Morton, D., 'The Supreme Penalty: Canadian Deaths by Firing Squad in the First World War', *Queen's Quarterly*, no. 79 (1972), pp. 345–52.

Mosse, G., 'National Cemeteries and National Revival: The Cult of the Fallen Soldiers in Germany', *Journal of Contemporary History*, vol. 14 (1979), pp. 1–20.

Mosse, G., 'Two World Wars and the Myth of War Experience', *Journal of Contemporary History*, vol. 21, no. 4 (1986), pp. 491–513.

Mosse, G., 'Shell-Shock as a Social Disease', *Journal of Contemporary History*, vol. 35, no. 1 (2000), pp. 101–8.

Offenstadt, N., 'Construction d'une "grande cause": La réhabilitation des "fusillés pour l'example" de la Grande Guerre', *Revue d'histoire moderne et contemporaine* vol. 44, no. 1 (janvier–mars 1997), pp. 68–85.

Offenstadt, N. 'Enquête sur les fusillés de 1914–1918', *L'histoire*, no. 237 (novembre 1999), pp. 64–9.

Oram, G., '"The administration of discipline by the English is very rigid": British Military Law and the Death Penalty 1868–1918', *Crime, Histoire & Sociétés/Crime, History & Societies*, (2001) vol. 5, no. 1, pp. 93–110.

Oram, G., 'Pious Perjury: Discipline and Morale in the British Force in Italy 1917–1918', *War in History*, vol. 9, no. 4 (2002) pp. 412–30.

Oram, G., '"The greatest efficiency": British and American Military Law 1866 to 1918', in B. Godfrey, C. Emsley and G. Dunstall (eds) *Comparative Histories of Crime* (Willan Publishing, Cullompton, Devon), forthcoming.

Peatty, J., 'Capital Courts-Martial during the First World War', in Bond, B. et al., *'Look to Your Front': Studies in the First World War by the British Commission for Military History* (Spellmount, Staplehurst, 1999), pp. 89–104.

Pedersen, P., 'Thou Shalt Not Kill: The Death Penalty in the Australian Imperial Force, 1914–18' in Oram, G. (ed.), *Unquiet Graves: Comparative Perspectives on*

Military Executions in the First World War and Modern Memory (Francis Boutle, London), forthcoming.

Philpott, W., 'Britain and France go to War: Anglo-French Relations on the Western Front 1914–1918, *War in History*, vol. 2, no. 1 (1995), pp. 43–64.

Porch, D., 'The French Army in the First World War', in Millett, A. and Murray, W. (eds), *Military Effectiveness, vol. 1: The First World War* (Unwin Hyman, London, 1989), pp. 190–228.

Reid, B. H. and White, J., 'Desertion in the American Civil War', in Freedman, L. (ed.), *War* (Oxford University Press, Oxford, 1994), pp. 139–43.

Roudebush, M., 'A Patient Fights Back: Neurology in the Court of Public Opinion in France during the First World War', *Journal of Contemporary History*, vol. 35, no. 1 (2000), pp. 29–38.

Rubin, G., 'Parliament, Prerogative and Military Law: Who had Legal Authority over the Army in the Later Nineteenth Century?', *Legal History*, vol. 18, no. 1 (April 1997), pp. 45–84.

Schaepdrijver, S. de, 'Theirs was Precisely to Reason Why: On Slaughter, Sacrifice and Shootings at Dawn', *In Flanders Fields Magazine*, vol. 2, no. 4 (July 2000), pp. 18–19.

Schleuter, Captain D. A., 'The Court-Martial: An Historical Survey', *Military Law Review*, vol. 87 (1980), pp. 129–66.

Sheffield, G., 'Officer–Man Relations, Discipline and Morale in the British Army of the Great War', in Cecil, H. and Liddle, P. (eds), *Facing Armageddon: The First World War Experienced* (Leo Cooper, London, 1997), pp. 413–24.

Sheffield, G., '"A very good type of Londoner and a very good type of colonial": Officer–Man Relations and Discipline in the 22nd Royal Fusiliers, 1914–18', in Bond, B. et al., *'Look to Your Front': Studies in the First World War by the British Commission for Military History* (Spellmount, Staplehurst, Kent, 1999), pp. 137–46.

Simkins, P., 'The Four Armies', in Chandler, D. (ed.), *The Oxford History of the British Army* (Oxford University Press, Oxford, 1996) pp. 235–55.

Smith, L., 'The Disciplinary Dilemma of French Military Justice, September 1914–April 1917: The Case of the 5e Division d'Infanterie', *Journal of Military History*, vol. 55 (January 1991), pp. 47–68.

Smith, L., 'War and Politics: The French Army Mutinies of 1917', *War in History*, vol. 2, no. 2 (1995), pp. 180–201.

Smith, L., 'Remobilizing the Citizen-Soldier through the French Army Mutinies of 1917', in Horne, J. (ed.), *State, Society and Mobilisation in Europe during the First World War* (Cambridge University Press, Cambridge, 1997), pp. 144–59.

Stone, M., 'Shellshock and the Psychologists', in Bynum, W. F., Porter, R. and Shepherd, M. (eds), *The Anatomy of Madness, Vol. II* (Tavistock Press, London, 1985), pp. 242–71.

Strachan, H., 'Military Modernization, 1789–1918', in Blanning, T. C. W. (ed.), *The Oxford Illustrated History of Modern Europe* (Oxford University Press, Oxford, 1996), pp. 69–93.

Strachan, H., 'The Morale of the German Army, 1917–18', in Cecil, H. and Liddle, P. (eds), *Facing Armageddon: The First World War Experienced* (Leo Cooper, London, 1997), pp. 383–98.

Stuart-Smith, J., 'Military Law: Its History, Administration and Practice', *Law Quarterly Review*, vol. 85 (1969), pp. 478–504.

Taylor, H., 'The Politics of the Rising Crime Statistics of England and Wales, 1914–1960', *Crime, Histoire & Sociétés/Crime, History & Societies*, vol. 2, no. 1 (1998), pp. 5–28.

Tombs, R., 'Crime and Security of the State: The "Dangerous Classes" and Insurrection in Nineteenth-Century Paris', in Gattrell, V. A. C., Lenman, B. and Parker, G. (eds), *Crime and the Law: The Social History of Crime in Western Europe since 1500* (Europa Publications, London, 1980), pp. 214–37.

Travers, T. H. E., 'Technology, Tactics and Morale: Jean de Bloch, the Boer War, and British Military Theory, 1900–1914', *Journal of Modern History*, vol. 51 (June 1979), pp. 264–86.

Travers, T. H. E., 'The Hidden Army: Structural Problems in the British Officer Corps, 1900–1918', *Journal of Contemporary History*, vol. 17 (1984), pp. 523–44.

Waites, B., 'Black Men in White Men's Wars', in Liddle, P. and Bourne, J. (eds), *Lightning Strikes Twice*, forthcoming.

Wawro, G., 'Morale in the Austro-Hungarian Army: The Evidence of Habsburg Army Campaign Reports and Allied Intelligence Officers', in Cecil, H. and Liddle, P. (eds), *Facing Armageddon: The First World War Experienced* (Leo Cooper, London, 1997), pp. 399–412.

Wilkinson, G. R., '"The Blessings of War": The Depiction of Military Force in Edwardian Newspapers', *Journal of Contemporary History*, vol. 33, no. 1 (1998), pp. 97–115.

Winter, J. M., 'Britain's "Lost Generation" of the First World War, *Population Studies*, vol. 31, no. 1 (1977), pp. 449–66.

Winter, J. M., 'The Impact of the First World War on Civilian Health in Britain', *Economic History Review*, vol. XXX, no. 3 (1977), pp. 485–507.

Winter, J. M., 'Military Fitness and Civilian Health in Britain during the First World War', *Journal of Contemporary History*, vol. 15 (1980), pp. 211–44.

Winter, J. M., 'Propaganda and the Mobilization of Consent', in Strachan, H. (ed.), *The Oxford Illustrated History of the First World War* (Oxford University Press, Oxford, 1998), pp. 216–26.

Winter, J. M., 'Shell-Shock and the Cultural History of the Great War', *Journal of Contemporary History*, vol. 35, no. 1 (2000), pp. 7–11.

Ziemann, B., 'Fahnenflucht im deutschen Heer 1914–1918', *Militärgeschichtliche Mitteilungen*, vol. 55 (1996), pp. 93–130.

Unpublished theses

Bowman, T., 'The Discipline and Morale of the British Expeditionary Force in France and Flanders 1914–18, with Particular Reference to Irish Units', PhD thesis, University of Luton (1999).

Collin, R. O., 'The Italian Police and Internal Security from Giolitti to Mussolini', PhD thesis, Oriel College, Oxford (1983).

Howe, G. D., 'West Indians and World War I: A Social History of the British West Indies Regiment', PhD thesis, University of London (1994).

Leese, P. J. 'A Social and Cultural History of Shellshock, with particular reference to the experience of British soldiers during and after the Great War', PhD thesis, Open University (1989).

Lynch, P. J., 'The Exploitation of Courage: Psychiatric Care in the British Army, 1914–1918', MPhil thesis, University College, London (1977).

Oram, G., 'Worthless Men: Death Sentences in the British Army during the First World War', MPhil thesis, University of Hertfordshire (1997).

Oram, G., '"What alternative punishment is there. . .?": Military Executions during World War One', PhD thesis, Open University, 2000.

Ralston, D. B., 'The Army and the Republic: The Place of the Military in the Political and Constitutional Evolution of France 1871–1914', PhD thesis, Columbia University (1964).

Sheffield, G. D., 'Officer–Man Relations, Morale and Discipline in the British Army, 1902–22', PhD thesis, King's College, London (1994).

Williams, R. 'A Social and Military History of the 1/8 Battalion, The Royal Warwickshire Regiment in the Great War', MPhil thesis, University of Birmingham, 2000.

Wilson, T. B., 'Morale and Discipline in the British Expeditionary Force, 1914–1918', MA thesis, University of New Brunswick (1978).

Index